Indian Travel Writing in the Age of Empire

Indian Travel Writing in the Age of Empire 1830–1940

Pramod K. Nayar

BLOOMSBURY
NEW DELHI • LONDON • OXFORD • NEW YORK • SYDNEY

BLOOMSBURY INDIA
Bloomsbury Publishing India Pvt. Ltd
Second Floor, LSC Building No. 4, DDA Complex, Pocket C – 6 & 7,
Vasant Kunj, New Delhi 110070

BLOOMSBURY, BLOOMSBURY ACADEMIC INDIA and the Diana logo
are trademarks of Bloomsbury Publishing Plc

First published in India 2020
This edition published 2020

Bloomsbury Academic
An imprint of Bloomsbury Publishing Plc

ISBN: HB: 978-93-89000-92-4; eBook: 978-93-89000-94-8

2 4 6 8 10 9 7 5 3 1

Typeset in Minion Pro by Manipal Technologies Limited
Digitally Printed and bound in India by Replika Press Pvt. Ltd. In 2019

Contents

Acknowledgements

I thank Chandra Sekhar of Bloomsbury India for inviting me to submit a book proposal, and for readily accepting this one—it has been in the pipelines for a long time, but it took Chandra Sekhar's insistence for it to take concrete shape.

Many thanks to the ecosystem in which most of my travels occur:

My parents; parents-in-law; Nandini and Pranav, and their ever-reliable, loving support for these academic itineraries;

Friends—Ibrahim, Josy, Ajeet, Neelu, Vaishali, Haneef, Savitha, Naveed, Premlata, Shruti, Soma for their unfailing enquiries about my perambulations;

Nandana—gentle, affectionate and ever-present contributor to the traffic of ideas, and for insistence on proper localizing and historicizing of 'Theory';

Molly, a.k.a. Chechu, for her prayers, when I set out every time;

Mentor, teacher, biblio-reference desk (also available for online help and consultation), K. Narayana Chandran (KNC), whose knowledge of routes into the most unexpected, and unsuspected, of realms (from St Augustine to *Udta Punjab*) is matched only by his wit and generosity in being pathfinder—to KNC, I owe reams of pages filled with gratitude;

Gratitude, boundless, to my loving interlocutor and friend, Anna Kurian, who flags off the journey, clears the route and ensures my safe run—especially in terms of dodging disasters such as the potholes and obstacles of bad verb forms and thinking—to the destined destination. *This one is for you, Anna, fellow traveller through my, what, 40+ books?*

To Soma Ghosh, Librarian—English, of the Salar Jung Museum (SJM) Library, I express my special gratitude for finding these texts and for making my Library visits and research so comfortable and fun. Soma was not only thrilled that somebody actually wanted to use these texts, but also began her own project of digging them up and digitizing many of them;

Special mention must be made of the fact that the principal texts discussed here were discovered in a ledger-catalogue at SJM many years ago by Anna. This book's journey began with that serendipitous, Columbine moment of discovery; and

To Dinesh at SJM, for his constant good cheer and help, a separate 'Thank you'.

Parts of this book originated in the form of early essays, and I am very grateful to the editors and referees of these journals for their observations and suggestions:

1. 'Colonial Subjects and Aesthetic Understanding: Indian Travel Literature about England, 1870–1900', *South Asian Review* 33.1 (2012).
2. 'Beyond the Colonial Subject: Mobility, Cosmopolitanism and Self-fashioning in Sarat Chandra Das' *A Journey to Lhasa and Central Tibet*', *New Zealand Journal of Asian Studies* 14.2 (2012).

Excerpts from many of the travel narratives used in this book appeared in my edited collection, *Indian Travel Writing, 1830–1947* (5 volumes, Routledge, 2016).

To the reviewer of the manuscript, for incisive comments: this book is better for them, so thank you, wherever you are in the wide, wide world of Indian academia.

A part of Chapter Four, 'Vernacular Cosmopolitanism in the Age of Empire', was delivered as a plenary talk at the 'India in Travel Writings 1500–2000: Producing Knowledge, Fashioning Selves and Others' conference of the Nehru Memorial Museum and Library (NMML), New Delhi, August 2019. I gratefully acknowledge responses to my paper by Kate Teltscher and Joan-Pau Rubiés, and thank Rita Banerjee, Fellow of the NMML, for inviting me to the conference. The paper will appear in a volume on travel writing edited by Rita Banerjee.

1

Introduction

Travel and Self-fashioning in the Age of Empire

> *The chief value of travel in foreign countries ... is to enlarge one's ideas, to make them broad enough for approximation with the ideas of other nations—to make one* cosmopolitan, *in a word; cosmopolitan, not necessarily in habits and manners, but in sentiments, sympathies and aspirations.*
>
> —A.L. Roy, *Reminiscences English and American* (1888, emphasis added)

The myth that it was Europeans who travelled and discovered various peoples and places of the world has been demolished quite effectively with critical studies of travel writing by non-Europeans in the last few decades. Writing about the knowledge production by non-European and imperial travelling subjects, Paul Smethurst says:

> Mobility is the *sine qua non* of travel writing, and travel writers, having been granted mobility as imperial subjects, then assume the authority to narrate. The duty of imperial travelling subjects is then either to explore and extend the empire, or survey and reconfirm its territories and the 'within-bounds' of the places and peoples of empire. They fit experience and anecdotal evidence to existing structures, maintaining order by acting as intermediaries between the world of experience and accumulated knowledge—between the empirical and the imperial. (2009: 7)

Smethurst, therefore, sees the travelling imperial subject as 'fitting' into the imperial structures, reinforcing, mediating and translating it.

Work done on native travellers and presences in colonial England by Sukanya Banerjee (2010), Simonti Sen (2005) and Antoinette Burton (1996) has treated the Indian travellers as fitting the category of imperial citizens, and whose writings embody a certain 'guest discourse' (Codell 2007). Elleke Boehmer's *Indian Arrivals* (2015), examining the writings—travel, poetry, memoirs—produced by Indians in England in the 1870–1915 period, documents how the Indians were influential in English culture, as the metropolis began to engage with the 'imperial periphery' that had folded into its everyday processes and practices.

Others such as Javed Majeed (2007), however, argue that a mobility-driven identity is disruptive of the colonial mobility regime founded on the native-as-travellee (that is, the native is the one the Westerner travels *to*, to see and record as the object of the travel), the Westerner-as-traveller, the native traveller as labour, convict, soldiers of the Empire, among others. Mobility itself is an empowering condition for the colonial subject, and travel writing 'informs the development of global citizenry literacy because, as cultural texts, they recount an engagement in, and with, cosmopolitanism' (Johnson 2010: 80). Consequently, they 'transform themselves (variously, temporarily, and often unstably) from objects of metropolitan spectacle to exhibitors of Western mores … [and] in doing so … unsettle the boundaries of empire and remake power relations in imperial culture' (Burton 1998: 3). Elleke Boehmer has proposed that the Indian travellers

> did not see themselves as secondary or belated in relation to it [the Empire]. Rather, they mapped and decoded the city's [London's] streets with reference to a ready-made index of pre-existing images, geographical coordinates and spatial terms acquired as part of a colonial education and from the pages of colonial newspapers. (2015: 83)

From a different perspective, Sumathi Ramaswamy details the introduction and expansion of geographical knowledge embodied in the globe in Indian school textbooks, in English as well as in local languages. Ramaswamy's meticulous work shows us that, with all the chronic ailments of the English educational mission in India, 'geography was the one subject to which the [Indian] child was invariably introduced' (2018: 33). In many cases 'cartographic evangelism'—Ramaswamy's term—was linked to and embedded in Christian proselytizing—resulting in, she notes, local, vernacular efforts (such as Durgashaṇkar Pathak's in nineteenth-century Benares) to incorporate native (Hindu, Islamic) cosmologies with the European one (139–140).

That the Indian 'eye'—a trope in many Indian travel texts of the period—was capable of observing and commenting on English life itself was a marker of subjecthood that was not entirely constituted by the Empire. Antoinette Burton has argued that we consider:

> [The] Indian traveller as an 'I', a self—as the subject or see-er … rather than as merely the object of colonial rule. If the capacity to represent the western city conferred a certain kind of person—or subjecthood—on Indians, it also enables them to claim a kind of collective identity as well. (Burton 1996: 43)

Jayati Gupta argues along similar lines in her work on Indian travellers: 'the act of travel could transform a colonial subject into a "citizen of the world" … a new form of sharing and understanding that sustains the underlying rationale of becoming transnational.' (2008: 66). Gupta sees even domestic tourism narratives set in India, such as Bholanauth Chunder's, as embodying an interesting tension and vision 'of burgeoning nationhood as well as the potential of global expansion' (65). It was a cosmopolitan rather than a 'Hindoo' vision, argues Gupta (65). More importantly, travel, including travel through Europe, was an exploration of the interiority of the colonial subject, and Gupta finds an intense self-awareness in these Indian narratives. That this 'awareness of the self is problematized by the plurality of selves' (67) is a part of the cosmopolitanization of the Indian and colonial subject. Such cosmopolitan travellers were hybrids, argues Julie Codell, and as they traversed Europe, they reversed the Grand Tour's generic conventions:

> Western travel narrative naturalized 'ideal' travelers—male, privileged, and autonomous agents, possessing leisure and means to satisfy their wanderlust. Indian travelers fit this profile but were not on quests for self-discovery, which occupied Western authors. They wanted to see Britain and Europe firsthand, judge what their colonizers told them, discover what colonizers did not say, and transmit information to other Indians. They negotiated conventions of travel literature in resistance to *and* in compliance with generic expectations, creating hybrids that drew on guidebooks (in an age of guidebooks), local histories, autobiography, and ethnography.
>
> Hybridity fit their reversed Grand Tour throughout Great Britain, one of their many reversals of generic features, such as the Western smorgasbord descriptions of sights, tastes, and sounds. Most Western travelers explored the 'unexplored'—places Europeans had not been before, which they tried to dominate through heroic claims and notions of the 'other' as exotic, inferior, quaint, erotic, and picturesque. Indian travelers played with these conventions by applying them to the over-explored, over-discovered Western metropole, reversing the hierarchy of periphery and center, and recalling the aristocratic eighteenth-century Grand Tour of Europe. (2007: 174, emphasis in original)

This means, their travels deterritorialized them as Indian or British, or Anglophile Indian or Indian Briton, or Bengali-Indian-Briton, or other hybrid possibilities (175).

This book, written in the wake and influence of such studies, also envisions a different kind of imperial-subject traveller. It studies works by a variety of Indians, shipbuilders such as Jehangeer Nowrojee and Hirjeebhoy Merwanjee, who went to England to study their profession; princes and kings on a leisure tour through Europe (the Rajah of Kolhapur, and Jagatjit Singh, the Raja of Kapurthala); those who spent some time as students in England (Rakhal Das Haldar and Romesh Chunder Dutt); journalists who were also on a leisure trip to Europe (G.P. Pillai); officials of the civil services or judiciary in India or those employed in specific projects like the Colonial Exhibition (Lala Baijnath and A.L. Roy) and others. Some, such as Jagatjit Singh, went on a round-the-world tour, including in their journey, Australia, New Zealand, Ceylon, Japan, the USA, besides Europe (Rabindranath

Tagore has separate travelogues on Russia, the Middle East, Japan, South East Asia and Euro-America). Others, such as Dutt, explored England, primarily, although they would take a short trip to Paris or visit Germany, Switzerland, Austria and Norway. In most cases, though, England as the centre of the imperial world was the key site of travel.

The imperial-subject traveller arrives in England eager to see the land. His, and in many cases, her, enthusiasm for the land of the 'master', as some term England, is palpable. The traveller is awestruck at London's crowds, busyness, museums and countryside. When travelling through Europe, they pay particular attention to the natural landscape but also the people and cultural practices, dress and museums. The imperial-subject traveller also travels aware of European history and identifies monuments and memorials. The traveller negotiates the physical and cultural landscape of these nations armed with information in the form of historical knowledge and a considerable number of literary sources for the places visited. However, beginning the journey as an awestruck imperial subject, seeking nothing more than a sight of England, the Indian traveller slowly alters his—the majority of travellers examined here are men, with a couple of exceptions—identity. The Indian traveller refuses to be in just a state of wide-eyed wonder at both familiar England—familiar because most of the Indians come to England already well read about the country—and 'new' England—new because this is often their first physical encounter with England/Europe. Therefore, the Indian traveller engages with England/Europe in fascinating and diverse ways. This book is a study of the Indian travellers' forms of engagement.

It identifies four key modes through which the Indian traveller engaged with Europe and the world. By 'modes' I imply 'manner' and 'measure', a 'way' but also suggestive of 'fashion' and 'style'. The term, I believe, captures both form and content, carrying with it the nuance of specific processes and methods. 'Mode', then, signals in this book the forms of *narrative* (objective travelogue, subjective descriptions) and *experiential* (intellectual, affective) engagement with the places they travel through, the conventions of writing adopted, and the political and cultural discourses that inform the writing. It assumes that narrative and its discourses are constitutive of the identity of the traveller and the very experience of travel. It tracks, through the exploration of these modes, the several kinds of identity that the Indian traveller constructs for himself.

Thus, it demonstrates how the Indian traveller often defies the sole category of the 'imperial subject' and presents himself, via an engagement with England, Europe and the world, in particular identities. He is a nationalist cosmopolitan whose moral cosmopolitanism determines the way he perceives the English social order. He is an aesthete who is also interested in the natural as well as built-up landscape and its inhabitants embedded in an unequal society. He is a connoisseur of the exotic, but one whose attention is repeatedly drawn to the foreign-exotic within England's 'national' identity. He is enchanted by England, but transforms this enchantment into an informed one, and thereby refuses to be a wide-eyed native in the imperial capital. He examines England and Europe's history but not ascribing any superior valence, instead exploring it through its entanglements with the rest of the world. In short, the book shows the Indian traveller as remarkably well-equipped to deal with colonial and imperial cultures when, through these four modes, he sets out to alter his bestowed identity as an imperial subject and that of England as an imperial power.

The book opens with the travellers' aesthetic engagement with Europe and the world. In this, the first core chapter, it argues that the imperial subject, steeped in the conventions of the picturesque, employs it to reconstruct the England/Europe he encounters. First, the travellers insist on paying attention to social stratification, along with attention to the natural landscapes. Then, the imperial-subject traveller also includes maps, topographical data and statistics into his account when describing buildings, parks, open farmlands and homes—a variant the chapter identifies as the 'enumerative picturesque'. The Indian traveller also departs from the traditional picturesque's emphasis on the rural and the countryside in order to dwell upon the imperial centre, industrial cities and manufacturing sites in England, European cities and America, and thus invokes an 'engineered picturesque'. Documenting variety, difference and wonder in the form of statistics, the traveller compresses and packages the lands he visits and travels through into an enumerative narrative. The chapter also examines the travellers' interest in and focus on the deprived classes and the lower rungs of the social order within Europe and England. With this, the Indian traveller generates a 'subaltern picturesque'.

Through the construction of an 'Occidental exotic', the Indian travellers appropriate a method of exoticization in order to creolize Europe/England. I argue in this chapter that the traveller, even when paying attention to European history, art or places, reconstructs England as a space of the cultural Other. Exoticism here serves as an aesthetics of diversity, and in the process, the traveller deterritorializes an English countryside or European history by pointing to the presence of a non-English or non-European Other within it. Through this, the traveller overturns the ethnocentrism of the traditional European exotic and instead demonstrates its ethnodiversity. In the process, even as he admits to a sense of enchantment at the wonder that is Europe, the Indian traveller recalibrates this enchantment as an 'informed' one. Exoticism and enchantment then serve as modes of self-fashioning, whereby the traveller does not emerge as one overwhelmed by Europe but as one in control of the negotiations with European sights and in the *representations* of those sights in the form of his travelogue.

In the continuing engagement with the multiple cultures, ethnic identities and their material and symbolic presences within Europe's major cities, the Indian traveller exhibits a vernacular cosmopolitanism. Here, mediating between his sense of national identity and burgeoning nationalism, the traveller also extends his interest in Europe's subaltern Others to invoke a 'subaltern cosmopolitanism'. Appropriating both the sentimental and the moral dimensions of this cosmopolitanism, the traveller engages with Europe in a wholly different manner, as the chapter shows.

The final chapter examines the Indian traveller's portraits of 'connected histories' across Europe. It shows how the traveller asserts a different order of interpretation that gestures at the making of 'epistemic communities'. Mediating between the global and the national in the form of a dialectic—what Ngũgĩ wa Thiong'o termed the 'globalectic'—the Indian traveller thereby positions himself, yet again, at the cosmopolitan moment. Further, this traveller appropriates the traditional rhetorical device of ekphrasis to address the ruins, artwork and architectural sights he sees in Europe but modifies it in challenging and interesting ways. Positing a transnational ekphrasis that is mainly of the historical rather than the artistic kind, the chapter demonstrates how the Indian travellers' attention to the inequalities and their attendant brutalities that are inscribed into, say, Roman ruins, constitutes a politically edged historical-critical ekphrasis by the imperial subject.

In the conclusion, I suggest that antinomies constitute the self-fashioning of the traveller, rather than contradictions. Both the imperial-subject self and the nationalist-cosmopolitan self coexist within him. This is a productive tension because it enables the traveller to find re-enchantment in Europe but one that qualifies the enchantment through an attention to social inequalities or brutal histories of Europe embodied in its memorials and ruins. The antinomic self is a form of transculturation.

There are interconnections and overlaps across some of the features—thematic, formal—of the travel texts discussed here. Exoticism is a part of the aesthetics of travel writing and the globalectic imagination contributes to the cosmopolitan sensibilities of the traveller. Subaltern picturesque accounts do speak with subaltern, moral cosmopolitan approaches to the English or European people and places in the analyses of these texts. The chapters, therefore, are at once distinct and supplement each other intentionally. What I have tried to do, despite these anastomosing connections, is to draw out specific strands within each chapter's focal point, whether this is about the picturesque or the interest in tangled histories.

*

These four modes are integral to the self-fashioning of the imperial-subject traveller. The cosmopolitan whose cosmopolitanism emerges from affective and moral investments in the European poor or the English working classes, the vanquished in battle or the memories of the victims of ancient carnages and social inequality, is a complex figure indeed. There is no 'detachment' that characterizes such a cosmopolitanism. Rather, it is a cosmopolitanism rooted in the complicated position of being an imperial subject but also a member of the social elite in India, of being an imperial subject but also one who is well-versed in Western history, literature and politics and intensely aware of his own country's similarities with older colonies and oppressed nations. As an aesthete, the Indian traveller does not accord undiluted aesthetic power to the picturesque or the sublime, choosing, instead, to appropriate it in ways that demonstrate his affective spin, founded on an attention to political and social realities in England, upon the aesthetic. Reading a ruin for its chequered violent history enables the traveller to erode the English or European 'national sentiments' towards its rulers, heroes or military triumphs. Treating the exotic as a way of presenting a multicultural, multi-ethnic Europe allows the Indian traveller to represent himself as an alert outsider, appreciative of but not mesmerized by cultural difference.

These identities are to be *inferred* as emerging from the discourses and narrative modes adopted by the travellers. There are few direct representations of the self in these texts, although some attention is paid to proxemics and comportment of their embodied selves and that of their neighbours and fellow travellers in some of them. *The modes explored in this book are forms of self-fashioning by imperial subjects who would not be reduced to that subjecthood or subjectivity.*

Their selves—which Stephen Greenblatt defines as 'a sense of personal order, a characteristic mode of address to the world, a structure of bounded desires' (1980: 1)—are shaped in the 'formation and expression of identity' (1) when they engage with England and through specific modes, some of which this book explores. While the fact of being imperial subjects limits the autonomy with(in) which the Indian traveller can fashion a *different* self/identity, it does not hinder it endlessly or totally. Travel, and informed travel at that, marks the clearing of a space wherein, through specific modes of addressing England or Europe, the traveller asserts an identity as a nationalist cosmopolitan, aesthete or morally committed global citizen. Travel, in other words, proffers an alternative mode of perceiving, forming and expressing one's identity in the contexts of being in the imperial capital as a colonial subject, encountering the Englishman/woman on *his/her* own terrain, and of being an intensely self-aware subject who opts to turn the spotlight—the travelling gaze—upon the English, for a change. Attending to social inequalities or the melancholic history of oppression embedded in ruins in the form of the travel account invites us to read the account as an instantiation of the discursive art of self-fashioning.

The representation of the self in these travel accounts is complex and layered. We see, for instance, the traveller oscillating between wonder and informed wonder, admiration for English mercantile, imperial or industrial successes and empathy with those who paid the price or did not benefit from these successes. This produces for our consumption an alert imperial subject, whose engagement with the Empire is imbued with a healthy scepticism towards its triumphs and an awareness of the material realities beneath the picturesque properties, exotic exhibits or treasured ruins. The traveller experienced the social pressures of being an imperial subject but did not allow himself to be decimated by them. Assigning to himself the task of interpreting England, the traveller in the process transforms (fashions) himself as a critical observing eye, a subject of observation rather than the object of (imperial, white, racialized) observation of the European travelogue. When this interpretation was inflected by nationalist concerns, moral and sentimental views of humanity, an interest in 'the human condition', it enabled a self larger than the imperial-subject one.

This is not to say that the Indian traveller escapes the 'colonized native' tag in its entirety. Given the fact that his travel was made possible by the mobility regimes of the Empire, his own social status (privileged, socially connected, upper caste and upper-class Indian male, in most cases), such an escape is unthinkable. Hence, we see expressions of wonder at England, gratitude towards English benevolence, and an acceptance of English modernity and location at the top of the evolutionary scale, all of which point, or implicitly signal, an imperial-subject identity. Yet, what these travelogues also demonstrate is the impossibility of reducing the Indian traveller to this identity—and this is entirely the result of a very effective set of self-fashioning modes, in terms of the discursive constructions of the cosmopolitan, humanitarian or aesthetic self.

Self-fashioning, then, is the refusal to submit to an assigned identity, appropriating a set of discursive strategies—modes—that then create a different identity of the traveller, one that we can trace in their many-layered texts.

2

Colonial Subjects and Their Dislocated Aesthetics

I also paid a visit to St. Paul's Cathedral ... It is also a large stone structure with towers and a lofty dome, greatest of all the landmarks of London. On entering it I was struck with the vastness of the internal space, the part under the dome being quite a maze of lofty grand arches ... Their [the walls'] dirty grey look, caused probably by the soot deposited by the smoke of the London chimneys, was very disappointing. The walls of St Pauls in Calcutta look far cleaner and nicer, notwithstanding all the dust and damp of a tropical climate.

—N.L. Doss, *Reminiscences, English and Australasian* (1893: 49)

Indian travellers, particularly those travelling in the second half of the nineteenth century, demonstrating evidence of considerable reading in English literary and other texts, appear to have assimilated the cultural codes and grammar of a specific aesthetic when viewing the countries they travelled to, especially England. The picturesque, which reigned during the late eighteenth and through the nineteenth centuries in England, found strong resonances in the transatlantic world's travel texts and landscape writing as well (Bramen 2002). 'The picturesque mode', writes Silvia Marchetti, 'while it emerged and consolidated in the seventeenth and eighteenth centuries, was not only cosmopolitan in reach, but also incredibly lasting over time' (2009: 402). The aesthetic serves the Indian traveller with a framework within which to view the places he was travelling through.

I draw my informing assumption for reading these accounts from Tim Fulford's work in *Landscape, Liberty and Authority* (1996). Fulford argues that discourses of landscape—a 'representation which claims simply to describe nature, but also to writing which uses the motifs and scenes of landscape-description in the course of critical and political arguments'—conferred a certain authority upon their writers (1). Fulford writes: 'within the polite and tasteful description of a scene in which natural (and national) order could be viewed was a struggle for authorial power' (1). Among these descriptions and accounts Fulford discerns the debate over taste, especially among the propertied classes where

> the ability to distinguish and possess shared standards independent of self-interest (standards of aesthetic value or taste) in agreement about the beauty or sublimity of landscape seemed not only a mark of the viewer's gentlemanliness but a criterion for the exercise of legitimate social and political power. (3)

The larger concern in this chapter, building on Fulford's reading, is the appropriation of aesthetic modes when describing natural and built European/global landscapes by the imperial-subject traveller who, by definition, lacks social and political authority in the imperial capital. The thesis forwarded here is that such aesthetics, suitably modified, enabled a self-fashioning in and offered a measure of authority to the imperial-subject traveller. To this end, I examine the appropriation of the picturesque aesthetic in Indian travel writing in the nineteenth century. Admittedly, in the Indian travellers, the 'commanding view' would not afford them, in England or in Europe, either 'paternal authority' over the land or 'official and institutionalized supervision, by which the poor are as much controlled as relieved' as was the case in the traditional English picturesque (Fulford 1996: 10). However, I argue, landscape aesthetics did give the colonial travellers a chance to 'transform themselves (variously, temporarily, and often unstably) from objects of metropolitan spectacle to exhibitors of Western mores … [and] in doing so … unsettle the boundaries of empire and remake power relations in imperial culture' (Burton 1998: 3).

The picturesque was not a unified aesthetic within England or in its transatlantic form, and variants such as the metropolitan picturesque, the antiquarian picturesque, the engineered picturesque have been identified by commentators. The picturesque, argues Denys Van Renen, had an endless capacity to subsume various cultural practices, besides indigenes, animals, plants, and terrain into itself so that it effectively constrains 'our ability to disentangle natural processes from cultural ones' (2015: 167). Van Renen argues a case for 'the breathtaking power of the picturesque to disarticulate widely divergent natural and socio-cultural processes'. The picturesque as an aesthetic was concerned with, of course, the representation of landscapes in pictorially attractive modes and the 'improvement'—a key term in the discourse of the picturesque—of the land so that it approximated a picture. But this was also an aesthetic deeply concerned with the question of perception. Rosemary Hill notes that at least one dominant strand of thought within the picturesque debate, in the work of Richard Payne Knight, for example, argued that 'aesthetic experience was dependent on the beholder, on memory, association, and context' (Hill 2014: 123). That is to say, the picturesque as an aesthetic mode did provide for considerations of the observing eye, the contexts of observations and the various cultural factors and practices that informed perception. It meant that the subject-self of the observer would inform, but equally would be informed by the aesthetic. Aligning Van Renen's and Rosemary Hill's recent readings with Fulford's examination of the discourse of landscape, I suggest that the aesthetics of reading the lands they were travelling in was central to the self-fashioning of the imperial-subject.

While the picturesque was, traditionally, aligned with nationalist ideas and geocultural specificity, it was also possible to expand its terms to include other lands. Will Mackintosh speaks of this 'capaciousness' of the picturesque:

> For Gilpin, the beautiful described that which was well formed and human-scale; the contemplation of the beautiful was essentially a humanizing and pleasurable experience. By contrast, the sub-lime was characterized by a combination of astonishment and terror, and necessarily turned the viewer's thoughts to the almighty and the eternal. And the picturesque balanced the two in pleasing harmony. Gilpin's definitions were profoundly vague and contextual, especially compared to the philosophical rigor of Burke. But the vagueness of the picturesque was precisely its power; in its popular usage, it could be applied to any appealing landscape and was a sufficiently capacious concept to describe the cultural ambitions of many and diverse travelers on both sides of the Atlantic. (2014: 91)

Acquainted with the English aesthetic and poetic traditions, the imperial-subject traveller appropriated this capacious mode of landscape description for his own purposes, as Mackintosh claims was the case with the American picturesque writers.

The picturesque, as employed by the colonial subject offers us interesting new trajectories in landscape description and tourist accounts. N.L. Doss's passage for instance, while focusing on the splendour and majesty of its built environment, is also marked by an attention to the stained nature of these buildings, or their inadequacies. Others, such as Jehangeer Nowrojee and Hirjeebhoy Merwanjee, in the process of praising the London parks, which are, in the true picturesque tradition, 'inclosed in by iron railings with handsome gateways', note that 'more wealth, more respectability, more beauty is to be seen collected in one spot than is to be found congregated in any other part of the world', thereby noting the social stratification in English society even as they appreciate the landscape (1841: 100). With this, Nowrojee and Merwanjee set themselves up as men of taste and authority, with a clear humanitarian-social concern for the poor in the landscape.

The Indian travellers did pay attention to, and write about, England and Europe's natural picturesque in ways that clearly imply a knowledge of the grammar of such writings. Here, for instance, is an account of the natural picturesque:

> We kept ascending an eminence for four miles, when we came to a magnificent prospect from the top of what is called Blue Bell Hill ... From the top of the hill Mr Baldock pointed out to us a bungalow, or a countryhouse, erected by an intimate friend and relative of his … And as some of our happiest hours in India are spent in bungalows, this, and the extensive and varied view, and the strong gleam of sunshine, gladdened our hearts … The view from Blue Bell Hill, all the way to the Kitscottie House, is very pleasing; there was not, it is true, any of the grand features of picturesque scenery. There are, however, a long range of hills which bound the view; and in the bottom, the river Medway, which takes an immense number of circuits, and which adds much to the beauty of the view. Corn fields, green meadows, orchards, hop gardens, here were all blended together, and formed a varied scenery. (Nowrojee and Merwanjee 1841: 291–292)

Immediately after this, they would describe 'one of the prettiest pictures that can be imagined, embracing the picturesque bridge, the old fashioned church, and the village—all surrounded and shut in by beautiful green verdure, form a scene of quiet …' (293). That Nowrojee and Merwanjee are able to say that the scene lacked the 'grand features of picturesque scenery' implies an awareness of the aesthetic and landscape discourse of the time.

Romesh Dutt when travelling through Ireland pays particular attention to the natural scenery:

> We took a long drive in a car, and then had a ride through one of the wildest valleys that I have ever seen, the 'Gap of Dunloe'. It is not quite so bleak and barren as the vale of Glencoe in Scotland, but the mountains are quite as high and the whole scene is quite as wild and picturesque. Emerging from that valley we came to the lakes and took a boat. The scenes through which we then passed defy all description. Enough be it to say that it is the wildest and the most picturesque scene that can be made up of mountains, rivulets, lakes, islands, creeks, promontories, and wild vegetation. The lakes being surrounded on all sides by high mountains, every loud sound was echoed most distinctly. (1896: 76–77)

These are classic instantiations of the picturesque, complete with the 'prospect view' (Barrell 1992), the boundaries and the harmonious variety, with the wild included as well. Immediately after the above passage on the picturesque Dutt would invoke the sublime as well, speaking of 'Llanberis Pass … which in its aspect of bleak sublimity yields to none else that I have yet seen' (80). Dutt would employ the language of the picturesque in describing Sweden, Norway and other parts of Europe too (158, 188, 200 and elsewhere). Others such as Baijnath would also take recourse to the language of picturesque aesthetics when speaking of European cities and the countryside. P.C. Mozoomdar would employ the aesthetic to describe Niagara (1884: 88), Emerson's village of Concord (103), the city of Washington (110), and so on. T.N. Mukharji speaks of Edinburgh as 'one of the most picturesque towns ever built by man on the face of the earth' (1902: 271) and uses the term 'picturesque' to describe Perth (275), Oxford (303) and Florence (375).

My interest here is not limited, however, to the extent to which the Indian travellers fit into and employ the idiom and grammar of the natural or civic picturesque with a focus on people and their lives, with attention to constructed buildings, city spaces and social settings (rather than just landscape and topography, see Andrews 1994), or the sublime, as invoked in the passages from Dutt and Nowrojee and Merwanjee. Rather, I wish to examine what I take to be their major reformatting of the aesthetic itself, to serve the purposes of self-fashioning. This chapter proposes that Indian colonial subjects, when employing the picturesque in England, Europe or other regions, often modified it considerably. In the hands of the colonial travellers, different signifiers entered the picturesque narrative about England/Europe, from steel and concrete structures signifying engineering and human culture rather than nature, to England's deprived poor, signifying the ugliness (rather than the valourizing in the traditional mode) of the picturesque.

Three modifications, with attendant and appropriate signifiers and rhetorics, of the picturesque may be traced in the travel writings.

First, the travellers' insistence on paying attention to social stratification, urban poverty, tainted buildings, obscurity of vision and political economy, aligned with a sense of race-differentials (of being colonial subjects in the imperial centre) in the countries they travel through, generates a 'subaltern picturesque'. The 'subaltern' in the phrase refers to the racialized subaltern status of the Indian traveller within the imperial capital (even though these were very elite travellers). But it also signals their attention to subaltern conditions, contexts and populations within the Euro-American physical and sociocultural landscape. The subaltern picturesque in the hands of the colonial subject is not a mere aesthetic of landscape 'appreciation'. The aesthetic, while following the conventions of Euro-American picturesque tourism, deviates enough from the grammar to serve as a mode of social critique of England, European culture and the imperial. The aesthetic is modified to incorporate discordant elements—such as class tensions, real poverty—into itself and consequently, instead of the harmony that marks the picturesque, we perceive disruption and dissonance.

Commentators examining the aesthetics' dissemination on both sides of the Atlantic have observed that the praise of (picturesque) poverty—a hallmark of the English picturesque in Uvedale Price and others—is tempered by their attention to the reality of the poor, and often tied in with a certain paternalism towards this poor (Fulford 1996: 138). This divided attention, argues Josephine Baker, *detracts* from the picturesque (2016: 427). Michael Martin argues that in the case of American travel writing:

> The picturesque mode is marked by particular aesthetic characteristics that both Bryant and Strother invoke in subtle ways in their respective studies of the American landscape. Specifically, they gesture towards elite standards of taste and privilege while, at the same time, modifying its criteria to include the plebeian, or everyday, for a given aesthetic experience. (2015: 77)

Others have noted that an attention to the 'ruined subjects' (Mukherjee 2009: 27) alters the aesthetic vision of the picturesque. It was never, Baker observes of Hawthorne, a purely aesthetic vision, but one imbued with an awareness of social stratification and more importantly, of social inequalities in the picturesque city or gardens. My argument about the subaltern picturesque draws upon these theorists tracking the variants in the aesthetic resulting in the dislocated aesthetics of the chapter's title, or a fractured picturesque. It is the composition of this fracture that the chapter traces.

Second, the imperial-subject traveller also incorporates maps, topographical data and statistics into his account when describing buildings, parks, open farmlands and even homes. Jhinda Ram walking through London's zoological gardens is delighted at the fact that the 'native of the coldest country in the world and the natives of the hottest regions of the earth [are] placed within a few yards of each other' (1893: 43). But he also notes, in the same breath, that the ponds and dens are numbered (43). Nowrojee and Merwanjee, while appreciating the urban picturesque of London, spend considerable time describing the dimensions of buildings, dates of construction, topographical locations, etc. (1841: 216–231). Lala Baijnath gives us the number of hansoms and omnibuses (1893: 34), post offices (35), costs of memorials (37), among others. In this version of the picturesque, what one may term the 'statistical picturesque', we discern aesthetic descriptions seeking an approximation to the topographical map and the scientific account. Just as Dahlia Porter sees in certain nineteenth-century travelogues an attempt to eschew the picturesque's 'effusive sentimentality' in favour of topography to document the 'veracity and truth of the nation's geography out of the mists of its obscure past' (2013: 164), these travellers, though alert to the sentimental nature of their antiquarianism when looking at England, also seek to create a statistical account that would be more 'objective' and perhaps distanced. The statistical picturesque is a shorthand term for this intergenre of the aesthetic account and the topographical study where numbers and maps jostle for narrative space with sentimental antiquarianism and aesthetic appreciation. This emphasis on providing information in the work of Nowrojee and Merwanjee leads Michael Fisher to argue that they 'used the

British informational travel guide genre to inform future Indian visitors what to expect from their trip to Britain' (2006: 101).

Third, the colonial subject departs from the traditional picturesque's emphasis on the rural and the countryside in order to dwell upon the imperial centre and the metropolis in England, Europe and America. Doss devotes an entire chapter to the manufacturing districts of Leeds, Manchester, Bolton and Sheffield. He describes the city, the working conditions, the manufacturing processes and the quality of products. Admiring these great industrial centres and the power they embody, Doss writes:

> Their position as a nation, their power, their wealth, their superiority over others ... they owe these to their great industry, perseverance, energy, skill, and to a determined will to meet with success, as will be clearly noticed by every one visiting these manufacturing districts, the real seat of the power and greatness of England. (1893: 121)

Industry, as the very meaning of the word indicates, is both a descriptor of the quality of work of the people and the products of a technical, mechanized process. Accounts of parks and landscapes where natural settings are modelled and even altered through the inclusion of concrete structures and built environments come in for the fascinated attention of the colonial subject. Incorporating the industrial within the picturesque, I suggest, generates the third dominant mode of the aesthetic, the 'engineered picturesque'.

Together, the three forms of the picturesque as traced within Indian travel writing may be said to embody a dislocated aesthetic. I use the term 'dislocated' to emphasize both: the displaced location of the traveller away from his homeland and subsequent relocation as a mobile observer in a new land, and the modifying of the aesthetic at their hands into a different kind of picturesque. The latter is one that focuses on the engineered and incorporates discourses—such as topography or the statistical—that then construct the land they travel in very different ways from the conventional picturesque.

This chapter will examine the enumerative and the engineered picturesque before turning, in the last and lengthier section, to the subalternized picturesque.

The Enumerative Picturesque

As he seeks to capture England's greatness and variety, Jhinda Ram proffers a vast quantum of statistical, cartographic and topographic data. He first cites figures of London's population from the 1881 Census, followed by statistics of housing, coffee houses and pubs, the city's consumption of coffee, wheat, liquor, meats, and coal, the extent of sewage canals, the number of theatres, music halls and concert rooms, the incomes of the London Corporation, statistics of street accidents, and figures on missing children (1893: 17–18). He gives the timings (24) and extent of the omnibus network. Jhinda Ram's narrative at once captures the magnitude of London and the cognitive wonder at this. Seeking to impose some form of textual control over this magnitude, Jhinda Ram takes recourse to an enumerative narrative scheme where statistics encapsulate London's diversity, vastness and variety. His account of London's transport network reads as follows:

> Their 668 omnibuses work daily. In 1885 they carried 58,389,997 passengers, over 13,229,219 miles, and earned, at an average of about 2 1/2 d[imes] each passenger, the sum of 576,780. Each bus earned at the rate of £ 18 a week. The Company's stud of horses numbered 7242. (23–24)

He also offers information about the number of deliveries the postal system of London makes, and the names of the districts, with their abbreviations in the form of a table (25–26). Ram later on various pages lists the costs of the Albert Memorial (48) and the London docks (83). He even numbers the buildings destroyed in the great fire of London of 1666 (44). Lala Baijnath also provides statistics of the numbers of carriages (34), omnibuses (34), post offices and pillar boxes (35), as well as the number of letters delivered (36). He also offers us the statistics for the Bodleian Library (144), demographic data and statistics on lectures delivered in English universities (148–149), specific engineering feats such as the Victoria Station (185) and industrial production (193). Nowrojee and Merwanjee produce tables of data: about London's bridges and their span, materials, date of opening (1841: 55), population (59–61) and others.

This enumerative—by which I mean the statistical, topographic and cartographic—discourse in the imperial-subject's travelogue fractures the aesthetics of the traditional picturesque.

Dahlia Porter examining English picturesque writings from the late eighteenth century onwards notes a 'materialist bent to the antiquarian project' (2013: 167). The traditional picturesque in William Gilpin and others embodied a 'purified topography' wherein 'the focal point was shifted from human action in the foreground to an object (cattle, bridge, building, etc.) in the middle ground, with interest created by adding variety to the landscape features (multiplying types of trees, rocks, clouds, etc.)', (168). This traditional picturesque is inverted by the enumerative picturesque.

The enumerative picturesque swerves away from the older picturesque's melancholic antiquarianism towards a more impersonal narrative mode. The imperial-subject traveller with this mode of documentation appears keen to offer a different order of legitimacy to their work. That is, in the place of the sentimental view of and response to the vistas and variety of England and Europe, the traveller delivers a 'scientific' account that, while capturing the pleasant scenes of buildings, industry and landscape, does so in terms of quantitative data. With this, the imperial-subject traveller fractures the aesthetic by aligning his work with the representational techniques of topographical and physical geography conventions of the era rather than with the traditional sentimental picturesque.

The imperial-subject traveller positions himself in an entirely different relation to the land and its features through the enumerative picturesque. While appreciative of the sights, achievements and beauty of the diversity, distance and demographics of, say, London or Paris, the narrative simultaneously asserts a form of editorial and perspectival control over this variety through the quantitative mode.

Statistical discourse popular across various fields in the social sciences of the time was used as a means of persuading readers brought up on anecdote and sentimental rhetoric, while also contributing to the making of an 'imagined community'—with scientists, land surveyors, mathematicians, perhaps—in Europe/England. It also claimed a kind of transparent access to the object it represented (Poovey 1993). More importantly, as Poovey argues, such a discourse, even when it limited itself to what can be counted, depended on the 'unfigured', because its characteristics depended on the uncounted. Poovey's argument has primarily to do with the rise of statistical thinking and political arithmetic in 1830s England. But it does not seem too far-fetched, given their exposure to and education in, Western modes of thinking, that the Indian travellers were well aware of this shift from sentimental, anecdotal discourse to the mathematical, even though they do not entirely abandon the sentimental, as we shall see in the last section of this chapter and in the rise of a moral cosmopolitanism (in a latter chapter).

When Nowrojee and Merwanjee observe and record the expansion of the English and Irish rail network, they speculate on the economic advantages of the same. They write: 'in a commercial point of view, this railway will bring Ireland and London nearer each other', before citing extensively an essay from the *London Saturday Journal* that documents the connections and routes (83–86). Nowrojee and Merwanjee replace their words with that of an authoritative text. But they do more than just cite: they define their perspective on the railway network and align it with the prevalent discourse of the time when they say 'in a commercial point of view'. I propose, following Poovey, that Nowrojee and Merwanjee first concede the commercial benefits of the railways to England and Ireland, thereby presenting themselves as people capable of recognizing this specific advantage. In other words, their employment of the commercial perspective, or their insertion into circulating discourses of accounting in the form of the commercial benefits of the railways, is a mode of self-fashioning where they set themselves up as 'foreigners' who can see these advantages for England. This means, not only do they reveal themselves as capable of such understanding, but also locate themselves in an imagined community of English and Irish supporters of the railway development project. Their tone of admiration for the expanded network and the efforts being made is given statistical and economic legitimacy with this, resulting also in a tweaking of the traditional picturesque's sentimentality with the commercial and the geographical.

This tweaking and combining the picturesque with the statistical is employed throughout his narrative by Romesh Chunder Dutt. He describes the heights of hills and monuments in and around Edinburgh, in some cases describing them as 'magnificent', before giving us the dimensions (49). We get to hear of the population of Glasgow (61), Aberdeen (65), the unique Lapp population which attracts his attention in Norway, Sweden and Russia (169) and the dimensions of various historic buildings (185, 223). Picturesque appreciation shades into topographical and statistical narrative in each of these cases. Dutt's account, like Baijnath's already cited earlier, constitutes a narrative cartography. 'Narrative cartography' involves the use of actual maps within stories (including journalism or films), often as supporting evidence for the stories (Caquard and Cartwright 2014, Caquard and Fiset 2014, Cromley 2017). There are no actual maps in these texts, but there are interesting forms of the cartographic data that are introduced.

I suggest that the introduction of locations, distances, routes, costs of travel, time to traverse, boundaries and networks in these texts serve as 'cartographic signifiers' (Denis Wood, cited in Cromley 2017: 307) that are a part of the enumerative picturesque. The cartographic signifier, first and foremost, enables the imperial-subject traveller to establish authority through transparent access to the object he claims to describe, mainly because this is what the impersonal statistical discourse achieves. This authority draws upon and simultaneously constructs the traveller's practises of observation and documentation as aesthetic *and* epistemological: that is, at once as an appreciation of the views/sights and an evaluative, calculating, appraising kind of observation. Cartographic signifiers are steps towards the making of the knowledgeable traveller because it makes use of both the aesthetic and the epistemological observational modes of documenting the countries visited. Thus, when Sullaiman Mahomed offers us detailed descriptions of Chicago city, its trade fare and a variety of data, ranging from the price of cattle to costs incurred in constructing public buildings, from the number of rooms in hotels to the number of artesian wells, he is enacting a particular self (1895: 120–125). He is then no longer a wondering imperial-subject traveller overawed by the sights. Rather, he is one who delivers this same sense of wonder via 'impersonal' facts and figures.

Yet, cartographic signifiers are *not* impersonal or objective. As Mary Poovey has demonstrated, figures of speech and figures of arithmetic are often mutually supportive and supplement each other. Take, for instance, the enmeshing of the two in Mahomed's account.

> I was astonished to see a carving machine turn out four or five statues at a time in a few minutes. There were, besides, remarkable old clocks, a map of the world made 400 years ago, and some gigantic bells from Berlin, one of which was 7,000 pounds in weight, requiring the combined strength of three men to ring it. There was a monster gun by Krupp, 127 tons in weight. (125)

Or later, describing the traffic in London:

> Amidst such huge traffic, it is no easy matter for the bewildered stranger to cross the road. Equally busy with traffic is the old bridge across the Thames. It is stated that 500,000 persons and 20,000 carriages pass over it daily! (267)

Or about the Royal Albert Hall:

> Near this region is the Royal Albert Hall, with accommodation for 8,000. Here concerts and other entertainments take place. The hall has cost £ 200,000. I once went to a concert in which 1,000 persons took part, half the number of the performers being girls. I was awe-struck with the splendour and magnificence of the performance. The orchestra consisted of 125 persons. What charming music! How beautiful the female forms that danced and sung on the stage. How delicious the whole scene! (270)

More staid descriptions but of the enumerative kind occur elsewhere too. Here is Syed Ahmed Khan on Marseilles, opening with his emotions on his first view of the city: 'we were truly astounded as we had never seen such a beautifully decorated city …' (2011: 127–128). He concludes this letter with:

> It has a population of 3,00,131. Seven thousand men are employed at various engineering workshops, 52 steam machines make soaps and produce 16,80,000 units each year; there are 28 steam oil-pressing machines to macerate oil producing 1,12,000 tons every year. Every year 50,000 red Turkish caps are also produced. The city has churches, museums, public libraries, picture galleries, theatres and zoological gardens. (129)

Khan's astonishment at the city's industrialized modernity—traffic, lights, roads—a variant of the metropolitan picturesque, demands attention to the marvel of *quantity* as well. Elsewhere, viewing the landscape on a train journey, Khan would again admire the conjunction of nature and culture elsewhere:

> Human designs on nature's beauty doubly enhanced its character; as far as eyes could see, the land was turned into beautiful floral gardens and wainscots with lush green grass. The canal water reached each and every piece of the land, gardens and wainscots through channels. Water coming through those channels in grass planks looked delightful. Watching such wonderful spectacles of nature, we reached the Lyons Railway Station. (132. Also, for other instances, 144–145)

The liberal use of exclamations and descriptors such as 'bewildered' and tropes such as 'monster' disturbs the attempted objective tenor of the statistical narrative in Mahomed's account, and the statistical undermines the expressions of wonder and thrill. This mix of rhetorical modes in the passages cited is, I suggest, a major move in the self-fashioning of the Indian traveller.

The rhetoric of Mahomed's description merges both the language of sentiment, with the tropes of astonishment and awe, with the language of numbers and enumeration. Accounts such as Dutt's and Mahomed's that merge the affective-figurative with the enumerative offer a cartography of emotions of particular spaces. This cartography is often described as a 'cognitive cartography' that studies the 'emotional responses to various cartographic designs as well as … represent emotions perceived and expressed in certain places' (Caquard and Fiset 2014: 103). Documenting both statistics and sentiment, the Indian traveller has produced an extraordinary cognitive cartography of the places he travels in. The enumerative picturesque relies on such a cognitive cartography that merges numbers and sentiment, maps and affect, to produce an aesthetic that is fractured. The enumerative picturesque is a major step in the Indian traveller's self-fashioning as a rational being with an awareness of political arithmetic, economics and spatial organization because it flies in the face of the centuries-old stereotype of the sentimental Asian native.

The emphasis on rational mapping and documentation in the Indian travelogue of the nineteenth century recalls a similar tradition in the European examples of the genre, dating back to the eighteenth century and the Enlightenment. In the European case, this presumed rationality of observation was embedded within the context of imperialism. Thus, Paul Smethurst has proposed that what distinguished modern forms of imperialism was its emphasis on rationality:

> The innovation was the idea of enclosing, naming, and 'rationalising' geographical space on a planet-wide scale. This was what distinguished

> European imperialism from earlier symbolic geographies and structures of power … the scientific and rational approach, through which the 'truth-regime' of this imperialist order is effected … (2009: 5)

Further, as critics of travel writing note, the scientific travelogue and the adventure travelogue both seek to 'locate' the Oriental. Ali Behdad writes: 'The knowledge of geography enables the scientific traveller to situate the Orient in spatial terms, while his historical knowledge allows him to locate it in time' (2009: 86). Elsewhere, Smethurst would argue that the presumably scientific and rational forms of observation constitute the 'evidence of systematic practices for finding order in (and imposing order on) the space of nature' (2012: 20). Rationality, embodied as mapping and numbering, for instance, is then a characteristic of the *Western* traveller.

However, we can discern a similar *rationalizing* impulse and its accompanying representational strategies in the Indian traveller's texts as well. If Smethurst and Behdad are correct in their premises, then when the Indian traveller appropriates the Western travelogue's strategy of naming, numbering, dating and locating against the Western lands, as noted in the enumerative picturesque narratives cited above, what does he achieve? While not imperial in the European sense of territorial acquisition, the Indian traveller certainly produces an epistemological and editorial conquest of the foreign land.

It may be further argued that the aesthetics of the enumerative picturesque demonstrates a degree of intentionality on the part of the traveller. The traditional picturesque too, as Paul Carter argued (1987: 243), demonstrated an intentionality. My point, however, is slightly different. Here intentionality has a political agenda because intentionality in the attention paid to the object, implies (as art critics such as Barbara Maria Stafford propose, 2009) a connectedness to the outside world. This intentionality distinguishes, Stafford argues, cognition and attention, from just routine subjective consciousness. It is this connectedness implied in the attention and the intentionality that contributes to a whole new order of self-fashioning in the Indian traveller.

The travellers map with considerable care and meticulous documentation—often relying on and cross-checking with other sources, surely—the object's dimensions, locate its costs, uses and functions, situate it within histories *and* express their wonder at all of them, as Mahomed does. I suggest that the enumerative picturesque underscores this connectedness and situatedness of the imperial-subject traveller in foreign lands. This means, the Indian traveller presents himself, temporarily and implicitly rather than explicitly, as a man-of-this-*European*-world rather than just an outsider in England, Europe or America. In other words, the enumerative picturesque is instrumental in positioning the alien traveller as one who is connected to the land he is travelling through, implying both intentionality and a degree of immersive insiderhood.

The Engineered Picturesque

G.P. Pillai writes, 'Every five minutes there is a fresh train ... How surprising! And these trains are underground!' (2006: 9). Lala Baijnath is even more wonderstruck: 'The Metropolitan and District Railways of London ... are really triumphs of John Bull's energy and perseverance in the means of locomotion employed in his metropolis' (1893: 35). N.L. Doss exhibits a fair amount of anxious wonder at the crowded streets when he records, 'There is a ceaseless stream of vehicles pouring in from the several roads' (1893: 39). Jagatjit Singh's first comments on London include the now-mandatory one on its crowds: 'I greatly marvelled at the enormous traffic in the streets as I drove along' (1895: 60). The very first comment T.B. Pandian makes about London records bewilderment and anxiety. The setting, yet again, is the railway system:

> Alighting at one of the many platforms of the Victoria Station, London, the Oriental stranger is bewildered by the number of such landings he views about him, his unaccustomed eyes being familiar with no more than three on Indian lines. (1897: 4)

As tourists, while they undertook the usual countryside tours of England and Europe, the Indian travellers were fascinated by London. Many also visited industrial towns like Leeds, Birmingham and factories in various cities. This departure from the standard picturesque is worth exploring for what it achieves in the imperial-subject's travelogue.

The railways are a means of accessing the picturesque urban centres, countryside and landscapes of England and Europe. This makes the rail network integral to *how* the land is made available. The description of scenic routes in Europe that we find in these travellers may be seen as the mechanical equivalent of Wordsworth's walking tours through the Lake District. Second, 'riding on mechanized transportation was in itself an immersive aesthetic experience of landscape' (Mackintosh 2014: 92). When Dutt speaks of viewing Scotland's 'fertile lowlands', which are a relief from 'so much of the barren rocks and heaths and mountains of the highlands', he is not only speaking of the landscape, but the mode through which the landscape is experienced: from a train (1896: 69).[1]

Rakhal Das Haldar visits the town of Reading where he first observes the old buildings, the 'clean' corn market before turning to the biscuit factory. He is shown the processes and the various kinds of biscuits and cakes manufactured there. He terms the activities 'truly marvellous' (1903: 68). N.L. Doss visits a cutlery factory (1893: 120–121) and a jute factory (126). Like others, Doss is suitably impressed by the rail network (86–87). The Rajah of Kolhapur visits the Bank of England and observes the printing process (which he describes as 'a wonderful machine' [Rajah Ram Chuttraputtee 1872: 28]), a woollen factory (41), the fire-engine (56), a silk factory (58), among others. Nowrojee and Merwanjee visit sawmills (1841: 253–257), ordnance factories (309) and other industries (they were in England to learn shipbuilding, in fact).

This attention to industry, manufacturing and technology in England and Europe has been noted by critics. Simonti Sen notes that urbanism as an index of England's modernity was the focus of all travellers, and that most of them recorded their astonishment at the sights (2005: 76–77). But it was not just awe at England's industrial modernity that draws one's attention in these texts, but the narrative that treats these as forms of the 'engineered picturesque'.

Ann Komara writing of the construction and renovation of the Paris' Parc des Buttes Chaumont in the mid-nineteenth century uses the term 'engineered picturesque' to describe the 'transformation of the picturesque idiom from a residential to an urban aesthetic' with the use of new industrial materials (2004: 5). Komara also notes the popular 'acceptance of fabricated elements of this picturesque landscape; this quality was especially present in the various applications of concrete' (6). While Komara is referring specifically to the alteration of the picturesque garden aesthetic through the incorporation of concrete and industrial elements, I use the term 'engineered picturesque' to describe the apparent harmony between human bodies/labouring bodies, machinery and the landscape (rural or urban), a feature I see as echoing the harmony of humans, topography and life forms characteristic of the traditional picturesque. I take my cue for this reading of the picturesque from Mary-Ann Constantine's short entry on the 'industrial picturesque' on the British Library (London) website, in the series 'Picturing Places' (Constantine n.d.). Examining the work of John Hassell, William Havell and others, Constantine perceives the existence of an industrial picturesque where the artists 'portray a world of low-key, local industry, where nature, architecture and human activity appear in harmonious balance'. It is a balance, she reiterates, between 'human industry and nature'.

Nowrojee and Merwanjee visit a sawmill and are impressed at 'one of the simplest and prettiest pieces of mechanism' they ever saw (256). The machinery adapts to the elevated piece of land on which the mill is situated ('the building stands on an eminence' [256]):

> The ground on the north side of the mill is appropriated to the storage of timber. Rafts were floated from the river by means of a canal, which

> runs open about two hundred and fifty feet, and on entering the rising ground, becomes a tunnel about three hundred and thirty feet in length ... (1841: 256)

The whole operation, they term 'astonishing' (256). Other examples of such sights of industry occur elsewhere too (258). Nowrojee and Merwanjee refer here, Mary-Ann Constantine would say, to the way in which the land's topography and physical geography (hill, river), the machinery and the human bodies are integrated seamlessly to produce pretty and efficient industries. Labour and landscape are brought together and mediated by the machinery. Approximating to the picturesque's integration of a variety of fauna, flora, buildings and people, into a harmonious 'composition' that constitutes the pretty picture, Nowrojee and Merwanjee's account combines a wholly different set of diverse things, from machinery to man. That they then describe it as a 'pretty' sight recalls the nineteenth century's rhetoric of picturesque descriptions.

In another example, about Cromwell town, A.J. Appasamy has this to say:

> The climate of the town is very invigorating and wholesome. The town has risen to importance owing to the chief industry of Cromwell Gardens where a yearly average of five hundred employees are engaged in producing flowers and plants over an area of 500 acres of land and in several hundred greenhouses measuring 0 feet to 900 feet in length and 20 feet to 40 feet in breadth ...
>
> An added attraction is 'Cromwell Gardens Park'. It is situated in a valley above the greenhouses and is becoming "one of the interesting beauty spots of the country". A rose-garden of 4,000 plants and the largest Alpine garden in the country are important features of the tiny little park. Surrounding these, the evergreen nursery makes an attractive background, and a beautiful contrast with the small artificial lakes that have been added. (1929: 80–81)

Akin to what Komara argues about the Parisian park, Appasamy appreciates the industrial elements—greenhouses, artificial lakes—that transform a naturally fertile landscape (Cromwell's climate being part of the natural elements) into a pretty sight. One notes, in the wake of Constantine's and Komara's arguments, that the picturesque landscape described here is not entirely natural and demands the constant industrious labour of both men and machines, the infusion of non-natural materials such as lighting, glass, concrete and metal.

Syed Ahmed Khan, in his letters written from Europe and England 1869–1870, visiting the palaces in France notes the creation of lakes and waterbodies:

> I was astounded to see the beauty of ponds, streams, fountains and springs, the ingenious ways of springing fountains from natural-looking artificial items such as statues, and animal heads, beautiful twists and turns of waterways and streams, beautifully trimmed shrubs and big trees, sculptures representing men holding each other in arm with their hand joined, and flower beds and beautiful plants. (2011: 136)

Similar accounts are to be found in Sullaiman Mahomed as well. The Black Friars Bridge (London), says Mahomed, is 'pretty and light in appearance' (1895: 267). Walking through the Crystal Palace grounds, Mahomed records:

> I liked to lose myself in the grounds, listening to the sweetest of music, and enjoying the best and most interesting of sights. A peculiar charm is thrown over the whole scene, when it is illuminated at night with the electric light … The gardens are laid out beautifully, and are adorned with statues. There is also a museum of birds, beasts and fishes. Some of the fountains … are said to be the largest in the world … the things of beauty and wonder to be seen here are innumerable. (274)

Mahomed, like Appasamy, is drawn to the beauty of Crystal Palace because of the mixture of the natural and the man-made. The fauna and flora enclosed constituted nature tamed and organized. The artificial lighting lends splendour to the 'scene' (the word itself resonant of the traditional picturesque). Echoing Mahomed and Appasamy, Jhinda Ram seeing Paris observes: '[I]n night the innumerable gas jets, with which it [the square] is lighted, give it an exceedingly picturesque appearance' (1893: 99). Kshitish Banerjee wandering through Kew Gardens praises the 'two hot-houses housing different specimens of tropical plants and trees' (1938: 134). The Rajah of Kolhapur, likewise, admires the 'glass-houses in which cocoa-nut, palm, and the like trees are kept' (1872: 10). Tagore, however, is not quite impressed and makes a derisive comment that aligns India and the Paris Exhibition:

> We went to see the Paris Exhibition. You may have pricked up your ears with eagerness, thinking that I am about to describe to you who knows what of the Paris Exhibition. But alas! Quite like garnering an education at Calcutta University, I looked at everything at the Paris Exhibition but failed to see anything properly. (2008: 34)

Earlier in his narrative, Jhinda Ram visits the London zoological gardens. He inventories the animal cages and enclosures and observes that in this place 'animals of almost every country on the earth [are] brought together within a few acres' (42). Ram, having employed the picturesque's strategy of describing a harmonious and ordered variety, has this to say:

> Is it not most interesting to witness the rustic lodges of picturesque and pleasing style appropriated to the use and comfort of the different birds and animals, scattered here and there in the extensive gardens, which are laid out most tastefully with sweet flowers and the most healthy and beautiful shrubs and plants? Is it not tempting to visit the pleasing and picturesque islands clothed densely with thickets and foliage in the midst of pools used for water for it? (1893: 42)

Ram merges the natural with the engineered. He notes and inventories the animals, relocated from their natural habitats into London's zoo. This creates the exoticism essential for the zoo (the exotic is one that is distanced from its natural state into a more controlled setting, as Christa Knellwolf, Natasha Eaton and others have persuasively argued). However, adding to the intensity of the exotic is the merger of the natural with the concrete constructed setting so that the animals are located within the man-made pools, cages, enclosures and other structures. The picturesque, then, in Jhinda Ram's account, is the choreographed coexistence of the tamed natural with the concrete.

The engineered picturesque in the hands of the Indian traveller serves the dual function of appreciating the 'natural' advantages of English weather, landscape and topography. But it also serves the crucial function of introducing labour and man-made matter into this set of advantages. When, for instance, Pandian praises the 'modern marvels' of London, he speaks of them in terms adapted from the language of visual arts: 'vivid scenes in a grand panoramic view' (1897: 19). The engineered picturesque is thus a variant of the traditional picturesque in terms of the georgic landscape rather than the Arcadian idyll with its insistence on labour and productivity.[2] It is nature—*controlled* via human efforts such as the machines, or lights, installed in the landscape—that renders the land picturesque.

The engineered picturesque serves two purposes. First, it communicates a sense of wonder and admiration for the industrious English, which has enabled them to build what several travellers term a great nation. The wonder of/at the engineered picturesque is a wonder at man-made efforts, in other words. For Doss, Dutt, Mahomed and others, the English then serve as a model for India and Indians.

Second, it modifies the constitution of the picturesque by shifting the nature of the response. Rather than a simple admiration for a pretty landscape, the engineered picturesque elicits more nuanced, knowledgeable response wherein the traveller seeks to understand and document features like the industrial process and the elements that make up the landscape's constructed elements. They emphasize, therefore, that the picturesque here is not simply an aesthetic. The landscape is also the manifestation of an ideology where what they are looking at and recording is *designed* nature, with 'design' implying human intervention founded on specific principles and informed, very often in England, by the privileges of class. Unlike the traditional picturesque which pretended to erase human actions upon the land (although, clearly, landscapes such as the famous Stourhead, *were* the results of human intervention), the engineered landscape, say the travellers, highlights human interventions. That is, the imperial-subject traveller's response to the built picturesque is founded on acquiring a degree of knowledge about the mechanics of building, arranging and organizing the land, in the form of machinery, lighting or industrial process. It is not, in other words, open-eyed wonder as much as informed wonder. Where in the traditional picturesque the spectator was to experience an emotional moment at the unexpected turns, curves, structures s/he would witness in the landscape, the Indian traveller in the midst of the engineered landscape is called upon to decode and decipher the land. In this process, the traveller also sets himself up as one who is *able* to know these aspects of the landscape.

A further point, extending the one above. Interpreting and deciphering the landscape in terms of the industrial machinery installed in it, as the Indian travellers do, signals an alertness to modernization and change. Moreover, as Susan Herrington puts it in her study of contemporary versions of the picturesque that incorporate industrial ruins, it draws attention to the 'viewer's ability to give shape to this experience [of viewing the landscape]; framing the effects and the associations it portends in ways relevant to our own times' (2006: 36). When the Indian traveller pays so much attention to industrialization, machinery, the urban condition of picturesque English landscapes, they are in fact reading England in terms of the possibilities for India, too. I, of course, take a speculative leap when I propose that the appreciation of the English park is done as an evaluative, epistemological mode driven by the opening up of such a possible transformation for India. However, given the emphasis in Nowrojee-Merwanjee, Malabari, Doss, Haldar, Pandian and others on the theme of English labour—that is, the hard-working English—and the effects of this labour (prosperity for England), it does not appear mere speculation. The English landscape is evaluated as a cumulative result of labour and industriousness, and the emotive response of wonder is tinged, I suggest, with an awareness that similar industry could transform India, too.

The Subaltern Picturesque

This section demonstrates how the Indian traveller, the so-called 'imperial subject' appropriates the aesthetic of the picturesque and inverts it to devastating effect. I term this inverted picturesque the 'subaltern picturesque' for various reasons that will emerge in the course of this section.

The imperial subject travels, on many occasions, as a racially marked subaltern-subject in Europe, but much less so in Australia and the US. The mobility regimes that determine his travel are informed by the consciousness of being such a subaltern-subject. Many do not set out with confidence or a sense of authority—except, for obvious reasons, the Rajahs and the Nawabs. (Thus Jagatjit Singh, the Rajah of Kapurthala, meets the King of Belgium, the Emperor of Austria, the King and Queen of Greece, among others [Singh 1895: v–vi].)

Jehangeer Nowrojee and Hirjeebhoy Merwanjee open their 1841 account by speaking of England as 'a country on which their [Indians'] life and property depended' (1). On the voyage itself, they discover that 'there were no fowls on board, and only two sheep', so the captain informs them that 'he could not supply [them] with any meat', and that they would have to 'subsist upon rice, peas &c' till they reached Good Hope (12). Nowrojee and Merwanjee then make it a point to state 'this was no "unpleasant message" to us' (13). Whether this is a reference to the absence of appropriate meats or the attitude of the European captain is not very clear, but both Nowrojee and Merwanjee express their anxiety at the entire situation. In other cases, the Indian traveller is conscious of the fact that the Indians in other countries, especially those of the working or merchant classes, are held in low esteem. Here is Hajee Sullaiman Mahomed speaking of the Indians in New Zealand:

> There are here about two dozen Indians, mostly Bengali Mahomedans, who go about the country, selling articles as pedlers and hawkers. I am sorry that they are held—and not quite without reason—in very low

> estimation by the inhabitants. I found them very filthy in their habits. (1895: 66)

N.L. Doss emphasizes the fact that on the voyage, he was a passenger whom the others avoided:

> I turned physiognomist, and began to scan faces of my fellow passengers … if perchance I might find a friendly and good natured face, that I was so much longing for. Every one seemed to avoid me. The passengers, all English men and women, seemed to keep their distance from me; and what better could be expected from people who are in the habit of keeping the natives of this country at an arm's length from when on land … It was out of question to make friendship with me, a dark native. (1893: 2)

However, Doss finds a subaltern solidarity with other Europeans of a different social background, but also with his fellow countrymen and, perhaps, non-Europeans: 'There were others of humbler position in life. I found they were more accessible.' The others, he notes, treated him with disdain: 'Even at table, where by right I was the equal of any of my fellow-passengers, there was a reserve and coldness shown to me, while there was a conversation kept up among the Europeans themselves' (2).

Jhinda Ram documents that on the voyage out, he was treated well by 'Anglo-Indians' (meaning, Englishmen and Indians who served in India, 1893: 8). S. Natarajan, travelling and writing in the twentieth century also notes that his fellow-passengers 'looked reserved and disinclined for any social life'. But rather than attribute it to racism, he recategorizes them: 'a feeling of horror came over me at the thought that I was to spend eleven days with this unfriendly collection of freaks' (1938: 3), thus embodying a far more confident imperial subject than his predecessors about fifty years before him. Lala Baijnath notes that on the voyage out, the Anglo-Indians 'were rather reserved and exclusive' (1893: 2). Baijnath, on arriving in London, declares in the opening paragraph: 'of all foreigners I would choose Englishmen as my rulers', in a chapter titled 'To England—the Home of My Masters' (21). Behramji Malabari, the reformer, sees England as a place that he could learn and benefit from:

> With all its unattractiveness, London is still a Mecca for the traveller in search of truth, a Medina of rest for the persecuted or the perplexed in spirit … to the searcher after enlightenment it is a Buddha-Gaya; a Benares for the sinner in search of emancipation. (1895: 2)

Malabari's theme of native learning, and European 'sources' of this learning, does an interesting shift into the theme of 'concurrent histories' (of which more in a later chapter). One can compare and analogize England, Malabari's quote suggests, only in terms of *non-European* places of enormous religious and cultural significance: Mecca, Medina, Benares, Bodh Gaya. Making an implicit case for concurrent histories—'that lay claim to territorial and temporal landscapes of the past' (Gunlög Fur 2017: 40)—Malabari situates England, Arab and subcontinental places of learning on the same plane. I will have reasons to return to this in the chapter on concurrent histories.

Some, like Romesh Chunder Dutt, feel weighed down by the expectations placed on them, and the history of unproductive travels in the past:

> For we have left our home and our country, unknown to our friends, unknown to those who are nearest and dearest to us, staking our future, staking all, on success in an undertaking which past experience has proved to be more than difficult. (1896: 2)

Dutt ponders: 'Shall we achieve that success? Or shall we come back to our country, impoverished, socially cut off from our countrymen, and disappointed in our hopes, to face the reproaches of advisers and regrets of our friends?' (2)

Both Dutt and Malabari communicate a sense of uncertain dependency on England, treating it as the fount of their hopes and future.

Rabindranath Tagore is more self-reflexive when he describes his encounter with an Englishman on the voyage out:

> We had an out and out John Bull on board ship. He had a body like a palm tree, a moustache like a broom, hair like porcupine quills, the face like a cauldron, eyes dull and expressionless like those of a fish. I found him repulsive and kept my distance from him. There are a few who commit no crime yet their expressions are perpetually criminal. (2008: 27)

Most of the travellers, then, arrive in a state of anxiety and uncertainty, deeply conscious of racial-cultural Othering. It is within this subalternized position as an imperial-subject traveller, overawed, uncertain, self-conscious, that their aesthetic response to the sights is framed. Numerous norms and aesthetic codes of the picturesque are undermined by the imperial-subject traveller in Europe.

The Antiquarian Picturesque and the Ruin

In his tour of the 'sights' of London, Malabari visits several places that embody and contain British and European history. These are in the form of 'panoramas', paintings and architectural sights. Malabari observes that 'the Panorama of the Battle of Trafalgar disappoint[ed]' (1895: 214), while the Panorama 'Constantinople', about Turkey, is described as 'gorgeous … a marvel and mystery of art … the warmth and variety of the East sobering down the solid monotony of the West' (215). He then records that in the major art galleries it was not cheerful to 'see the fair sex jealously shut out' because 'there is not a single bust in the [Westminster] Abbey or the Cathedral … devoted to the memory of a woman' (217–218). N.L. Doss discerns some animal remains in the Abbey's Chapter House and is appalled that 'such things [are] deposited in a place connected with a sacred edifice like the Abbey' (1893: 49), clearly, for him, deflating the power of the place. T.B. Pandian, visiting the Tower of London concedes that

> it is a grand sight this gallery of arms worthy of a nation of dauntless warriors; but alas, for the visions of barbaric cruelty called by the sight of an array of instruments of torture which the same nation of braves were once wont to use upon prisoners condemned to torment! (1897: 28)

He then concludes: 'Looking at these now, one can hardly believe that the brave British nation could ever have resorted to such cruel barbarities as is indicated by these blood-curdling mementoes of their past savagery' (28).

Pandian then describes the 'solemn and majestic grandeur of the more ancient cathedrals and churches' (32). Then he says: 'there is something of picturesque or subjective interest to engage the attention of a reflective mind'. However, he evades the task of telling us what he reflects on by saying, 'it would take whole volumes to tell their tale for any purpose' (32). The Rajah of Kolhapur finds Manchester a 'fine town' but observes that 'the factories spoil the beauty of the town' (1872: 57), thereby serving up an iconoclastic picture of the town.

If Malabari is only impressed by Western art when it reflects the grandeur of the ancient East, and mourns the gender inequality of the Abbey, Pandian reads in the ancient spaces of Abbeys and galleries the signs of English depravity. When there arises the opportunity of detailing the picturesque churches and cathedrals, Pandian smoothly slides out of the narrative responsibility by clearly informing us of a *non-narrated* (as Gerald Prince would term those elements excluded from the narration, 'that which cannot be narrated or is not worth narrating', 1988: 1).

Pablo Mukherjee, writing about Emily Eden's inversion of the picturesque when she travels through India, argues that 'antiquarianism focused attention on ancient ruins, not to celebrate their splendour, but to view them with a mixture of nostalgia and melancholy about the inevitable passage of time and the cyclical rise and fall of civilizations' (2009: 25). Mukherjee proposes that 'the visual evidence of the inevitable decay of past civilizations brings to mind a salutary reminder of the fragility of the present dispensation, leading to dark musings about its apocalyptic slide into oblivion' (25). Such a focus, for Mukherjee, '*exceeds* the domesticating boundaries of the picturesque mode' (25, emphasis in original) leading to what he terms an 'uneven picturesque' (26). *Contra* Eden in Mukherjee's reading, the imperial-subject traveller generates an uneven picturesque when writing about England by focusing on not the inevitability of human frailty and destruction but on the angularities of the so-called picturesque modes, angularities that suggest a far-from-pleasant history or even a worthy story associated with the monuments.

The moments wherein the imperial-subject traveller focuses on the more troubling, disturbing, unfair and non-worthy aspects of antiquarian and historically significant structures approximates to this inversion of the picturesque aesthetic. It is inverted into an uneven picturesque, one that admits to an aesthetic appeal of the European scene, but an aesthetic that is quickly enmeshed in a deflationary narrative that draws attention to cruel histories, the non-narratable and the socially unjust in Pandian and Malabari. Even though he employs it as a variation of the 'modesty trope' of travel writing (Sell 2006) wherein the traveller would claim he was unworthy of writing an account, Pandian's rhetorical move implies something more. He suggests that one could, if s/he *chooses*, reflect on the ruins and the architectural antiquarian spaces. His refusal to document these reflections however as a narrative choice implies one, that he himself did not reflect on them, or two, though he may have reflected on them, it was subject matter unworthy of narration, or sharing with the world. One traveller (Malabari) documents the inequality of English society embodied in its artwork, and one traveller (Pandian) notes the barbaric history encoded as greatness and then the non-narrated in the English museums and antiquarian spaces.

There are other ways of representing European history and its hoary antiquarian sites/sights. Rakhal Das Haldar passing through Paris first documents the city this way:

> Reached Paris, the so-called capital of the civilized world. Passed by the splendid bronze column of July where once the infamous Bastile stood. I was so very tired that my senses had become dull, and I appreciated little the magnificence of Paris. (1903: 19)

Several features of the above description arrest us here. First, there is Haldar's sceptical-ironic 'so-called' that alerts us to his attitude towards the 'civilized' Western world and its major city. Then, he draws attention to the symbolic value of the French Revolution by describing the Bastile as 'infamous', thus gesturing at its continuing iconicity, even in its remains, as a reminder of social change. Third, even the 'capital of the civilized world' does not attract him so much as to stave off his tiredness, and his 'dull' senses do not register its 'magnificence'. To be drawn to the subtexts such as social change and revolution is the very antithesis of the picturesque which, commentators have noted (Andrews), was mainly concerned with order and harmony. Then, the refusal to be impressed by and the employing of an ironic aesthetics at the presumed great sights of the Western world are signs of a deflationary picturesque, blunting the attractiveness potential considerably, even if the ironic stance is only temporary and unstable (as Burton describes the colonial subject's self-fashioning and power relations with the imperial centre).

Later, Haldar visits Stapleton Grove in Bristol town. Bristol, for Haldar, is a site of 'pilgrimage', as he puts it (29). Stapleton Grove is the site of Raja Ram Mohan Roy's death, and is marked by a gravestone for him. Haldar records the picturesqueness of Stapleton Grove in interesting ways. He notes that it is a 'most lovely spot'. He continues:

> I thought that the Rajah's death had taken place [in] a paradise ...The natural sceneries without the windows were indeed enchanting ... I could easily picture to myself the calm and glorious moon-light night of the 27th September, when the Rajah lay stretched on his bed in a strange land ... (31)

Haldar then visits Roy's burial site and quotes one D.L. Carpenter's elegy on Roy which speaks of 'shadowing elms their drooping boughs incline' (32). Beyond this 'pilgrimage', Haldar records visiting only a soap factory at Bristol, and does not offer any other account of his visit to the town. Haldar's emphasis on the melancholic nature of the visit and the site are well in tune with the picturesque's emphasis on ruination, passage of time and human mortality. However, it is important to note that the entire bustling town is *reduced* to Roy's grave, with Haldar going so far as to imagine the picturesque scene of Roy's dying, complete with a speculation of the calm, moonlit night. Further, the landscape's reduction and deflation into the grave is compounded by the fact that Haldar is speaking of the death-site of another imperial-subject traveller, his fellow countryman. The entire landscape, I suggest, is in Haldar's account transformed into a subaltern picturesque through this dual emphasis: as a space of death and mourning, and as the space where an imperial-subject traveller had died and lies buried.

I take my cue here from Diana Kontsevaia who, speaking of mass graves, writes:

> dead bodies occupy a specific physical space, claiming the territory for the group of people who are related to the deceased ... Despite attempts to deemphasize territory, it continues to play an important role in the politics of the living, especially in the reburial of past victims. As a result, the territory a memorial occupies is significant because it re-organizes the territorial boundaries of an ethnic group. (2013: 17–18)

That is, the picturesque English landscape is transformed into the topos of mourning for an imperial-subject traveller rather than for any Englishman or woman. By citing an Englishman's elegy for Roy, Haldar further underscores a (reverse) colonization: of the topographical and cultural space of Bristol and Stapleton Grove by the buried Roy. Even the English, suggests Haldar, recognise the greatness of Roy. This melancholic picturesque made possible by the burial site of an imperial-subject also serves, in Haldar's narrative, to imply the cosmopolitan sensibility of the English: the Englishman accepts the cultural icon from a different context and composes an English elegy for him (Roy), to be cited by another Indian (Haldar).

That the mourning requires an *Englishman's* elegy also renders the entire anecdote unstable. The Indian mourns the fellow-countryman, Roy, *via* the citation of an English elegy. That is, the discourse of native mourning requires, in Haldar's case, the grammar of an English genre (elegy) and the English language. It could also, then, be argued that the elegy confers a certain honour upon the dead imperial-subject, in the eyes of the later traveller. If Roy's dead body and tomb produce a colonized space within England, the employment of the English elegy in Haldar's mourning signals the consolidation of the genre as a universal one through the incorporation of Roy into it. That is, the English elegy can serve, the anecdote suggests, the purpose of non-English mourning too. In this fashion, the English elegiac tradition universalizes itself when Haldar deems it appropriate for mourning a fellow-Indian.

Like Haldar, Romesh Chunder Dutt invokes the melancholy associated with the picturesque ruin when describing Melrose Abbey:

> We could not fail being impressed with the grandeur of this ruined edifice with its loft and imposing windows, its venerable ivy-covered walls, its beautifully carved and ornamented columns, its fretted vaults and the lonesome graves all around. After the lapse of ages, after all the ravages of time, and the cruel ravages of war what remains still challenges the admiration of visitors ... (1896: 67)

The passage of time that the ruin reminds Dutt of is etched in stone but is also ineluctably embodied in the graves. Dutt's invocation of a 'bloody' history in terms of war links mutability to human acts in this account.

When travelling in other places, some picturesque accounts focus on the reorganization of the land, especially where local/native cultures are replaced by European modernity. We see this in N.L. Doss's accounts of New Zealand. Doss proposes that European settlers have introduced a variety of fauna and flora into New Zealand—'making it look more and more like the country from which they originally came'. He then expands on this transformation:

> The Maori of former days was a savage. He lived on the roots of trees and ferns, the animals he found in the woods, and the coarse fish that swarmed the coast, but he had no taste of corn and fruit, neither had

> he ever seen what is called a garden flower, nor possessed a single domestic animal ... The New Zealand of today is very different from the New Zealand of fifty years ago, when it was merely the wild home of the savage and the cannibal. (1893: 161–162)

For Doss, then, colonization and Europeanization transform the space into a picturesque, secure and safe setting, although this has been effected through the eviction of the Maori. The transformation of the landscape into an aesthetic idyll is coded in the form of an evolutionary scheme: from savage to civilized, from primitive to modern, and from native to European. That is, the aesthetic transformation of the country is read as an analogy with both domestication and 'civilization'.

The Civic Picturesque

When he visits Stoke Poges, Rakhal Das Haldar visits the churchyard where Thomas Gray composed his famous elegy. Haldar recalls the poem now, which, he says, he had 'read with tears in [his] eyes' (1903: 75). Then he notes that 'the monument [to Gray is] by no means an elegant one' (76). Interestingly, then, Haldar writes: 'As we drove back, I looked longingly on the picturesque church-steeple and regretted that the tolling of the curfew and the parting day were wanting to complete the picture in the Elegy' (76).

The entire episode is a fascinating instantiation of the imperial-subject traveller's politics of the picturesque.

First, Haldar's anecdote signals the dependence of the imperial-subject traveller on the English vocabulary (poetic, aesthetic) to document the subjective experience of the scene. In other words, the English cultural codes gleaned through a cultural training in poetry and aesthetic description mediate the imperial-subject traveller's experience of the landscape. This may be cultural training and colonization of the native who cannot view and experience the land except through the frames of the English aesthetic.

However, an interesting instability is introduced into the aesthetic experience.

Haldar suggests that the full comparison of the Elegy's description of the land with the visceral experience of the land remained *incomplete* due to his departure from the scene. The ocular limits demanded by and of the picturesque in the form of a dimming of daylight (also a theme in Gray's poem with referencing to fading light) is necessary for the complete visceral experience of a well-known picturesque scene, the churchyard. In a neat tweak of the mutability and temporality theme that underwrites the picturesque's melancholia (Mukherjee), Haldar mourns the impossibility, due to the sheer lack of time and daylight, to properly *eyewitness* the true picturesque because of his departure. I suggest that his disappointment arises because, as one who knows the literary-cultural tradition of the English and European picturesque, he has been trained to look for experiences of a certain quality of the picturesque. He finds it difficult, then, to reconcile the aesthetic experience with the visceral one: a feature Alan Vardy notes, of certain picturesque accounts: 'the difficulty of aesthetic experience as visceral lived experience' (2013: 195).

In the place of the picturesque's traditional emphasis on temporal limitations and mortality, Haldar focuses on the temporal limitation on *eyewitnessing*, that is, in person, the picturesque itself, thus rendering the very *English* aesthetic incomplete and unstable. The references to the 'curfew' and 'parting day' (phrases taken from the first line of Gray's elegy), suggestive of sunset/twilight, shifts the picturesque closer to the obscurity and shadowy perceptions that characterize the uncanny (Giblett 1996), but also of a 'picturesque gone awry' (Vardy 2013). Adapting Gray's own phrasing to describe his experience of the scene, and then documenting the dissonance between the traditional aesthetic discourse and the visceral experience, Haldar renders the melancholic picturesque both unstable and uneven—and the imperial-subject traveller is the one who constructs the instability and awryness of the aesthetic.

By drawing attention to the sad state of the Gray memorial he repeats the theme of Gray's own poem about 'neglected spots' where 'mem'ry o'er their tomb no trophies raises'. The melancholy generated by the recalled Elegy is matched by the discovery of the very material embodiment of the Elegy's themes in Haldar's description and serves up the uneven picturesque. A further point to be made is related to the fact that it is the imperial-subject traveller who reads Gray into the landscape of mourning, thus revealing a formidable knowledge of the poetry but also the aesthetic conventions of the picturesque. That is, the imperial-subject detects the irony of Gray's themes when he connects it to the very *English* countryside complete with churchyard, steeples and spires, and thereby reveals the unevenness of the picturesque.

Then, given that Gray spoke in the same poem of paths of glory that lead to the grave, the inelegance of the Gray memorial, as Haldar presents it, is his reflection on the validity of Gray's own argument. The imperial-subject traveller links the philosophy of the poem to the life and death of the poet through the material medium of the grave. Bringing together aesthetics, philosophy and material remains, Haldar adjudicates on them, and thereby fashions himself as an interpreter of all three. If the sentiments of the poem, in English, were meant to move the English reading public, Haldar positions himself as a traveller from a distant land equally practised in decoding the affect in the poem and the material contexts in which he *recalls* the poem.

Lala Baijnath also subtly shifts the aesthetic ideals of the picturesque away from pretty landscapes to their human content, generating the *civic* picturesque rather than a natural picturesque. When speaking of Leamington and Warwick, he is all praise for the former. 'Here', writes Baijnath, 'one gets some idea of what English scenery is like' (1893: 188). But he prefaces his account in a wholly awkward manner: 'The former [Leamington] is noted both for its natural scenery as well as for its medicinal springs. Lovers of the picturesque, as well as those with deranged livers, visit it in very large numbers' (188).

Baijnath aligns two contrasting rhetorical moves here: the aesthetic and the biomedical. Leamington is both the site of picturesque views and the site for medical cures. The aesthete and the ill both participate as the human element, he suggests, in the landscape. If the former is the connoisseur distantly appreciative of a pretty-as-a-picture landscape, the latter is the utilitarian in the land. The former fits the landscape because he focuses on the natural *scenery*, the second is an interloper whose focus is a cure from the natural *springs*. In effect, the presence of the humans with 'deranged livers' renders the picturesque a mere biomedically useful land rather than the 'landskip' of the picturesque tradition and may be treated as a subalternization because of the emphasis on the ailing body and its cures rather than the aesthete's body.

But Baijnath does not stop at this form of subalternization. We are not given an account of his experience of the picturesque beauty of Leamington. Instead, Baijnath cites an entire passage from the *Guide to Leamington* (188). This displacement of the picturesque from visceral experience of the landscape to a citational-textual iteration is both curious and interesting (even in the traditional picturesque, though, there was a trend where new places encountered during the tour would be judged 'in relation to standards of taste defined in previous tour narratives', Fulford 1996: 184). Two contrasting effects emerge as a result of this strategy in Baijnath's text.

In the first, the citation renders the views, the landscape and the observer at least partially irrelevant and redolent. The guidebook stands in for the observer, Baijnath. The guidebook was meant to be an objective, impersonal document and the personal travelogue 'freed from the guidebook burden, could now specialise in recording an individual traveller's distinctive reactions to the stimuli of the tour' (Buzard 2002: 49). When Baijnath replaces the 'distinctive reactions' with the objective guidebook tone and mode, he effectively effaces himself as the recorder of the picturesque. First, it does away with the observational eye and the observing body of the traveller. Second, it replaces the visceral with the textual, and makes the latter stand in for the former as a mode of 'seeing' itself. The erasure of the traveller and his replacement by a citation alters the account of the picturesque because the visual and ocular component—and authority—so central to the picturesque are done away with. The reliance on a textual guide could be read as either replacing the visceral experience or providing the vocabulary and discourse that completely encapsulates the visceral experience. Third, if 'the travelogue outranks the factual descriptions exemplified by the pedantic guidebook' (Lisle 2006: 31), the lapse into the factual account seems to be an attempt to showcase textual and useful knowledge rather than the experiential one. Inadvertently, then, Baijnath *relinquishes* his authority over the landscape description when he replaces his experience with the textual citation, at least in this instance. He therefore creates a new form of the non-narrated when he chooses to *not* give us his view, preferring to fall back on an established guidebook, almost as though he did not wish to spend his energies documenting his own responses to the land—an inversion of the very foundations of the picturesque aesthetic.

The second effect of this narrative move complicates the question of the imperial-subject traveller's authority which, as argued above, is diminished. The citing of a guidebook is integral to Baijnath's self-fashioning because he uses the strategy of the *antecedent literarios* for his purpose. In order to site the present Baijnath cites the past in a clear case of what Mary Louise Pratt terms '*antecedent literarios*', or prior literary productions. In this act of citing *antecedent literarios*, the contemporary traveller 'express[es] recognition of what he has learnt to know is there' (2007: 228). Paul Smethurst has argued that 'Nature, in effect, disappears from the scene as the travellers (George Sand and William Hazlitt) regard the natural world through the already written' (2012: 6). This is a *deflation* of the picturesque in the process of avoiding an eyewitness/experiential account of nature. However, with this move, Baijnath also demonstrates his knowledge of the picturesque conventions, the guidebook to the area and uses it to *affirm* what he sees. It is an act of recognition of the textual as manifest in the material that Baijnath documents when he cites the guidebook. He appears as a migrant to the textual tradition of landscape description, but by being able to immediately use the text to describe the picturesque scene—he has used the term 'picturesque' *prior* to the citation—he in fact invokes the authority of predecessor texts to situate himself as a knowing reader-traveller. Smethurst proposes:

> The theme of finding order and structure in nature is continued here as the picturesque connects aesthetic codes to mercantilism and land reform in a process of *territorialisation*: a practice which replicates patterns of nationalism and imperialism. Although romantic travel writing supposedly begins with mental structures rather than external templates, forms of order and structure emerge in the representation of the natural world which connect it with systems of museum order and latent imperialism. (6, emphasis in original)

Here it is the imperial-subject traveller who seeks and finds order in the English countryside, and often, like Baijnath, cites textual sources to communicate description, appreciation or commentary on the order he sees in England. In such cases, one can argue that the Indian traveller undertakes a process of reverse colonization and territorialization, *at least of the discursive variety*, and may be seen as embodying Burton's argument about the destabilizing, however temporary, of power relations between imperial centre and colonized native subject. If, as Kate Teltscher argued in her work on early modern travel writings on India (1997), the genre is an attempt to impose textual control over the new worlds seen and travelled in, the Indian traveller embodies the subaltern's discursive construction and control, via aesthetics, of the imperial cities of Europe.

Both the above constitute a subalternization of the aesthetics. The appropriation of the vocabulary of the guidebook to both relinquish and claim authority in Baijnath alerts us to the impossibility of seeing these aesthetics as restricted to a singular, monolithic iteration by Englishmen and women. Indeed, Paul Smethurst has noted about travel writing:

> The production of an abstract nature ranged across local and global space. The impact of overseas discoveries played a significant role in forming attitudes to the natural world … A global, if Eurocentric, map of nature (and mankind) was therefore being assembled which would have considerable impact on domestic space through, for example, the redistributions of plants, museum collections and exotic influences in the design of gardens. Landscape aesthetics and scenic tourism, as recorded in romantic and picturesque travel writing, reveal inner reflections of a geopolitical vision. An increased sense of national and, by extension, imperial belonging was a significant purpose and outcome of the domestic tour in Britain. (9–10)

The precise *obverse* of the above observation is what we see embodied in Baijnath. It is the overseas' (imperial-subject traveller's) discoveries of English (and other) nature, countryside, plants and animals that generate the Indian's geopolitical vision as a cosmopolitan (this book's ur-argument). While Baijnath and other travellers do exhibit a sense of imperial belonging (as already noted), they also reposition themselves as figures of authority when they are able to 'read' the English, and by definition, alien, landscape into and against the *English* guidebook, or via their visceral experience of the same. The iteration of aesthetics codes, such as the picturesque's, therefore, speaks not only of a relinquishing of aesthetic and experiential authority but also as a re-statement of the traveller's authority adapted and appropriated from the correct *textual* sources with which he demonstrates remarkable familiarity. He does not always need to cite his personal experience because he practises a shorthand when he simply cites the appropriate textual resource, vocabulary and resource. (I shall return to this theme of the 'informed enchantment' of the imperial-subject traveller later in the book.)

There is one further device in some of these authors that demands examination, and that is the inclusion of the disempowered into the accounts of picturesque landscapes. Travelling through Warwick, Baijnath notes the beauty and scale of the gardens. Baijnath comments:

> Nothing but *persistent human effort* could have produced those lawns of velvet green, those groves of trees with their luxuriant foliage, those trim hedges, those high railed fields with their dark green but not bright plants, those neat and exquisite flower-beds and grassplots which everywhere embellish the country and the cottage in England ... The appearance of the fields was less than that of India, and the whole seemed to partake *more of art than of nature*. (1893: 189–190, emphasis added)

One notes here the emphasis on fields as the product of 'art' and labour rather than 'nature'. The shift towards labour, worker and human effort denaturalizes the picturesque scene, instead projecting it as a sight of embodied human *work*. Baijnath does not present an English arcadia but a *georgic* landscape, one effected through labour. In sharp contrast to the pastoral picturesque that emphasized an Arcadian idyll devoid of human intervention and presence (as argued by Raymond Williams), Baijnath prefers to treat the picturesque land as artifice and the end-product of human *labour*. He thus *brings back the (subaltern) working class into the picture*, so to speak. Where the traditional English picturesque 'gave middle-class tourists an analogous means of distancing themselves from vulgarity', it 'made inconceivable ... [the] people's connection to the land they live on and from' (Bohls 1997: 97). This 'aligns the tourist with the proprietorial classes' increasing refusal to acknowledge or take responsibility for agricultural labourers' struggles' (97). This convention of the English picturesque—distancing from labour and the poor except, on occasion, to aestheticize poverty—is precisely what is destabilized in the imperial-subject traveller's account.

At one point, Baijnath would explicitly reference the London poor, although he claims their misery is partly because they drink and refuse to work (1893: 32–33). Malabari would refer to the urchins as 'the street arabs [sic] of London' (1895: 237). Romesh Chunder Dutt writing about the London poor declares that 'the lower classes ... are in many respects very far from what they ought to be' (1896: 27). He blames their wretched conditions on their lack of education, habits of drinking and 'imprudent marriages' (27). The public houses, he says, are full of drunken working classes and the unemployed (28). However, in rural England, the sight of the poor is not too 'displeasing': 'You see the mother and her children living in peace, though alas! Often in poverty, and robust healthy-looking village-girls with roses and carnations blooming on their cheeks' (29). Dutt also records that the gentry complain that 'merchants and tradespeople are following them too close and are treading on their heels, and allusion is sometimes made to those "good old times" when it was something to be born a gentleman' (37). Dutt endorses the social mobility, though:

> But the daily increasing Enlightenment of England is fast closing up such silly distinctions, and every change in institutions leads to further equalization. This equalization is to the tradespeople a consummation devoutly to be wished for, and this class therefore is never averse to change. (37)

Visiting Ireland, Dutt writes:

> As one is hurried on through the open country by the train, his eye is refreshed by the deep-green fields and plains which surround him on every side ... As for the villagers they are poor indeed. Man, woman, and children and a good round number in all, are often seen working in the same field in sun and rain, and are housed together in the night probably with their pigs and geese in the same wretched hut. This is not the only fertile country in which the cultivators are exceedingly poor! (78)

But, says Dutt, in Switzerland, the poor are happy (95). Similar attention to the economic state of the people is noticeable in Kshitish Banerjee's account of rural England:

> I hardly found anything in the villages to be impressed with ... The houses lie scattered, one here and another there, showing no signs of order. But the abodes of the villagers look quite decent; they are all

> buildings with tiles on. The exterior of the houses of even the poor villagers is hardly a true index of the economic condition of the owners. (1938: 103)

Banerjee then makes the claim that 'it appears from their clothes and houses that they are not much poorer than our small zemindars' (103–104). First, Banerjee disrupts the traditional picturesque's account of the scenic English village. Then he claims that the outward appearance of the village and houses bely the true economic status within. Finally, he believes the English rural poor to be at par with the smaller landlords of India. The attention to the gap between appearance and economic realities is a major swerve in Banerjee's employment of the picturesque. Mixing aesthetic and social observation, Banerjee resists the 'nature' only mode of the picturesque. Noting the cultural and economic struggles of the inhabitants of the village, travellers like Kshitish Banerjee force us to look at the landscape in entirely different terms, such as history and political economy.[3]

T.N. Mukharji is impressed by the order and method of English society, as also its organized spaces and its poetry.

> To an oriental, however, the artistic surroundings of English life seem to have too much of method in them, and therefore look stiff and tiring. As if all things have received an impress of the strong character of the English constitution. Artistic beauty there glares upon you like a full blown rose, and does not know like a bashful bud how softly to peep through emerald leaves in all its maidenly sweetness. Such is our art. But, oh my countrymen! do not glory in it. It is rather our misfortune that we can yet produce such art. For it is all poetry, a fairy dream delineated in all its picturesque sweetness. Such poetry ill-fits this hard hungry world, which plucks the sweet lotus and would not allow it to play with the Zephyr on the blue bosom of the wide lake, fleeces and slaughters the sporting lamb that does no harm, shoots the soft-eyed gazelle, and enchains the mild elephant that browses like a cloud on our hillside jungles. Prosy wakefulness thrives in this world of ours, my countrymen! not the trance of poetry ... (1902: 322)

Here Mukharji erodes the power of what he perceives as the artistic order of English society by proposing that any such art is far too rigid and 'tiring'. He then proposes that any poetry that is dedicated to 'picturesque sweetness' is, in fact, a denial of the material realities of the word. With this Mukharji has disputed the foundations of literary and spatial picturesque aesthetics (the picturesque, as we know, meant literally, 'pretty as a picture', thus uniting in its semantic scope the spatial and the art forms of the pictorial or verbal variety).

When speaking of picturesque country-sides, more importantly, and in a clear departure from the English picturesque tradition, the Indian traveller does not detect any paternalism in the landowners. Where the traditional picturesque, in at least one strand (represented by William Gilpin), excluded the poor from the landscape painting but sought to put in place a certain paternalistic and limited incorporation (by way of visits and views of the poor to the landowner's lands, for instance), the imperial-subject traveller's subaltern picturesque notes the lack of any sympathy for the absent (or, if present, damaged and vulnerable) poor.

Like Baijnath drawing attention to labour, in a slightly different key, here is G. Parameswaran Pillai (1897) describing the sights of London's streets at night. The metropolitan picturesque (Andrews 1994) is transformed, as Pillai describes it:

> The big buildings appear bigger, the tall chimneys look taller and the dome that dominates London holds majestic sway over its silent surroundings. It is an enchanting night. As you walk on, you become deeply impressed by the silence. There are no men or women in the streets, there is no rattling of wheels and the only figure you meet with … is the policeman. (32)

Then Pillai alters the above idyllic picturesque setting, thus far devoid of human elements. He writes:

> But stay, here is a mass of human flesh animate or inanimate you don't know, which on nearer examination resolves itself into half a dozen individuals, sleeping in the most fantastic positions, sitting, lying, half

> sitting, half-laying, knees above head, hands beneath legs, pinched cheeks and ragged limbs, hatless, shoeless, bearing unmistakable marks of misery. They are perfect strangers to the comforts of home. Some of them are averse to toil. Others are victims of the fierce competition of the overcrowded labour market. The parks are closed against them at dead of night … They betake themselves … to the benches outside parks or to the bare earth and try to go through the function of sleep, hungry and shivering with cold … The sight of men of hungry and hunted look, women bonnetless and with dishevelled hair and children extremely dirty and shoeless, all members of the great army of rags amongst whom are a large number of thieves, pick-pockets and rogues … (32–33)

Like Baijnath, Jhinda Ram tempers his account of majestic and picturesque London through a focalization on the poor. He writes:

> But stop for one moment. While you enjoy the magnificence and splendour of the Great Metropolis, do not fail to see the misery and wretchedness in its streets. Little children clothed in rags, and having neither shoes nor stockings on their feet, meet your eye. A ragged urchin here, with a lot of flowers in his hand, thrusts the flowers up under the gentleman or lady passer-by … There a poor woman, with an array of children before her, offers matches, but silently appeals for alms. (1893: 13)

Sullaiman Mahomed's first description of London opens with this sentence: 'You can have an idea of the greatness of England, and of the source of that greatness, from London, the first city in the world' (1895: 265). After a few sentences about its 'teeming population', of it being the 'center of world-wide commerce', Mahomed writes:

> Its enormous wealth is in painful contrast with the extremes of poverty and wretchedness … The same city which boasts of proud mansions, immense trade and untold riches, is also the abode of squalid poverty, and of the crimes which degradation and poverty bring with them. The poorest of the poor are living most miserably, on unwholesome and insufficient food, in wretched holes, where the light of heaven is dim, and its breath is charged with the impurities of the surroundings. (265–266)

A few decades later, Kshitish Chandra Banerjee is appalled to see beggars in London: 'such poverty in a Land of Plenty—a Land which has the biggest empire to rule over' (1938: 117). He then rails 'bitterly against the Government of the country which could not solve the problem of the poor' (117). Tagore observes beggars in the Brindisi streets (2008: 32). S. Natarajan is disappointed at London: 'Frankly, I did not like the place. The sooty air one breathed in with every breath, the untidiness of the roads, the food—either at the Indian or the English restaurants—the begging on the streets …' (1938: 96).

Pandian devotes an entire chapter (Chapter Three) to 'working class homes' in which he demonstrates how, due to their low income levels ('two shillings or so a day', 1897: 17), one sees 'disorder and untidiness' (17), before describing the homeless poor: 'foodless, half-clothed, lying through the live-long night on the bare surface of these stony bedsteads … life to the houseless poor of London must seem nothing more than an intolerable condition of agonizing cursedness!' (18).

N.L. Doss, like the others, observes the large numbers of 'boys of the shoe-black brigade', the 'crossing sweepers … generally boys, and sometimes grown men too, who are idle or unfortunate not to find any other work for themselves' on the streets of London (1893: 40). When he travels through France en route to England, Rakhal Das Haldar notes that 'the whole country seemed a garden' (1903: 19). Then, instead of imaging this garden—a staple of the picturesque aesthetic, traditionally—as a pretty sight alone, Haldar interrupts the scenic narrative with a set of two questions: 'Where do the poor people live? Underground?' (19). Haldar's narrative points to the missing elements, the poor, in the topography and in the process *insinuates* that all is not well in the artifice of beauty the land represents (a theme Raymond Williams discussed in connection with the English pastoral poem, where the labour had to be evicted from the narrative to render the land pastoral and Arcadian).[4] Soon after, when visiting a memorial column, Haldar notes the 'old invalid soldiers' who had offered souvenirs at the site (20). Kshitish Banerjee at the War Museum notes that 'India alone contributed as many as 1,338,620 soldiers out of the total number of 9,296,691 soldiers of the whole British Empire who had participated in the War' (1938: 121).

The inclusion of the working class, the broken and the poor—the subalterns—into these accounts constitute a reterritorialization of the landscape. It alters, I suggest, the traditional picturesque mode of landscape description, makes it 'uneven', when it repositions the subaltern within the language of landscape description itself. Jonathan Paquette and Aurélie Lacassagne studying the 'aesthetics of mining' in Canada argue that the inclusion of miners in the accounts changes the aesthetics of the land because the workers, working to different rhythms and bodily dynamics underground are themselves deterritorialized. About a poet's account of such a space they write:

> His aesthetics of the mine are reflected in his landscape, but also in his poetry where the cartography of the subterranean world appears as an ambivalent contemplation of terror and boredom in a time 'suspended' from the human time above-ground. (2013: 250)

This deterritorialization is precisely what is effected in the Baijnath and Pillai texts when the workers, urban poor and disempowered 'appear', so to speak, on the otherwise picturesque scene. Even the engineered picturesque is tempered through the intrusion of the subaltern focus of the Indian traveller, as in the case of Nowrojee and Merwanjee. Documenting a visit to a cloth mill in Scotland, they write:

> In all the mills, women and children are principally employed; but their appearance excited our compassion, as we noticed almost all that were thus employed, were meagre and pale looking creatures, and their health is soon injured from the heat and impure atmosphere of the rooms in which they work ... (1841: 441)

This deterritorialization of the mill's landscape through a focus on the damaged bodies embedded within the machinery that operates in it erodes any admiration for the economic and social picturesque the industry may represent.

In some cases, we see another kind of deterritorialized picturesque. For instance, Malabari locates London's picturesque in the Asians and other nationals walking its streets.

> Here goes a Parsi gentleman at large, in evening suit capped by his conical paper turban, followed by ladies of his family, dressed in the height of the season, with the saris thrown airily round, drawing half of Oxford Street behind them. They seem to enjoy the attention.
>
> More picturesque than this party are Rao Sahib Moro Punt and the Rao Sahiba, dressed impartially, half in the English, half in the Indian style, in which the buff-coloured sari, the scarlet shawl, and the cartwheel of a *puggri* play a prominent part. From the hotel, where they have put up, to the private drawing room or the public hall, the shop, the theatre, the hospital or the park, do Mr. and Mrs. Moro Punt repair, a pair of 'Indian princes,' taking all they meet into confidence, asking queer questions, and drinking in the doubtful admiration which the London mob knows how and on whom to bestow. (1895: 240)

As Rogers would say, it is squalor (as already noted) and an unprecedent cultural and racial diversity in and of the city in Malabari that generates in the picturesque of metropolitan London.

The deterritorialization of the picturesque, both rural and metropolitan, effected through the careful inclusion of the subaltern into the narrative may be termed an anti-*Concordia discors*. *Concordia discors* was an influential Enlightenment ideology of encirclement and universal cartographics (Cosgrove 2001: 195–199). It has been argued that *Concordia discors* was a key trope in the nineteenth-century colonial missionary's rhetorical and narrative construction of India. It suggested that variety needed to be subsumed into some measure of order in order to generate the picturesque (Nayar 2008: 117–131). I suggest that in the imperial-subject traveller's narrative, the harmony expected of the picturesque where variety is subsumed into a favourable, pleasing, organized space is denied. Instead of such a harmonious social order that delivers the picturesque, in these texts the subaltern picturesque is one where the discordant appears in the form of London's poor, and it inverts the aesthetic.

What this means is: in contrast to the traditional picturesque which demands a clear harmony within the variety of elements and social classes, the appearance of the socially disenfranchised shifts the focus towards discontinuities. The conventional picturesque, writes Johan Andersson, which had 'its origins in the period of the enclosures of the English countryside tends to aestheticize suffering and dispossession, while the pastoral is an idealizing mode of representation with roots in bucolic poetry' (2017: 540) and ignored exploitative social relations. In a parallel argument, working with Nathaniel Hawthorne's travel writings, Jennifer Baker has argued that the American picturesque aligned the aesthetic with social stratification and social mobility. She writes that such views

> were not always compatible with traditional picturesque conventions, and his [Hawthorne's] picturesque depictions of the *social* landscape often raise troubling questions about class relations and attendant questions about regional and race relations in a fractured nation. (2016: 413, emphasis in original)

She notes that, unlike the traditional English picturesque (notably in Uvedale Price, William Gilpin and others) which elevated poverty itself into an aesthetic ideal, Hawthorne's notebooks 'emphatically juxtapose picturesque depictions of the poor with frank statements about the reality of their conditions' (427). Baker points us to the inherent problems of an aesthetic that idealizes poverty by ignoring the 'pervading ugliness' (Hawthorne, cited in Baker 427. Also see Martin 2015 for a similar argument about the proletariats in the picturesque) of the material conditions of slaves and workers in a picturesque landscape. Other commentators have also noted such variations in the picturesque tradition when adopted elsewhere. Thus, Brandon Rogers in his essay on the American picturesque argues:

> the concept of the picturesque functions as a political tool for Realism, not only to place the artistic observer in a position superior to the

> observed object, but also to perform a Hegelian synthesis for the dialectics of 'civility versus squalor' and 'beauty versus reality' in order to impose a structure on an increasingly diverse city. (2002: 77)

Rogers is signalling the shift away from an aesthetics of beauty and harmonious diversity towards an aesthetics wherein poverty is *not beautiful* and social diversity is the cause of friction rather than harmony and multicultural balance.

Adapting this argument to the imperial-subject traveller's aesthetic, I suggest that this is precisely what can be termed the subaltern picturesque: the attention to unequal social relations, economic deprivation and poverty provide Baijnath, Doss, Pillai and others the countervailing measures to the aesthetics of the picturesque. England and Europe were not, then, seen as through the conventional aesthetics of the picturesque. Rather, this aesthetic was subalternized through the attention to the ill-fitting, disruptive figures of labour and the poor.

There is no shared aesthetic ideal here between the Indian traveller and the nineteenth-century English landscape artist because the Indian traveller imbues the aesthetic with questions of political economy and welfare. Yet there is an awareness across cultural differences, of economic hardship and social inequalities. This cross-cultural awareness, and discourses built around it, of humanitarianism for instance, positions the imperial-subject traveller as a passing insider in the English landscape, particularly due to his sensitivity (real or feigned) to the social aspects of the landscape. In a meditation on the state of the poor in England, Romesh Chunder Dutt moves from the specific to the general condition of humanity:

> It is really painful to reflect on the amount of suffering of the poor in this country in this inclement weather. Thousands of poor people live here in ill-constructed houses, with broken windows which hardly keep off the cold blast, with no coals to warm their rooms, no sufficient clothing to keep themselves warm, and in many cases with hardly sufficient food to give them due nourishment. Many people die in this country in winter either of hunger and cold or through diseases

> generated through insufficient nourishment and exposure to cold. Were we to sympathize with every sufferer in this world, our life would be one long tissue of woe. It is only by forgetting, nay, closing our eyes to what is going on around us, by smothering the ready sympathy of childhood, and steeling our heart against emotions of pity, that we live and work on unconcerned as we do. It is only in moments of astounding calamities (the present war is an instance) that people take a due cognizance of the sufferings of their fellowmen; but every day and every hour there are sufferers around us by hundreds and thousands. The civilization of ages has done much to mitigate the privations of mankind, but how much more has it yet to do! (1896: 43–44)

Dutt here moves from poverty and suffering in the English countryside to the general conditions of abjection in the world. Avoiding localizing the description, even as he begins with it, enables Dutt to extrapolate the human condition itself. The picturesque English countryside under which lurks this extent of poverty and deprivation is then no longer the source of a simple aesthetic account, but rather the means of meditating on things beyond national borders. This move via attention to political, social and economic issues alters considerably the traditional picturesque's national emphasis (wherein the picturesque enhanced a sense of community and national identity). Instead, it uses England's picturesque as a means of thinking of 'human civilization' and 'humanity' itself. The erosion and erasure of the 'national' dimension in favour of the global humanitarian is once again an inversion of the canonical picturesque.

It may be argued that the Indian traveller presents the poor in the English/European landscape as a disruption in the order of nature, one that disturbs any purely aesthetic evaluation of the land. The application of social and economic *value*, often drawing on political economy and an awareness of social organization in European society, to the sights and views by the Indian tourist ensures that the English or European land is not treated solely as a series of consumable 'scenes'. If the metropolitan picturesque aestheticized the urban spaces cities such as London, the subaltern perspective that the imperial-subject traveller brings to this aesthetic on his travels achieves something else. The metropolitan picturesque had conventionally transformed the city into a landscape to be consumed as an aesthetic object. That is, the picturesque traditionally commodified the land as an 'attraction' and enabled the erasure of political, economic and social relations that were connected to that land. The imperial-subject traveller ensures the social dimensions of the land are retained in their accounts so that the commodification is resisted, at least temporarily. Further, the insinuation of the humanitarian and economic discourses and tropes into aesthetic accounts of the European landscape-as-commodity by the Indian tourist sets him up in a way so that 'wealth (expressed as the collection of as many scenes or views as possible) rather than landed property (a single landscape owned, governed and inheritable) becomes the source of power' (Fulford 1996: 142). That is, the lack of ownership (of the lands he traverses) does *not* render the Indian traveller powerless to describe the landscape. Rather, it is the mobility through diverse lands, collecting and recording 'scenes', imbuing his aesthetic vision with social and humanitarian concerns that renders him powerful. In other words, it is the mobility that fuels the accumulation of landscape scenes but via a merger of the 'disinterested' aesthetic of the traditional picturesque with humanitarian, economic and social ideals, politics and concerns that leads, first, to a democratization and subalternization of landscape aesthetics and, second, to a self-fashioning of the Indian traveller.[5] In the process the imperial-subject traveller resists the hegemonic approach—the picturesque—to the English/European landscape by inserting a humanitarian (maybe even moral?) perspective and judgement into their own approach. It could be argued that this approach imbued with a humanitarian perspective towards the poor figures in the landscape was more internationalist and universal than European or English—the imperial subject traveller was making a larger point about industrialized modern nations and their social iniquities. (I shall return to this point in a different way in a later chapter when looking at subaltern and moral cosmopolitanism.)

Whether the famous 'intentionality' of the picturesque (Carter 1987) is built into the imperial-subject traveller's accounts of the poor is a moot point, as is the question whether their incessant attention, in many cases, to the English/European poor and working classes signals a subtle attempt to build an imagined community: the colonial subject who has no ownership claims over the picturesque English lands aligned with the white working class and poor who also have no such claims. In short, the cultural hegemony of the aesthetic is eroded by the imperial-subject traveller through the introduction of social analyses alongside the aesthetic. Retaining the subjective viewpoint of the picturesque but infusing it with the social and economic analysis of poverty, class differences or the status of the underclass enabled the imperial-subject traveller to erode the hegemony. What started off as a regional-national aesthetic to valourize the land *by* Europeans/English—with, of course, the broad emphasis on a 'taste' for the landscape—shades into an instrument of multiple perspectives and deterritorialized aesthetics.

*

From the employment of cartographic signifiers and the enumerative picturesque that sets up the knowledgeable imperial-subject traveller, through the attention to the engineered picturesque's emphasis on modernization, industry and possibilities for India, to the humanitarian critique underlying the subalternized picturesque, the imperial-subject traveller dislocates the traditional aesthetics. In the process, I suggest, the narrative also destabilizes the identity of the imperial-subject, who now emerges as a knowing, evaluating, calculating and humanitarian aesthete who is no longer offering a simple emotive response to the wonders of the English landscape. This is the inversion or dislocation of the aesthetic mode for their own purposes.

Notes

1. The manner in which canals, roadways and railway lines transformed the English landscape has been well documented in W.G. Hoskins's *The Making of the English Landscape* (1955). See, in particular the chapter 'Roads, Canals, and Railways'. He also records the comments of literary figures like Charles Dickens, Dr Johnson, John Clare, William Wordsworth and others, many sharply critical to the appearance of these massive constructions. But Hoskins also notes that the railway's 'embankments and viaducts changed the prospects [of towns like Bath]' and viaducts often 'brought a fine geometrical composition into the urban landscape' (205–206). Hoskins writes:

   > Even in [John] Clare's own country, the railways has been absorbed into the landscape, and one can enjoy the consequent pleasure of trundling through Rutland in a stopping-train on a fine summer morning: the barley fields shaking in the wind, the slow sedgy streams shading meditative cattle, the elegant limestone spires across the meadows … true that the railways did not invent much of this beauty, but it gave us new vistas of it. (206)

   Dutt's description instantiates the Hoskins point about how the railways changed the way the landscape was perceived, and this applied as much to the imperial-subject traveller as the native, English traveller.
2. Laurent Folliot treats the 'georgic element, distinct from the picturesque in its much-greater insistence on depicting human activity', particularly in terms of tracing signs of inhabitation (2011: 202).
3. Kristin Lozanski (2013) has argued in a fascinating account of the Western/First World traveller in India that the encounter with beggars in Indian cities often left the traveller 'disoriented' and exposed their own vulnerability. Lozanski treats such a disorientation as embodied and as problematizing the traveller's notions and intentions of intercultural understanding. It might be interesting to study the imperial-subject travellers' texts from this perspective, examining the proxemics of their encounters, including encounters with the European and American poor.

4. Raymond Williams' reading of the pastoral poem in *The Country and the City*, which is what I am citing here, also resonates with Ronald Paulson's account of the rise of the picturesque. Paulson writes:

> The Picturesque only shifted emphasis to the distinctive landscape form of the national and local, of property with or without the presence of its owners. The furniture and works of art in the interiors became the agricultural improvements and landscape gardening. Enclosed fields and (by the use of ha-has) apparently unenclosed lawns. (1996: 233. Also, Fulford 1996: 129)

5. A parallel from post-industrial landscapes has been studied by Anthony Fassi who notes how the abandoned industrial site now houses the homeless. Those who photograph these industrial ruins ignore the material realities of these spaces when they were up and running:

> While they engage in a form of cultural resistance by encouraging awareness of defamed industrial ruins, they also risk transforming these ruins into artistic commodities. A number of examples will demonstrate that even the modern, urban, industrial ruins of the late twentieth century submit to the picturesque gaze. When foregrounding familiar aesthetic qualities of the ruins they explore, urban explorers risk obscuring the material realities of economic decline, joblessness, and urban despair. (2010: 145–146)

However, Fassi argues that images from photographers such as Camilo José Vergara carry a different subtext:

> Vergara's photographs of such ruins bear witness to the negative forces of deindustrialization: the demise of the urban, working class and the plight of homeless residents living among the abandoned centers of American industry. These spaces are rarely thought to have any value at all and seem at odds with picturesque ruins nestled within municipal, state, and national parks. (145)

3

The Occidental Exotic

Romesh Chunder Dutt wandering through Eastbourne visits the village of Pevensy. Here he sees 'Martello Towers', and about this historical structure, Dutt writes: 'built by the English in 1804, when they feared the descent of Bonaparte on the English coast. They are a line of fortified towers with drawbridges and moats, along the southern coast of Kent and Sussex' (1896: 22).

A few decades before Dutt, Nowrojee and Merwanjee viewing a Panorama in Leicester Square, 'saw a representation of Jean de Acre and the bombardment of it by the British fleet' before writing an account of the destruction of Egyptian troops in the war (1841: 215).[1]

These texts alert us to a shift: it is not just *English* victories or martial exploits represented in the image that arrest the Indian traveller emotionally, it is also the destruction of the Egyptians or the threat of the foreigner that 'produces', so to speak, the English memorial and the panorama. Thus, they undercut the spectacle and the English space of the performance by focusing on (*a*) the ethnicity of victims in the spectacle and, (*b*) their own, that is non-European, affective response to this. The passages from Dutt and Nowrojee-Merwanjee invite the investigation this chapter is concerned with: the exoticization of Europe in Indian travel writing of the period.

Traditional views of European exoticism in literary-cultural and even scientific texts have consistently underscored the links between exotic representations and imperialism (Maria Baine Campbell 1988, Rousseau and Porter 1990, Knellwolf 2002, Eaton 2006, Schmidt 2015, among others). Exoticism, they all agree, was instrumental in Othering the racially, ethnically and geopolitically different peoples and cultures. Bernard Smith links exoticism and empire: '[Exoticism] was a category of accommodation by means of which the European perceived and interpreted the Other according to the limits and constraints of European understanding' (cited in Knellwolf 2002: 11). As Knellwolf summarizes it, 'the "exotic" thus describes fantasies as well as historical responses to otherness, both permeated with the attempt to contain it within the intellectual and real boundaries of empire' (11). It served the purpose of creating colonialist fantasies about the distant too, she notes.

Contemporary reconsiderations of the European exotic conclude, as Eugenia Zuroski Jenkins (2012) notes, that exoticism need not end in Eurocentrism, dehumanization and imperialism. Exoticism can also serve the purpose of generating 'cosmopolitan possibilities' (Rosenthal 2012) for the European self. Such re-evaluations of the exotic propose an 'aesthetics of diversity' (Jenkins). This chapter takes such a re-evaluation of exoticism as an approach to the Other seriously and traces its many manifestations in Indian travel writing of the 1830–1940 period. It takes as its point of departure a question: What does exoticism, traditionally seen as an approach appropriated and professionalized by Europeans towards non-European Others, achieve when directed at Europeans by Indian travellers and observers? Unlike centre/periphery, the term 'exotic' has no 'overt counterpart' (Knellwolf 10–11). However, an inversion of European exoticism, by turning the exoticizing gaze on Europe itself, is discernible in Indian travel writing.

That exoticism relies considerably on the visual text is now a truism (Schmidt 2015, Chapter 2). The Indian traveller visited the National Gallery, Madame Tussaud's, numerous museums in the course of the trip. Then he visited palaces, ruins and memorials. Here he saw images and material objects that were radically distinct from his home culture. How he assimilates the distinctly different—the exotic—into a frame of knowledge and meaning-making is the key concern here.

Together, the siting of the foreign in Romesh Dutt and Nowrojee-Merwanjee, one in the form of a monument, the other in the form of a spectacle and its responses, within English geocultural topoi and its contact zones—tourist spaces, theatre, antiquarian ruins—gestures at what Christopher Pinney calls 'Creole Europe'. Such a creolization is made possible through the presence of the foreigner, the exotic (from *exo*—outside), within England: a 'xeno-figure'. Pinney defines the 'xeno-figure' as the 'material, "figural" history of this encounter [between the self and the Other] and the everyday material creolization of Europe' (2002: 131). Such a xeno-figure, writes Natasha Eaton following the work of Victor Segalen and Pinney, 'is the exotic object moving between sometimes hazardous contexts, accruing value precisely because of its volatile status' (2018: 14).

The Occidental exotic, as I characterize the Indian travellers' appropriation of the form, creolizes Europe/England through its attention to the xeno-figure (which, as Pinney notes, is *figural* too) within Europe/England. It constitutes an aesthetics of diversity in the process of deterritorializing and reterritorializng Europe/England. The ethnocentrism that underwrites European exoticism and its informing geopolitical and discursive ethos—that is, imperialism—is undone in the Occidental exotic through its foregrounding of alterity *within* Europe. The Occidental exotic at the hands of Indian travellers remains enchanted by Europe/England but this is a reconfigured enchantment, one which I term 'informed enchantment'. This discourse of enchantment by the European exotic is an instrument of self-fashioning when the Indian traveller represents himself, first, as a romantic cosmopolitan and later modulates this enchantment into an 'informed' one. It is a cosmopolitanism that combines within it the appeal of the (European) exotic and the possibilities of the exotic's diversity. The recourse to authoritative English/European texts and sources, ironically, enables a degree of assimilation of the exotic—the exotic is, by definition, what remains singular and unassimilable—by the Indian traveller in the form of informed enchantment. But it also signals the traveller's alertness to his own knowledge of how this so-called English or European picturesque was put together—that is, the sources of England's exotic. Thus, the chapter documents the rise of an occidental exotic *and* the Indian traveller's response, informed by both wide-eyed wonder and cultural literacy about England and Europe, or what I term 'informed enchantment'.

The Occidental Exotic and the Creolization of Europe

T.B. Pandian's chapter on Jews in England opens with this sentence: 'No race of aliens in England has greater cause to be grateful to the British nation than have the now dispersed and almost universally derided tribes of the ancient Jewish nation' (1897: 79). He then observes that 'they are allowed to hold honourable seats in both Houses of Parliament ... also taking a personal and am active part in directing the affairs of the British Empire at large' (80). Jewish synagogues, Pandian adds, 'are no longer hidden in obscure corners, but they stand out, richly adorned, to public view' (82). Earlier in his text, Pandian documents encountering an English Squire who tells him: 'Your countrymen spoil our wheat trade by being able to bring their Indian produce into the English market at cheaper rates than we can afford to sell at' (40).

Pandian's observations are not about a foreign object 'controlled by museological structures of knowledge and display, abstracted in a space beyond touch', but rather it is 'a part of an everyday tactility and sensuousness' of society (Pinney 140). In the first case, he shows how the Jews have benefitted from being in England. But his sustained emphasis, it is clear, is on how the Jews are a part of England's legislative and imperial mechanisms. By locating the Jew at the heart of the imperial project, 'directing the affairs' (even if, surely, they did not *entirely* control the imperial offices), Pandian, I suggest, creolizes the English imperial and civilizational missions. Refusing to accept the ethnocentrism of the English/British imperial structure, Pandian introduces a foreign presence at its core, thereby de- and reterritorializing it. This exoticization—the process of locating the foreign and the different, sometimes outside its originary context—is, in sharp contrast to European exoticism, not imperial in tone or effect. Rather, it dismantles the illusion of control, power and authority of the British Empire by implying a multiracial and multi-ethnic imperial formation.

This introduction of xeno-figures is the first major step in the exoticization of England/Europe in Indian travel writing in the age of Empire.

Xeno-figures at the Heart of England

Elleke Boehmer, studying Indian literary figures such as Toru Dutt, Sarojini Naidu and others in late nineteenth- and early twentieth-century England, presciently discerns a 'multilayered and interconnected, as well as divided and interconnected' empire in their writings (2015: 7), with a 'distinct impression on British cultural and literary life' (6). This leads, Boehmer notes, to an Indian influence on literary networks such as the Bloomsbury group—so much so that Boehmer terms it 'Indian Bloomsbury' (214). My interest, related but not identical with Boehmer's project in *Indian Arrivals*, is the rhetorical and discursive strategies through which the Indian travellers achieve this multilayering. Following Christopher Pinney, I suggest that the Indian travellers' insistence on locating what Pinney terms 'xeno-figures' within English landscapes—physical, topographical, cultural—exoticizes England in ways that alter its racial and cultural patterns significantly.

There is a considerable amount of interest in the colonial reconfiguration of the British Empire in many of the Indian travelogues. In the chapter on Aesthetics (Chapter 2), I cited Kshitish Banerjee's recording of the Indian soldiers fighting in the British army in the World Wars, thereby drawing attention to the 'foreign' at the heart of the British imperial project. N.L. Doss in the Picture Gallery of the Crystal Palace exhibition, records seeing a gallery labelled 'To the Victoria Cross Section'.[2] He writes:

> To my great surprise I noticed, that in almost every one of them, the scene of battle or of the deed of daring represented in each picture, lay in eastern soil, mostly Indian. The men combating with the English heroes who afterwards won the soldier's much coveted Victoria Cross for their valour, wore turbans and were of dark complexion. (1893: 60)

Then there are the instances wherein the Indian traveller records memorials and emblems of British imperial progress. This is Dutt's previously cited account of 'Martello Towers' in Eastbourne: '... built by the English in 1804, when they feared the descent of Bonaparte on the English coast. They are a line of fortified towers with drawbridges and moats, along the southern coast of Kent and Sussex' (22).

And Nowrojee and Merwanjee viewing a Panorama in Leicester Square (also cited earlier):

> The scene we beheld was awful, we observed some of the Egyptian troops lying here and there killed, and wounded … The blowing up of the powder magazine … killed nearly 3000 Egyptian, it was a terrible sight as we saw hands, legs, heads, & c of these unfortunate beings flung into the air. The town of Acre also presented a galling and heart-rending spectacle, it was a mass of ruin and every house was shattered to bits.

Jhinda Ram, like Dutt and Nowrojee-Merwanjee, observes war memorials and relics:

> On the Eastern side there is a relic showing the bombardment of Copenhagen ... Nelson is seen sealing his despatch to send it by a flag of truce, in the foreground are the wounded, in the distance, Copenhagen is in flames. (1893: 46)

Dutt's brief account detains us here because it draws attention to the origins of a famous English tourist attraction. These origins are linked to the foreign, the imminent arrival of the overseas/foreign conquistador, Napoleon. A monument to *English* history, tinged undoubtedly with nationalist hues, recalls the foreign at the heart of England, even if the foreign is available only in the form of a strange absent presence, and a haunting reminder of that architecture's teleology. Nowrojee-Merwanjee's documentation of their sentimental response to the scenes of war, death and destruction underscores the fact that the war's primary victims were *Egyptians*—who had been depicted in an English Panorama.

Where Dutt noted that the forts, now English tourist attractions, were a direct response to the threat of a foreign invader and Nowrojee-Merwanjee observe England's triumph over the foreign (Egyptian) troops, Ram locates the military triumphs of the British within a xeno-figure, this time, Denmark. Ram then moves on to another memorial, this time 'erected in honour of the victory of British arms in the Crimea' (48). At Madame Tussaud's, Ram encounters

> the most horrible thing ... a melancholy relic of the First French Revolution, the most extraordinary relic in the world, the original knife and Lunette the identical instrument that decapitated 22,000 persons and shed the best and worst blood of France, bought by Madame Tussaud from the grandson of the original executioner. (52–53).

Jagatjit Singh also records 'relics from Napoleon the First' in Madame Tussaud's (1895: 74).

Hazel Hanh has argued that the illustrated periodical press of the 1880–1905 period in England and France was full of visual and verbal details of colonial wars in various parts of the Empire. Hanh argues that these descriptions were significant for two reasons:

> images of wars and battles in far-flung corners of the empires conveyed senses of patriotism, adventure, and the cause of civilization, as well as the visual pleasure of exotic locales ... Colonial wars instigated illustrated magazines' coverage of local cultures simply because, as a result of the fascination with colonial wars, relevant regions were in focus. Representations of military heroism, violence, and local culture appeared simultaneously. (2012: 78–79)

Hanh's point is that the discourse was layered with both regional/national concerns and an interest in the exotic distant Other. This discourse is precisely what the Indian traveller undermines when he focuses on these colonial conquests and wars, by pointing to the non-European elements that determined the necessity of such wars (territorial conquests) and contributed to both, the success of the wars and the sense of European/English national identity. Thus, by directing attention to these creolized wars—by which I mean the centrality of the xeno in the making of European nation- and empire-building wars—the Indian travellers demonstrate how the discourse of national identity, national triumphs and national territory are always already constituted by the Other. This is an inversion of the periodical press's project of documenting English success in the distant exotic land because the Indian traveller points to the exotic *within* even ultra-nationalist projects such as war.

Dutt, Ram, Nowrojee-Merwanjee and Banerjee, among others, in the act of documenting British triumphs, are in fact demonstrating what Michael Rothberg terms 'multidirectional memory'. For Rothberg, 'collective memories of seemingly distinct histories—such as those of slavery, the Holocaust, and colonialism—are not so easily separable from one another' (2011: 524). For Rothberg, there is an urgent need to include 'differentiated empirical history, moral solidarity with victims of diverse injustices and an ethics of comparison that coordinates the asymmetrical claims of those victims' (526). Such a memory-work includes processes of transcultural borrowing, exchange and adaptation (524). More importantly, Rothberg suggests that such a memory is marked by a 'multidirectional sensibility—a tendency to see history as relational and as woven from similar, but not identical fabrics' (528). He sees both comparison and political affect as central to this process (525).

Following Rothberg, I suggest that the Indian traveller, first, refuses to accord undisputed pride of place to English memories of their military conquests by interweaving it with memories of valour by other races, or ruin and destruction of the foreign. Second, and following from the first, the traveller locates this triumph within a comparative history of colonial empires such as those of Russia and France, through the invocation of Napoleon and Crimea, among others.

The first signals the traveller's multidirectional memory of English conquest *and* mourning—for the foreign (France, Crimea, Copenhagen) destroyed as a result of England's triumph. Even the triumphal relic, then, serves the Indian traveller as a means of recalling who lost when England won. Thus, the relics of the nation's great wars and the memorials around these that Ram, Dutt and the others describe are not solely defined within the rubric of 'Englishness'. The second, a more distant point, invokes a trans-European phenomenon of imperial greed and resultant violence.

The Indian traveller responds, I suggest, in the form of 'political affect' when he deflects the discourse away from any putative admiration of English triumph by expressing horror at the sight of injured Egyptian bodies or Copenhagen in flames, or taking pride in the contribution of non-English races to Britain's imperial progress. Thus, Doss erodes any potential evaluation of representations of English military prowess by documenting the role played by brave Indian soldiers. The Victoria Cross, he notes, went to many Indian soldiers serving in the British army. In the process, I suggest, some of the heroism of the English to be found in the popular press of the age (see Hanh 2012) is eroded in the counter-narrative provided by the Indian traveller. That the sentimentality is turned towards and is invested in non-English events from the past as well when viewing the celebratory *English* paintings and relics may be then construed as the imperial-subject traveller's inversion of the traditional European exotic.

The attention travellers like Doss and Banerjee pay to Indian soldiers in the imperial machinery are instantiations of multidirectional memory, instantiations that approximate to the Occidental exotic without succumbing to the European exotic's easy binarism of us/them. The Occidental exotic in the Indian traveller is one committed to the multilayered nature of European identity, where the layers originate in several cultural exchanges and appropriations. The Occidental exotic enunciates these appropriations when pointing to the xeno at the heart of the Empire. In the Occidental exotic of the Indian traveller, there is no *one* England.

With multidirectional memories that foreground xeno-figures, the Indian travellers reterritorialize the English space and English spectacle with their focus on the foreign (Egyptian) bodies and the foreign audience's (themselves) response. There is no longer an ethnocentrism of the English spectacle because the foreign takes centre stage, in the Panorama and in the audience's response to it. Whether, as Daniel O'Quinn (2012) argues in the case of the Arab Abul Hassan's affective response to the *Ta'ziyeh* performance in early nineteenth-century London, this constitutes the 'staging of affect and community affiliation' is a moot point. But what is clear is that the Indian travellers do foreground the intractable foreign at the heart of London.

Other instances and modes of such de- and reterritorializing of London and England via the invocation of xeno-figures may also be found in these texts.

Romesh Chunder Dutt explicitly links Britain's imperial dreams with the process itself. Dutt writes:

> England is great, not as a military power in Europe,—but in her colonies. To display in a focus as it were the vast resources of her various colonies, to display to Europe and to the world the strength which she derives from her connection with various nations to the ends of the world, and to draw closer the bonds of sympathy and fellow-feeling which bind these colonies to her,—this was the idea of the Exhibition,—and of the reception of the Indian and Colonial visitors. England desired that these visitors should go back to their countries full of sympathy and affection for her, and every English town, every alderman and mayor in every corporation, worked nobly towards this common end … The idea of a sort of federation of all these colonies and dependencies with England was in the heart of hosts and guests alike, and was expressed forcibly in many an eloquent speech ... (1896: 145–146)

These exhibitions have been studied for the ways in which they produced in miniature the extent and expanse of imperial Britain for the consumption of the English visiting them (Flyn and Barringer 1998, Mathur 2011), and therefore need not detain us here for repetition. However, what I wish to draw attention to is Dutt's keywords: *strength, bonds of sympathy and fellow-feeling, affection.* Several rhetorical flourishes are at work in Dutt's codes here.

Britain's strength, he declares at the very outset, is 'in her colonies'. Centring the foreign and the distant at the heart of the Empire, Dutt deterritorializes metropolitan imperial discourse. The accent on 'strength', aligned with 'colonies', shifts the solidity of imperial power and formation away from London, the British Government and the British people towards a non-European space, geopolitical, demographic and cultural. Dutt's introduction of the colonies is a narrative and discursive xenotransplantation which appears exotic and therefore, by definition, distant and untouchable.

Yet, he qualifies this xenotransplantation narrative by adding the tropes of sentimentality—affection, sympathy—with a biological reference ('heart') to the earlier symbolism of 'strength'. Dutt's reference to Britain's strength may be fruitfully read as Britain's *vitality*. Thus, Dutt's insistence on England's 'strength' is, I suggest, a code for England's *life* itself. Imperial and English life, then, says Dutt, can only live with the colonies. England receives its life from the colonies who are held to it with 'bonds of sympathy' and 'affection'. The idea of such a cohesive lifeform ('federation') was in the 'heart', says Dutt, of 'hosts and guests'. Strength, or life, that draws on the external colonies then is no longer truly exo- or outside. It is a *part* of England and is a fact people recognize in their 'hearts'.

Writing about his heart transplant in his famous *L'Intrus*, Jean-Luc Nancy says:

> A life 'proper' that resides in no one organ but that without them is nothing. A life that not only lives on [survit], but that still lives properly, within the three-fold grip of the stranger/the foreign: that of the decision, of the organ, and of the transplant's effects. (2002: 8)

Nancy would go on to say, like Dutt's image of a linked 'federation', that life is polymorphic, embedded and enmeshed in networks:

> [T]here comes a certain continuity of intrusion, its permanent regime: added to the more-than-daily doses of medication, and being monitored in the hospital, are the dental effects of radiation therapy, the loss of saliva, alimentary supervision as well as that of contacts that may be contagious, the weakening of muscles and kidneys, the diminution of memory and of the strength to work, the reading of medical analyses, the insidious returns of mucositis, candidiasis, polyneuritis, and the general feeling of no longer being dissociable from a network of measurements, observations, and of chemical, institutional, and symbolic connections, which do not allow themselves to be ignored, as can be those of which ordinary life is always woven. On the contrary, these connections deliberately keep life constantly alert to their presence and surveillance. I become indissociable from a polymorphous dissociation. (12)

Appropriating Nancy's account of a biomedical condition and process to read Dutt's discourse is, at first sight, bizarre. Nancy pays attention to the connections between man and machines, moving the focus from *exo-* (the heart coming from outside) to *endo-* (transplanted into him). His account elsewhere on the heart as the seat of emotions, such as sympathy, resonates with Dutt's insistence on networks that keep Britain alive and strong, and his own trope of the feelings in the 'heart' of English and Indian populations. Dutt implies that England's lifeline is supplied by nourishment from the colonies, who are outside yet within England. It is the network of colonies that keeps life *alive*. Hence there is no possibility of speaking of England as a self-contained autonomous imperial centre without a reference to its polymorphous nature.

Further, in this same passage, Dutt categorizes the visitors to the exhibition as 'hosts and guests'. He quickly deconstructs this dichotomy by observing that the 'idea of a sort of federation of all these colonies and dependencies with England' was in the 'heart of hosts and guests alike'. If we assume the hosts are the organizers of the exhibition and the visitors would be other Englishmen and women, then Dutt is claiming that *all* English/Europeans feel the need for such a federation where England and her colonies would be organically linked. If we assume that at least some of the visitors/guests were people like Dutt (that is, non-English, colonial subjects) and other Indians, then the above passage's use of the dichotomy alongside the presumed commonality of feeling—'in the heart'—may be interpreted differently.

Dutt has already shown us that England's life depends on its external colonies which, consequently, are no longer external to her, being her very 'strength'. Visitors from the colonies, like Dutt, who believe in and feel for the federation of England and the colonies, as supposedly all English (hosts) do, are then not *guests*, because it is their homelands that are now intrinsic to England. That is, if what Dutt says is true, and the colonies (one of which is India) are now a part of England's strength, then Dutt is not a guest but a part of the host body. He has already demolished here the dichotomy of host/guest with his preceding description of 'dependencies'. Then, by suggesting the same structure of feeling across *English hosts* and *Indian/non-English guests*, he further deconstructs the binary by linking them in affective affinities, namely, sympathy and affection, whose seat, tropologically, is their 'heart'. In my reading, Dutt not only makes the colonies, including India, indispensable to England's life, he also refuses to retain any hierarchy/dichotomy as host/guest. In short, the xeno-figure at the heart of the Empire is not an intruder but is the veritable lifeline that keeps the Empire alive, and with which the Empire has a polymorphous relation. There are only networks linking, embedding, the xeno-figures within England's body.

T.N. Mukharji would retain Dutt's organicist metaphors with a slight variation. This time London is the 'heart' of the world, supplying 'life-blood' to the rest of the globe:

> It is the centre of the earth, the heart that supplies the life-blood to the commerce of the world, and sends forth the impulse by force

> of which the Esquimaux hunts the seals among the icebergs on the Greenland coast, the whaler braves the perils of the polar seas, the Chinaman's ape plucks the tea from the steepest hills, and the savage Negro pursues the fleet ostrich in the boundless deserts of Central Africa. (1902: 40)

Mukharji may have altered the biomedical trope a fraction by asserting that England is the heart of the world, but the circulatory metaphor (life-blood that reaches the colonies and even places that are *not* its colonies—such as Greenland and China) *implies* that there is a necessary linkage that keeps the body and body politic alive. That is, even if Mukharji does not claim outright that the colonies keep the heart going, the very use of the trope suggests Mukharji's awareness of the Empire's dependency.

Tagore would use the same organicist metaphor in his *Diary of a Westward Voyage*:

> If this improper over-abundance of material goods is considered the chief element of civilization, then that civilization definitely becomes man-destroying. This worldwide cultivation of the steady draining of the human blood will surely lead man one day to a suicidal end ... (1962: 68)

Others too make this dependency clear. Lala Baijnath would phrase it in simpler and direct terms: 'the possession of India is thus a valuable acquisition to England' (1893: 69). Rabindranath Tagore would say in his *Journey to Persia and Iraq*:

> The fatal arrow for Europe lies in the weakness of Asia. The heavy load of suspicion, hostility and hatred, of untruthful diplomacy and spying which Europe carries on her back is due to her grabbing for pieces and portions of the weak Asiatic continent. (2003: 29)

Taken together, Dutt, Tagore, Baijnath and Mukharji, some explicitly and the others implicitly, locate England's life in its extraterritorial linkages, thereby suggesting that the foreign is integral to England's health.

Exotic Diversity and the Collection

In his reading of exoticism Victor Segalen argues that exoticism is an aesthetics of diversity (2002). Segalen's focus on ontological and epistemological diversity, freeing exoticism from the commodity fetishism and colonial cultures, unsettles power relations between the representing European power and the represented, claim contemporary critics (Aravamudan 2012: 240, Jenkins 2012). Such a diversity interpreted within imperial geocultural formation—embodied in amusement parks, exhibitions, literature—by the Indian traveller produces a global cultural discourse where it is no longer simply centre/periphery, Europe/India. That is, instead of a mere 'appeal of the exotic' in terms of binary pairs such as Europe/India, such an exoticism would involve multiple cultures within the same frame. The self/other relation which Segalen identifies as the key element in the aesthetics of diversity could also be reworked with *more than one racial/cultural Other* when it is enunciated by the Indian traveller.

We see such an insistence on the aesthetics of diversity in Kshitish Banerjee's account of seeing an African woman masquerading as an Indian dancer in a London 'amusement hall'. Banerjee first notes that the board announcing the event said 'Indian romantic magic and dance. The vivid picture of an Indian village'. There were some 'Bengali musicians who were playing on a harmonium, a flute, a *tabla* and several other musical instruments'.

> Then the dance-programme began. Now a young lady, an African Negro, appeared on the platform. She wore an Indian costume. So short was her sari that neither her upper body nor her legs beneath the knees were properly covered. Attended by the Indian music she began to dance, in the course of which she was making ugly postures by moving her breast, waist and eyes. It irritated me so much that I rose to my feet just after she had finished her dance and gave the audience to understand that the girl was not Indian and her dance too was not in any sense Indian. I requested them not to form an impression of the Indian music and dance from what they had seen there. (1938: 138–139)

Banerjee is clearly upset at the masquerade and what he sees as the vulgar impersonation of Indian art. The entire spectacle alters the English perception of Indian art, he argues, with the audience.

Writing about his visit to Europe a few decades before Banerjee, T.N. Mukharji records how he was mistaken for a West Indian. A young girl, a visitor to the Crystal Palace exhibition, he writes, 'complimented me for the performance of the band brought from my country, 'via [sic] the West Indian band composed of Negroes and Mulattos' (1902: 105). Mukharji admits that despite this obvious error on the girl's part, he went 'on chattering for a quarter of an hour' (105), but also says he 'wince[d]' at the mistake. Mukharji, more forgiving than Banerjee, is gesturing at the homogenizing of race.

Banerjee and Mukharji point to the portability of both race and culture in colonial representations of Europe's Other. For the white audience and visitor, the black woman *is* Indian, and the dance *is* Indian. Imperial amusement, then, Banerjee points out, hinges not on any clear binary or distinction between races but in a remarkably naïve denial of difference and diversity *between* races. For English audiences, the globe is being served up but cast as a racial *binary*: white, non-white. This proclivity for fluid racial identities ensures that, while the imperial centre may be peopled by *many* races, the discourse and representations ignore these differences in mass spectacles which are primarily about the managing of difference. It at once destroys the uniqueness of each racial-cultural group but also invokes an exoticism based solely on the English/Indian binary (in this case). The black woman, exotic in and of herself, is exoticized as an Indian performer. Thus, the exotic Other (race) is mobile, with exoticism being distributed across a continuum on which both African and Indian women are located. Banerjee is, in fact, underscoring the homogenizing tendency of Empire which does not bother to distinguish, at least at the level of the consumer/everyday, African and Indian identities. For the white audience, the black performer from Africa, the Caribbean or India are fungible in the homogenizing space that is London. In other words, Banerjee's critique of England's mass entertainments such as the dance and Mukharji's annoyance is directed at precisely this racial portability where a rich diversity is subsumed into a flattening binary.

This flattening also means that the performers are disconnected from their original homes and nations and relocated into incongruous settings such as the English stage. In this overtly synthetic (campy?) setting, the 'native', dark-skinned dancer is 'incongruously out of keeping with the … [dancer's] world, but expressive nonetheless of fantasies of imperial control over space, landscape and interior' (McClintock 1995: 125).

We also, however, have very different approaches to the exotic. The Indian traveller is more understanding and tolerant of exoticism, and thrilled to see various cultures packaged and showcased on the English stage. Take, for instance, Jhinda Ram's experience of the English stage. He watches the performance of 'The Mikado' or 'The Town of Titipu … a Japanese play'. It was 'a brilliant and triumphant success', he writes. After the play, the 'Japanese nobles were discovered standing and sitting on the stage in their native attitudes' and they 'sang the chorus in a splendid way':

> If you want to know who we are,
> We are gentlemen of Japan:
> On many a vase and jar,
> On many a screen and fan,
> We figure in lively paint:
> Our attitudes queer and quaint,
> You're wrong if you think it ain't. (1893: 23)

Ram records oriental entertainment at the heart of London, where the Japanese self-reflexively advertise themselves as 'queer and quaint'. He sees London's exotic entertainments as splendid and spectacular. Undisturbed by anxieties that there may be a fair amount of stereotyping and ethnic chic marketing involved, Ram is more accepting of the cosmetic cosmopolitanism being sold on the English stage.

Sullaiman Mahomed had noted that London's 'teeming population, forming a vast beehive, numbers among its representatives from all parts of the world' (1895: 265). Windsor Castle, he writes with the enthusiasm of a tourist, is magnificent in its 'royal pomp, magnificence and splendour' before itemizing the 'costly jewellery, invaluable pictures, furniture of the very best, rich hangings and tapestry and the richest embroidery and painting'. He concludes this inventory of Windsor's glory with 'there are three or four big rooms, full of treasures received from India, including the famous Peacock Throne' (271). A few pages later he would document the treasures in the Tower of London: the Kohinoor, 'guns taken from Tippoo Sultan and Napoleon Bonaparte' (275). Jhinda Ram in the South Kensington Museums inventories the items in the India segment (1893: 40–41). Doss notes, in a wistful tone, that in the 'State Jewel House', he saw the 'Koh-i-noor, the diamond of unparalleled beauty and value, which once belonged to Runjeet Singh king of the Punjab, but is now the property of Queen Victoria' (1893: 59). Syed Ahmed Khan observes two features of the Zoological Gardens in Marseilles: 'Giraffe walked around in an enclosure where a small shed is built for the winter season. The shed has signs of Islamic flags etched on it and the Arabic inscription underneath it says …' (2011: 130).[3]

The Indian traveller's focus on diversity is structured around people, places and objects, as we can see in the above examples from Mahomed, Ram and others. On their inevitable tourist trip through the British Museum, the Indian travellers inventory the collection and recognize it as a globalized space with items from all parts of the world. Susan Stewart argues in *On Longing* that the collection does not seek the 'restoration of the context of origin, but rather the creation of a new context' (1993: 152). In the case of the collection, Stewart argues, the question is not whose labour made the collection possible but rather what is inside the collection (152). Further, the objects, no longer connected to their origins, are 'naturalized into the landscape of the collection itself' (156). Steward's arguments resonate with the work of commentators on the exotic, where the exotic, too, is viewed delinked from its origins (see Eaton 2006). In many ways, then, the museum and the exhibition freeze the exhibit in a past.

Take, for instance, the Colonial and Indian Exhibition of 1886, which 'staged for its visitors an elaborate encounter with a timeless and traditional India from within the "wild, mad whirl" of industrial modernity' when it showcased Indian village-life, artisans and craftsmen (Mathur 2011: 57). It was an India frozen in time, in a past that the 'West' had left far behind in its own evolution into modernity. Thus, India, embodied in its products, was located at an *early* stage in evolution with this focus on artisans and craftsmen rather than industry and modern technology, on its villages rather than on its cities.

However, the Indian traveller does not observe only the India exhibits.

In the British Museum, such a traveller finds Greek, Egyptian, English, European *and* Indian exhibits. Commentators argue that the textual inscriptions of the various artefacts onto paper, into an archive, results in a 'semiotic homogeneity' (David Jenkins, cited in Bennett et al. 2017: 38). For Bennett et al., the ordering of the world's artefacts into the museum is a sign of imperial domination and control. In the heyday of Empire, they argue, the 'different class fractions' organized into the museum, generates an 'ethnographic capital' and enables the 'epistemological authority' preliminary to governance (42–43).

However, the above project of colonial governmentality via the museum does not always work to impose this semiotic homogeneity. The Indian traveller encounters a *semiotic heterogeneity*, often quite cheerily and welcomingly. He sees, arranged in room after room, the world's difference and variety. First, the Indian traveller in his tourist peregrinations experiences a serial exoticism: from the ancient Greeks to the contemporary West. Second, this serial exoticism is no wide-eyed wonder, but hedged within a prior knowledge, however minimal, of these exotic cultures through their Westernized education and knowledge of the globe (as Sumathi Ramaswamy has argued in

Terrestrial Lessons [2018]). Third, the serial exoticism enables the traveller, passing from room to room in the museums, to locate himself, India and his civilization within this variety of humanity (especially in evolutionary and natural history museums). Fourth, in the process, he also locates mankind itself among other species and non-living materials on earth. Combined, these four do not produce a dominated subjectivity of the colonial traveller. He partakes of the ethnographic capital embodied in the museum, as a member of the human race and not only as imperial subject. It is also the first stage in a certain informed enchantment and cosmopolitanism.

Serial exoticism is the often-rapid experience of moving across what Anne McClintock described as panoptical time and anachronistic space. It signals the 'image of global history consumed—at a glance—in a single spectacle from a point of privileged invisibility' (1995: 37). In this human (social) and natural times were mapped onto each other so that human evolution was mapped to show how Western civilization represented the pinnacle of human progress, as opposed to the primitive (non-European) cultures. As Tony Bennett puts it:

> panoptical time and anachronistic space functioned as an administrative and regulatory technology whose principal mechanism was, paradoxically, one of freezing history by denying the agency of those subjects whose political perspectives threatened to make the bourgeois, male and imperial culture of the late Victorian era merely a stage in history rather than its end or telos. (2004: 25)

The 'far away could now be equated with the distant pasts which had been excavated in Europe' (62). That said, there is no 'point of privileged invisibility' in the Indian traveller's account of his visit to these museums. This is because the Indian traveller is aware of the museum as a pedagogic tool and his own position as a learner. T.B. Pandian, for instance, relates the artefacts he perceives in the British Museum to the textual inscriptions of these. He writes:

> The British Museum, where all that history has recorded, all that Science has taught, and all that Art has accomplished, is effectively illustrated in

> concrete forms by all manner of exhibits brought together and set forth like so many silent 'object lessons' taken from the Book of Nature and the archives of *universal* literature. The Museum contains the largest and richest general library in the world … (1897: 30, emphasis added)

Pandian aligns several aspects of the museum here. He sees the museum as an embodiment of *human* history, of 'universal literature' itself. This history, which includes the histories to be found in both arts and sciences, has a material dimension in the form of the objects displayed. There is a slide between the 'Book of Nature', presumably studied by science, and 'universal literature'. Pandian refuses to privilege European and English civilization. It refuses to accept any civilizational hierarchy that the viewer was supposed to learn (if Tony Bennett, McClintock and others are to be believed). That is, Pandian foregrounds the collection in the museum as *an index of humanity's diversity and progress as a whole*. He also mutes the presumed 'scientific' hierarchization or theories by simultaneously speaking of the knowledge to be found in *literature*. These moves, I suggest, when faced with serial exoticism, reject England's 'scientific' ordering of human civilization by proposing that the imaginative world of literature from around the world has also offered insights into the human. It pits, then, the scientism of England's anthropological museums against 'universal literature'.

Jhinda Ram appears to fulfil the purposes, as Bennett and others studying the politics of museum culture have defined it, of the collection when he writes 'we may gain in practical fashion, an idea of the successive dates of civilization' (1893: 55). Here, Ram appears to have conceded the hierarchy of civilizations implicit in the museum's ordering of various cultural collections. Ram then goes on to describe the Egyptian, Greek, Byzantine, Roman, Renaissance, Elizabethan 'courts' (rooms) before moving on to the industrial and technological exhibits. He also underscores that several of the exhibits are copies: '… a dark tomb copied from one at Beni Hassan … a model of the Acropolis … copies of the Apollo Belvedere' (56). Whether this inventory of cultures and civilizations in their metonymic variety is also serialized as a hierarchy is not very clear in Ram's account. He is, however, conscious of the museum as a place of simulacra: attesting to the 'copies' placed therein, Ram implies that the museum neither captures the original nor presents the entire civilizational story. It is, he suggests, partial (metonymic) and a simulacrum.

Kshitish Banerjee viewing the Natural History Museum writes:

> How delightful it is to see the varieties of people in their natural forms and how interesting it is to make a comparative study of different parts of man and those of a gibbon which are kept side by side ... In the geological world there are precious stones, different kinds of soils and rocks including even gold and silver rocks, and these are the things among others which interest the visitors. (1938: 130–131)

Sullaiman Mahomed observes that 'there is a grand museum of countless specimens of art and industry from all parts of the world', which, for him, makes the entire Crystal Palace 'a gigantic school for instruction as well as amusement' (1895: 273). Behramji Malabari at Tussaud's makes sure he 'begin[s] the tour with the Indian, Anglo-Indian and Afghan celebrities' (1895: 227). S.K. Bhuyan is impressed by the 'whole of ancient and medieval history and civilisation of the world' that were 'brought together by the patient and patriotic labours of generations of scholars and antiquarians' (1979: 60) in the museums of Britain. They represent, he says, 'the attainments of the civilised world' (61). Among these 'attainments of the civilised world', Bhuyan lists the 'the Magna Carta, the Rosetta Stone, the tablet of the Laws of Hammurabi, the Elgin Marbles and the Egyptian mummies' (60). One notes Bhuyan's emphasis on the transnational collection, which he reads in universalist terms and within global time frames. Egyptian and English materials are both part of this universal inventory of human achievements. The refusal to concede or invoke civilizational hierarchy by putting all of these into one series is a semiotic *heterogeneity* that disrupts any narrative that privileges the European modern over the non-modern Indian or African.

Serial exoticism in these cases emphasized through the saccadic movement of/by the Indian traveller across time and space (in the museum) generates an awareness of this semiotic heterogeneity when he focuses on the various chambers within which civilizational remnants are placed. That is, the Indian traveller is *aware* of his serially arranged viewing of cultural artefacts from different places (hence the mention of various rooms). He treats these as instances of heterogeneity and diversity rather than accept any imperial ordering of the same—there is no sense in the travelogues that the traveller sees the collection as anything other than embodying the glorious diversity of the world itself and humanity *in its entirety*.

The attempt to freeze time in a museum and to present certain parts of the world as non-modern—such as India—are noted by astute Indian travellers. Thus, Romesh Chunder Dutt wandering through the Crystal Palace writes:

> As a sight the Indian Court far surpassed the other Courts; and backward as India is in machinery and in practical and useful modern products, her ancient arts, her exquisite workmanship in gold, silver and ivory, and her fabrics of fine texture and unsurpassed beauty, are still the wonder of the modern world, and were the theme of unbounded admiration among hundreds of thousands of English ladies who visited these Courts. (1896)

Dutt concedes that India is not an industrial nation, that she has little by way of 'practical and useful modern products'. However, this does not, in Dutt's view, assign India to the primitive and ancient. In fact, he argues that these so-called non-modern crafts, skills and products are 'the wonder of the modern world'. That is, Dutt rejects the teleology and civilizational hierarchy (the lower/primitive Indian and the higher/advanced West) the museum implies, according to Bennett et al., by firmly claiming the label of the 'modern' for India.

T.N. Mukharji spends the better part of a chapter on the 'Colonial and Indian Exhibition'. He begins by noting the 'clay models of the military races that uphold the power of England in the East' (1902: 69).

He quickly moves on to the vessels, cutlery and jewellery from India, 'which from time immemorial excited the wonder and commanded the admiration of the western nations' (69). From this 'vast panorama of India's artistic wealth', Mukharji moves to representations of 'jungle life in India' (69–71). After this account, Mukharji turns to the anthropological: the 'various aboriginal races were interspersed among the products and manufactures of India'. This is Mukharji's commentary on the ethnological exhibits:

> … shortstatured Andamanese woman, bedecked with shells and leaves, the white skull of a near relation dangling on her jet black breast. Her husband stood near, spear in hand, his hair frizzled according to the most approved modern fashion …
>
> The Negrito type of the Andamanese bore a strong contrast to his neighbour, the Nicobarese, in whom the Malay element is predominant, although there seem to exist a strong admixture of the Mongolian blood in his veins. The Mongolian element grew stronger as the visitor passed on to the next group of models, consisting of the Burmans of the Irawady Delta and the Karens of the hills …
>
> That most interesting assemblage of tribes that people the North-east frontier of India, all belonging to the Mongolian family of the human race. There stood the tawny Sinpho, his head adorned with a helmet made of plaited rattan cane, and the everlasting Dao in his hand, with which he fights, chops off the head of his fallen foe, clears the forest land, cuts his scanty crop on the hillside, and does all sorts of household work. The proud Naga was there, fully equipped for war, dyed tufts of feather waving over his head, dyed human and goat's hair adorning his breast … The Naga is a savage. His insignia of honour are therefore so crude and primitive. Had he been civilised he would have prided in stars and ribbons … On the side of the Naga stood the Hill Miri of Assam. The customs and manners of this tribe agree in many respects with those of the Hindus of Lower Bengal … (71–74)

Mukharji goes on to discuss various other tribes and ethnic groups as well (74–75). After this, he expounds on the progress of Europe:

> The myriads of visitors that daily flocked to the Exhibition revealed to us the great mysterious cause of European progress. It is discontent.

> It is the constant search after knowledge and the constant readiness to accept a better state of things, whenever that is discovered and understood. (75–76)

Mukharji concedes the colonial-imperial construction of comparative history, which locates the European at the advanced levels of civilization and the non-European at the beginning moments of historical time when he writes:

> So far as material condition and intellect as applied to practical life go, the present of the European nations will be our future perhaps many centuries ... He [the Indian] has always done his best to shut his eyes against the influence of modern enlightenment. (77–78)

In one space—the Exhibition—Mukharji maps India and the 'West', and places and people within India. Sullaiman Mahomed too, like Mukharji, pays attention to the exhibition's ethnographic collection. He visits exhibits from the Arab world, the Caribbean, Java, Sumatra, Borneo, Fiji, New Zealand and 'many other places'. He terms some of them 'real savages', and they 'have their own wild dance', consisting, he says, of 'yelling and gesticulating' (126).

The exhibition functions, in Tony Bennett's phrase, as an 'evolutionary accumulator':

> accumulating all past times within itself, the evolutionary museum—by providing a summation of previous development (natural, cultural, scientific and technological), pointing a way forward and providing an instructional programme that would contribute to the realisation of this dynamic—functioned as a historical technology for operating on the present. It did so by activating the historical tension within the make-up of the modern person, giving this a progressive but gradualist momentum. This was clear enough in the programme proposed for the ethnological museum which, by means of the typological method, was to function as an evolutionary accumulator, storing—by means of their survivals—a record of each painstaking step in the processes of cultural and technological evolution, and thus providing a template for future social development as an equally painstaking and gradual process ... the museum accumulates the past to both retain it and initiate a movement beyond it. (2004: 106–107)

These 'centres of accumulation' (Bruno Latour's term, adapted by Bennett, 123), the museum, located the 'museum at the centre of a set of distributive networks through which the new forms of knowledge that had been made possible through its operations as a centre of accumulation could be brought to bear on the governmental task of shaping future citizens' (123). For Bennett and other museologists, the museum and the exhibition are places for the gathering of 'ethnographic capital' for the colonial government (2017: 42).

Ethnographic accounts, Joan-Pau Rubiés has argued, were integral to the (European) travel writing genre after the sixteenth century because geography (or cosmography) was a means of an 'encyclopedic synthesis for the description of the world' (2002: 242). Ethnographic discourses, which are part of almost every early modern as well as later travel narratives, 'convert the linear historicity of a foreign culture into a timeless present serving the historicity and narrative identity of the European writer/consumer' (Campbell 1999: 226). The Indian traveller provides a distanced ethnographic account: he is observing the various races and cultures within the synthetic narrative of the Exhibition. Cultural differences become coded and represented as racialized hierarchies when Mahomed or Mukharji dismiss the non-Europeans exhibited in London or Paris as 'savages'. The non-European becomes the object of consumption by other non-Europeans such as the Indian traveller, within the European space of the Exhibition.

Bennett's argument about the pedagogic and political dimensions of the museum is borne out by imperial subjects such as Mukharji, but their 'schooling' via the ethnographic exhibits in the European museum is not as complete or effective as Bennett implies. Thus, having conceded the superior modernity, technology and material progress of England as embodied in the museum and exhibition, Mukharji undertakes what I see as a spectacular shift in his account. This shift occurs in the form of short evaluative statements he inserts into his account:

> The poor Naga has therefore to be content with the short-lived honour of being privileged to wear the necklace of human hair round his neck.

> But he kills not so much for that distinction as for the pleasure which the act of killing affords to most men of all nations, except, all honour to him, the Hindu. The greatest pleasure which wild tribes in all ages and in all parts of the world found in life was in exterminating their fellow-men living on the opposite side of a river or a hill. Civilised men in Europe, restrained from cutting the throats of their neighbours, enjoy innocent pleasure by hunting to death the poor little fox, or by shooting the deer, or the pheasants and pigeons specially reared for the sake of being killed. The rich among them go to all parts of the world to kill. (1902: 73)

He then adds:

> Of all nations in the world, the Hindu alone feels sorrow to shed blood, and is able to realise the fact that such acts are against the dictates of mercy, for his religion teaches him to look upon every-living thing as his own self. (73–74)

And subsequently: 'The power to relish destruction of life is developed in the Naga in as lush a degree as it is in the European' (74).

The shift in Mukharji's discourse when speaking of the comparative history of the world's peoples—the 'image of global history' that McClintock talks of (already cited)—has two stages.

The first stage is his positioning of the Nagas, whom he has characterized as 'savage' (like Sullaiman Mahomed does, of Caribbean peoples exhibited in the Crystal Palace) in the passage quoted above, alongside the European. Thus, Mukharji undermines the discourse of European modernity, progress and civilizational superiority which, supposedly, is embedded in the exhibition by equating the 'savage' and the 'civilized'. In the centre of accumulation—London—where the exotic savage is presented to the world, Mukharji overturns the hierarchy when he views the exhibits.

The second stage is visible in Mukharji's comparative 'study', so to speak, of bloodlust. Mukharji's statement about the Hindu who 'alone feels sorrow to shed blood' is an assertion of a *moral* civilizational superiority in the exhibition. Thus, even as he concedes England and Europe's *material* progress and advancement, he assigns the position of the moral superior to the Hindu. Inserting a stereotype of the 'spiritual East' into his discourse, Mukharji reads the entire history embodied in the museum through an entirely different lens in these statements.

Behramji Malabari also expresses a similar view of English bloodlust:

> A military career seems to be the ambition of many a well-born youth who can afford it. Even Anglo-Indian parents, who have the means, find their sons more inclined to that line than to others. Do the boys like it best? Is it the savage instinct for killing that stirs them, or is it their destiny? Who can say if England is not preparing for a very big war? (1895: 133)

Both Malabari and Mukharji when viewing the museums in England in particular and English society in general, offer interpretations that effectively undermine the civilized English/savage colonized binary. At one point, Mukharji would even refer to the British as 'civilised savages' (146). This suggests that, although the exhibition of the variety of human races, tribes, ethnicities and their cultural practices under one roof is a pedagogic project envisioned by the English to train the colonial subjects into accepting the advanced European, Mukharji inverts this intention.[4] The quest for and accumulation of ethnographic capital that may have been the goal of the exhibition then becomes the imperial subject's when he shifts the focus to instances of shared savagery (Nagas, Europeans) and moral superiority over a material one (Hindu over European). To phrase it differently, it is the imperial subject who generates an unexpected kind and quantity of ethnographic capital precisely because the centre of accumulation placed all cultures under one roof and enabled Mukharji's comparative study and musings. The imperial subject at the heart of the Empire proffers a variant lesson from the one the exhibition sets out to deliver to its visitors from the colonies.

Exotic diversity, therefore, prepares the grounds for the imperial-subject traveller to overturn, or at least erode, the power of the discourse embodied in the museum and the collection. It allows him to speak in universalizing terms rather than England/India binaries when speaking of diversity. Then, as we have just seen in Dutt, Mukharji and others, they also invert the discourse of civilizational hierarchies.

When Malabari, Dutt, Mukharji and other travellers experience the exhibitions of London or Paris, they are initially embedded as imperial subjects within the circulation of ethnographic objects that, first, communicate to the subjects the power of the imperial centres of accumulation. Second, as they traverse the exhibition and examine the collection, they develop comparative histories such as the ones cited above. These histories do not follow the logic of the imperial collection but pursue a trajectory independent of the collection. Thus, the sight of Nagas or Maoris in London/Paris enables Mahomed, Mukharji and Malabari to also incorporate other histories into their narratives, especially that of English bloodletting, imperial wars, among others. That is, the collections may be seen as enabling what Ricardo Roque has termed 'epistemic circulation'. Roque writes:

> This colonial economy did not just move objects from place to place more or less violently or simply trade objects as gifts or commodities, but these networks also moved and traded documents and information. Therefore, together with objects, miniature histories were circulated, so that such epistemic circulation drew trajectories that were not necessarily coincidental to the physical movements of objects. (2011: 15)

The Indian traveller's exposure to the exotic diversity of the museum collections marks the epistemic circulation around the objects on display—from Maori persons to material products from various nations—and not always within the logic of the colonial collection or ethnographic capital. This does not, of course, mean that the collection's ethnographic capital is eroded. Epistemic circulation is the unexpected production and transmission of information in the form of other histories and cultural knowledge that is engendered by the colonial exhibition but not limited to it. The objects in the museum may have been collected by imperial collectors but they produce or lead to knowledge not always determined by these processes of collecting, cataloguing and display. When, for instance, the Indian traveller is exposed to the Maori or Naga 'bodies' or artefacts within the space of the museum, he moves on to tangential histories and comparisons with England and/or Europe. Thus, we can see epistemic circulation as a rupture in the colonial pedagogic project of both, the history narrated by the museum collection and of the imperial subject who is to be taught this history. Epistemic circulation is the natural outcome of the colonial museum's exotic diversity. Its trajectory (as Roque terms it) is unpredictable and evades regulation as merely 'colonial' knowledge or colonial pedagogy. Epistemic circulation also renders the Indian traveller a cosmopolitan rather than just an imperial subject through the consumption and production of these multiple stories and histories of different peoples and cultures.

The impression one gets from reading these passages is that the Indian traveller is enchanted by the sights of London and the other European cities but tempers this enchantment in various ways. Having been entranced by the variety and splendour of the museum and gardens, they explain it in ways that are unexpected and subversive. It is to the specific enchanted subject that we now turn.

Informed Enchantment

In this section, I suggest that a certain cosmopolitanism emerges in the Indian travellers' negotiations with the variety, novelty and exotic in England/Europe. This cosmopolitanism is undoubtedly a romantic one, with wonder, curiosity and pleasure at the sights he observes. The appreciation of the wonders of the Western world that one sees in these texts marks a fascination with the exotic. Yet, this appeal of the exotic is not merely wide-eyed wonder. It is wonder imbued with a clear knowledge of what he is perceiving, and for which the imperial-subject traveller is *prepared*.

For Srinivas Aravamudan following Tzvetan Todorov, exoticism and knowledge are incompatible. Aravamudan writes:

> A non-exoticist sensibility would systematically assimilate novelty into the observer's life experience. To allow the exotic to linger, novelty has to be placed in a framework that resists assimilation and revels in the perceived unavailability of the sensibilities produced by the exotic object. (2012: 228)

Linking exoticism with cosmopolitanism, Aravamudan argues:

> If the exotic implies a free-floating object or person that delivers strange effects—whether frissons of delight or shivers of danger—the cosmopolitan denotes a free-floating subject who connects hitherto distinct spheres. In some ways, it could be argued that the cosmopolitan subject arose by being able to harness the unproductive remainders of exoticism into a kind of comparative engine. The cosmopolitan was a new kind of subject who could rise above specific objects, properties, and principles. (229)

The Indian traveller in Europe achieves precisely a mixture of all these effects. First, he retains the absolute singularity of English sights, people and artefacts, treating them as unassimilable into his daily life. He is a 'proper' colonial subject, in awe of the imperial metropolis, enchanted by all things English. He has, indeed, come to England and travels across Europe in search of the singularity. That said, he then proceeds to demonstrate remarkable knowledge of the objects he sees, the places he visits and the culture he encounters. We now see a shift, in which the Indian traveller offers us a different engagement with England, one that might be called a rationalization of the enchantment—what I term 'informed enchantment'—of the first moment. If the exotic enchants the traveller, we discover that the traveller also undertakes a cosmopolitan position of making comparisons, connecting histories and, in general, assimilating these different singularities into his life. He romanticizes it and then assimilates it.

The Aesthetics of Enchantment

> You may read of London all your life, but you will never know what it is like, unless you see it. (Pillai 2006: 9)

Pillai here warns the armchair traveller that nothing, no reading about nor textual familiarity with London, prepares one for the city. Pillai is only rehearsing an old trope in travel literature: the authenticity of the eyewitness; it is embodied cognition that authenticates the sights. It is in the cognitive engagement with the sights of the imperial metropolis that the colonial subject first demonstrates the sense of enchantment in his narrative documentation of his experiences.

Now, enchantment and wonder, commentators tell us, are about the *cognition* of wondrous events and things, and the emotional response to them. Narratives of wonder demand, Jonathan Sell notes, a bodily inscription of the eyewitness into the event being narrated so that the cognitive and emotional states may be conveyed to the reader who is located in a 'contextual disparity' from the traveller (2006: 135–136). In London, the colonial subject encounters, cognitively, an industrialized modernity. What these colonial subjects are enchanted by is the focus in this section.

It is with enchantment that the aesthetic negotiation and understanding of England by the colonial subject begins, and it is this enchantment that will later modulate into a more 'informed' engagement with the cognitively *new*. Every Indian traveller of the age marvels at and offers fulsome details of the extensive (modern) mobilities in England, its great museums, monuments and galleries, and finally, its present cultural scene, specifically the theatre.

Antoinette Burton has pointed to the descriptions of English railway systems as a generic feature of these narratives (1996: 129). Simonti Sen also notes that urbanism as an index of England's modernity was the focus of all travellers and that most of them recorded their astonishment at the sights (2005: 76–77). Burton and Sen are right: these descriptions exhibit a sense of wonder at London's sights. Flowing crowds, the efficiency of the London railways, the helpful cabby and the sights from the top of the omnibus are features that elicit wonder in each of these narratives, suggesting that the colonial subject, above all else, is fascinated by the mobility that the English in general and London in particular embody. This mobility is the marker of the imperial *present* that the traveller is enchanted by.

G.P. Pillai writes: 'every five minutes there is a fresh train … How surprising! And these trains are underground!' (2006: 9). Lala Baijnath is even more wonderstruck: 'The Metropolitan and District Railways of London … are really triumphs of John Bull's energy and perseverance in the means of locomotion employed in his metropolis' (1893: 35). N.L. Doss exhibits a fair amount of anxious wonder at the crowded streets when he records: 'there is a ceaseless stream of vehicles pouring in from the several roads' (1893: 39). Jagatjit Singh's first comments on London include the now-mandatory one on its crowds: 'I greatly marvelled at the enormous traffic in the streets as I drove along' (1895: 60). The very first comment T.B. Pandian makes about London records bewilderment and anxiety. The setting, yet again, is the railway system:

> Alighting at one of the many platforms of the Victoria Station, London, the Oriental stranger is bewildered by the number of such landings he views about him, his unaccustomed eyes being familiar with no more than three on Indian lines. (1897: 4)

By presenting himself as a 'stranger', and the sights as strange to his Indian eyes, Pandian inaugurates the trope of the wonder-struck colonial subject.

The bodily inscription of wonder, we can see, takes the form of the personal anecdote. Anecdotes, Stephen Greenblatt argues, are 'registers of the singularity of the contingent'; they are not history, they are provisional and can be retold (1991: 3).

Pillai narrates the train's movement in terms of the sheer physical experience of it:

> You feel you are perpetually travelling. You find you are beginning to see the same stations, the same porters, and you realise you have been

> travelling in a circle ... You may read of London all your life, but you will never know what it is like, unless you see it. (2006: 9)

N.L. Doss wakes up to the quiet of the London morning, and records his cognitive disorientation at the stillness:

> I waked up in the morning, and thought it was too early to wake up, for I saw no sign of daybreak as I was accustomed to ... I thought I would lie in bed, until I would hear the crows sing out their accustomed melody in the morning ... I afterwards learned that a crow or any other bird, except sparrows, is seldom seen in London ... (1893: 36)

Doss is here recording the startling, wondrous difference in the experience of waking up, a difference that brings home to him the difference in settings, environments and cities.

To capture the wonder of London's crowds, Doss again resorts to the anecdotal mode, where it is his personal experience that is foregrounded:

> I often walked along this street, and the constant throng of vehicles of all descriptions that passed along this road, and the immense crowd of foot-passengers that walked on the footpaths on its two sides, made me quite nervous about my own safety, when I first saw this ever moving mass of men, horses, and carriages. (39)

Jagatjit Singh, upon perceiving the sombre buildings of London, notes that they 'give an impression of gloom and sadness'—which is the impression they make on his emotional faculties at that moment (1895: 59). Jhinda Ram confesses that, having seen the crowded London streets, he 'yielded to the temptation of plunging recklessly into the thick of English life' (1893: 11), even though, he says he did not know where he was 'going to, or how far, or why' (11). It was, he notes, 'a most difficult task to cross the roads' (11).

These anecdotes, the *petit histoires* of London's modernity as perceived by the colonial subject, constitute the first *cognitive* moments of the aesthetics of enchantment. The enchantment is not simply constituted by viewing, but by the very physical experience of mobility, of the rush of London life. The enchantment references London's present, its modernity.

The second set of objects that comes in for sustained attention from the traveller is the monumental-memorial-museum culture of England. The Indian traveller, while drawn to the modernity of England's metropolis, is more enthusiastic about its past. If, as Nigel Leask argues, English and European romanticism 'imported the antique, the curious, and the picturesque to the metropolis, as modernity, technology, rationalism, and 'universalist' aesthetics were exported to the periphery' (2002: 52–53), we perceive a reversal in the Indian traveller's narrative. If India is the periphery, then the traveller from India who chooses to focus on England's antiquity wonders at the antiquity at the heart of modern London. The traveller from the margins, therefore, is less moved by the efficiency of modernity than by the existence of the picturesque—exotic—antiquity within this modernity. It is not, it must be noted, the English metropolis that alone focuses on the picturesque and the ancient, but a traveller from the periphery who does so.

The interest in Macaulay, the English poets, philosophers and statesmen like Carlyle and J.S. Mill constitutes a part of this antiquarian impulse. Pandian is all praise for the 'solemn and majestic grandeur of the more ancient cathedrals and churches', and prefers the 'sacred shrines of Old England' for being 'a study in themselves' for instance (1897: 32). The mandatory viewing of Westminster and the castles suggests an equal, if not greater, engagement with England's antiquity than with its present. Even when traversing the wealth of the British Museum, Doss confesses, what interests him is the collection of 'numerous antiquarian and ethnological collections ... the signatures of some of the ancient kings and queens of England ... old charters ...' (1893: 56) and in Scotland, the grave of John Knox (124), even though he is sceptical of the supposed blood stains from a murder committed three hundred years ago (125). Jhinda Ram opens his chapter on memorials and monuments in London with fulsome praise—'to do honor to their names and to show respect to their memory' (1893: 45)—before going on to detail the attractions of the ancient civilization exhibited at Crystal Palace (56) and later Westminster Abbey (65–69) and the Tower of London (69–75). The enchantment with Madame Tussauds, another commonplace in every travelogue along with the theatre, the memorials and museums, clearly marks the colonial subject as a cultural tourist, a spectator, in imperial London (Baijnath 25, Doss 69, Ram 50–53, Singh 74).

Finally, every single traveller is enchanted by the English theatre scene. For example, the Rajah of Kolhapur seems to have gone to practically every theatre in Drury Lane and Covent Gardens (Rajah Ram Chuttraputtee 1872: 23–24, 36). Pandian refers with considerable awe to the 'temples of drama', the London theatres, before listing them (1897: 24). Baijnath, too, is all praise for the London theatre scene, where watching the staging of *Much Ado About Nothing*, he says, made him 'realize what Shakespeare is' (51). Jagatjit Singh claims he enjoyed the Prince of Wales's theatre 'very much' (63).

However, as we shall see, this cultural tourist role is not the only one occupied by the imperial subject. Displacing this identity is that of the cultured tourist, and this tourist's aesthetic engagement with London is of a wholly different kind.

The Aesthetics of Recognition

Thus far I have argued that the enchantment with things English is characterized by an emphasis on the sheer cognitive pleasures of 'seeing' England. But 'seeing' as a tourist is not the only way the Indians perceive England. Combined with the role of the passive gazer is that of the enquiring observer. Jonathan Crary has persuasively demonstrated that to be an observer is to follow 'codes, rules, practices'. An observer is one who 'sees within a prescribed set of possibilities, embedded in a system of convention' (1990: 5–6). The Indian traveller is enchanted by England, but he is also viewing England from within specific codes and a specific 'set of possibilities'.

These codes, I now argue, construct a wholly different subject-position of the imperial subject.

N.L. Doss, in the first lines of his narrative, presents himself as a man eager to see England: 'the idea of visiting England and seeing its wonders and its still more wonderful people in their native home, was very exciting' (1893: 1). Baijnath claims: 'It is now-a-days the ambition—the dream of every educated Indian, to pay a visit to the home of his rulers, to those lands of civilization and liberty of which he has read so much, or which he wishes his country to come up to' (1893: 1). Jagatjit Singh admits, 'ever since I can remember it was my great ambition to travel in Western countries, and judge for myself of the marvellous things that were told me concerning them' (1895: iii). Each of them, therefore, opens with the sense of wonder, eager anticipation at seeing a long-awaited nation. But how exactly is the sense of anticipation created for the colonial subject? And how does it alter his ways of seeing?

The Indian travel narrative moves from an expression of cognitive enchantment to one of *recognition*. The first is the domain of wonder and admiration that constitutes a part of aesthetic understanding. The aesthetics of recognition is primarily an aesthetics of knowing and constitutes the second part of the aesthetic understanding of the traveller. The aesthetics of recognition, importantly, displaces the primary identity of 'colonial subject' occupied by the Indian and offers another identity: that of an informed, cosmopolitan cultural insider which is made possible by the traveller's 'memory citizenship' in English culture. But before this identity is forged, the narrative sets out to 'enclose' the wonders registered cognitively.

There are two stages to be examined here: the modes of textually 'enclosing' the wonders of England in the travellers, and the 'informed enchantment' that tempers and modifies the wonders the colonial subject experiences in England. We see a particular brand of cosmopolitanism here that characterizes these accounts in which the colonial subject has acquired a fair measure of textual, epistemological and aesthetic understanding of the 'wonders' of

England. There is, therefore, a move from the textual comprehension of wonder to the self-fashioning of the imperial-subject traveller as a 'knowing' subject and cultural insider. We have already studied the 'enumerative picturesque' in the preceding chapter—this can now be extended to make a related argument.

The perambulations through the city that then awes them with its scale is a means of embodied enchantment that is then managed through the enumeration narrative. 'Enchantment' is the 'childlike excitement about life' (Jane Bennett 2001: 5). Critics examining photo-walks and their role in producing enchantment argue:

> The relationship between movement, cognition, and knowledge is central here, since this embodied thinking happens in practice with one's surroundings. The photo-walks are thus to be understood as creative encounters, rather than as a means of 'collecting' information about the city. Here, attention is focused on the practice of walking and taking photographs, and the reflection to which this immersion with the environment may give a 'push.' This reflection, which might happen via enchantment, is a surprising momentary state in-between: an interlude of sorts. It is impossible to know whether or not these moments took place, but forming a creative relationship with one's surroundings can allow one to see the world anew. (Pyyry 2016: 111)

It is a *heightened* awareness of their setting, argues Pyyry. Pyyry concludes:

> Moments of enchantment are accidental, but they can sometimes be produced with artistic methods ... photo-walking as one potential way to produce these moments. During the photo-walks, sensing and thinking happened 'with' photography and by participating in the world. (112)

Thus, the effort at documenting the sights through the multisensory apparatus of the human eye, ear, skin but aided by the camera produces, as Pyyry suggests, a whole new degree of enchantment with the settings and route the traveller takes. Many Indian travellers did take photographs during their journey, especially of buildings, parks and landscapes. Following Pyyry, it is possible to see these images incorporated into their travelogue as a means of producing enchantment of a different order.

However, another route to enchantment may be discerned in these texts: enumeration and the statistical documentation of the sights they see. The inventory and numbers draw our attention to the scale—physical dimensions, volume, costs—of whatever they were seeing, and, in the process, as to *how* they were seeing and documenting it. That is, the observation accompanied by details such as dimensions is a different order of enchantment with the sights of London or Paris. It contains within itself processes and stages such as cognition, affect and reflection. This form of enchantment is at once 'childlike wonder' and knowledgeable wonder.

With this enumeration, the Indian traveller manages to not only deliver the magnitude of the culture/country but to also reduce, enclose and encompass the complexity of England into manageable data. The statistical account does, of course, convey the vastness and variety, but makes it less threatening when catalogued and numbered because the traveller imposes a pattern, a certain order, on the vastness. From this point, the traveller is also in a position to temper his wonder with understanding and evaluation, or 'recognition'.

The Indian traveller, having expressed awe and admiration for the English railway system—which is paradigmatic of their encounter with English modernity itself—also moves toward *enclosing* the wonder in a particular way: through an enumeration narrative. By 'enclosing', I mean the apprehension and comprehension of wonder, imposing a measure of textual control by casting objects and events that invoked cognitive surprise into a more manageable set of numbers and tables.

Take Jhinda Ram's narrative for instance. He first cites figures of London's population from the 1881 Census, followed by statistics of housing, coffee houses and pubs, the city's consumption of coffee, wheat, liquor, meats, and coal, the extent of sewage canals, the number of theatres, music halls and concert rooms, the incomes of the London Corporation, statistics of street accidents and figures on missing children (1893: 17–18). He gives the timings (24) and the extent of the omnibus network. Jhinda Ram's narrative at once captures the magnitude of London and the cognitive wonder at this. Seeking to impose some form of textual control over this magnitude, Jhinda Ram takes recourse to an enumerative narrative scheme where statistics encapsulate London's diversity, vastness and variety. His account of London's transport network reads as follows:

> Their 668 omnibuses work daily. In 1885 they carried 58,389,997 passengers, over 13,229,219 miles, and earned, at an average of about 2 1/2 d [d—for pence] each passenger, the sum of 576,780. Each bus earned at the rate of £ 18 a week. The Company's stud of horses numbered 7242. (23–24)

He also offers information about the number of deliveries the postal system of London makes, and the names of the districts, with their abbreviations in the form of a table (25–26). Ram later lists the costs of the Albert Memorial (48) and the London docks (83). He even numbers the buildings destroyed in the great fire of London of 1666 (44). Baijnath (1893) also provides statistics of the numbers of carriages (34), omnibuses (34), post offices and pillar boxes (35), as well as the number of letters delivered (36). T.N Mukharji, along the same lines, estimates the number of hansom cabs in London at around 13,000 (1902: 37), the dimensions of the Royal Albert Hall and its construction costs (67–68), the number of books in the Cambridge University Library (248) and other libraries (262).

The statistical account and inventory is a form of assertion and comprehension, the imperial-subject traveller circumscribing the vastness of London into an inventory. Critics such as Daniel Martin (2011) have proposed that in the early modern era the 'sophistication of multiple subject-object relationships based on resemblances and sympathies ... had once given wonder, enchantment, and curiosity free rein' (189). Post-Enlightenment, we see 'the flat, visually based tables of scientific classification' that introduces the disenchantment of the world (189). Heterogeneity is replaced by the homogenizing collection, Martin notes, and this 'repressed heterogeneity' (xvi) is a key shift in the sense of enchantment.

However, within the aesthetics of statistical recognition as embodied in the heterogeneous data uncovered and documented by the Indian traveller, there is a sense of enchantment not limited by the table or the classification. The spectacle of large buildings, library collections or cabs in the city of London are sources of enchantment through their sheer plenitude and variety, but these are shaped into a narrative that allows the enchantment to be experienced but in restrained ways. The 'recognition' is the casting into manageable diversity and variety the incomprehensible—sublime—vastness of London or Europe. Thus, it is possible to argue that the act of enumeration is an assertion of this agential recognition that, while retaining the enchantment invoked by the heterogeneity of things seen in Europe/England, manages to harness it into a restrained enchantment. Rather than leave the heterogeneity to produce a cognitive unsettlement by virtue of sheer scale and numbers, the Indian travellers' aesthetics of recognition retains and restrains the heterogeneous as statistics.

Cultural-Aesthetic Insiderness and Informed Enchantment

The 'stranger' that Pandian opened with is no more visible after the initial moments. He is now an informed visitor. The 'codes' of observation are those the traveller has assimilated from his elite background, with English education, the English language and English culture. These codes ensure that the enchantment of the first moment modulates into something else altogether, a condition of 'informed enchantment', prepared for by the aesthetics of enchantment, of recognition

G.P. Pillai, upon observing the countryside, breaks into poetry:

> The sudden appearance of the sun in the sky amidst rain, reminds one of the following patriotic lines by Ireland's greatest poet:
>
> Erin! The tear and the smile in thine eyes Blend like the rainbow that hangs in the skies; Shining through sorrow's stream, sadd'ning thro' pleasure's beam ... (2006: 60)

Pillai here is able to function in a Wordsworthian mode, where the sight of nature—Irish nature—immediately invokes poetry, even if in the form of quotations from an Irish poet. The enchantment with the sights seems to be almost prepared for, and the verse is right at hand to capture the scenery in words. This form of enchantment constitutes the apotheosis of the colonial subject as observer.

Each individual is writing after the travel. He casts his act of cognition within an aesthetic that, in his view, presumably indicates the appropriate response of enchantment. This suggests a slippage from cognition to recognition, where the latter is the self-conscious aesthetics—and an act of memory—mediating the recollection of the sights.

When Pillai quotes English poetry, or when Doss identifies the monuments at Westminster 'referred to by Irving in his Sketch Book' (1893: 48), or when Pandian invokes a 'Scotch bard' (1897: 6), they exhibit not just pleasure that the truth of the books and literature has been borne out by the physical sights, but also a certain informed enchantment at this truth. The traveller also takes pleasure in discovering the original 'home' of the products he is familiar with in India. Thus, Doss is joyful at seeing the factory of Bryant and May, 'our Old Acquaintances', as he calls them as soon as he arrives in London (34). None of this is about cognition. Rather, these instances suggest a *recognition* on the part of the colonial subject who proudly—at least in the narrative he prepares for later readers—presents himself as a cultural insider.

Describing the neo-colonial traveller, Mary Louise Pratt suggests that s/he 'does not claim the authority to represent, but only to express recognition of what he has learnt to know is there' (2007: 228). But the expression of recognition is a mode of establishing oneself as a learned traveller, as opposed to an uninformed one. Visitors who speak knowledgably of Christopher Wren and the making of St Paul's Cathedral or the bloody events of English history, or cite poetic descriptions of the landscape are positioning themselves not as individuals who lack authority, but as members of an elite group (of imperial subjects) who have *learnt* something about British culture and can therefore express opinions instead of just awe.

Informed enchantment erodes at least temporarily the sense of surprise and novelty and replaces it with the wonder of the strangely familiar. Thus, Pillai is able to say of Edinburgh Castle—'to foreigners the Castle has already been rendered familiar by the popular poet of Scotland'—and goes on to quote lines of verse from Scott (2006: 56). He maps London in terms of its great literary figures: Milton, Byron, Monk Lewis, Macaulay, Dickens, Ben Jonson, David Garrick, among others (45–46). He then maps Edinburgh similarly, in terms of its literary-historical geography, identifying places of birth or residence of Robert Burns, James Ballantyne, Walter Scott, Adam Ferguson, David Allen, and others (57). T.B. Pandian describes Fleet Street as 'inseparably associated with the names of such "Giants of Literature" as Samuel Johnson, Thackeray and Charles Dickens!' (1897: 21). He also quotes Goldsmith (64) and uses literary analogues such as 'Pickwickian dispensation' (66). Jagatjit Singh watches *Alladin* and *Chicago* at the Alhambra and finds them to be 'beautifully mounted' (1895: 82). Baijnath even offers a few lines of Shakespeare criticism and references to the authorship problem of Shakespeare's texts (1893: 52–53). He quotes Tennyson (62), George III, the ancient Greeks (63) and Swinburne (107–108), before listing a set of authors 'worthy of serious study' by Indians (109). Jhinda Ram also quotes Charles Kingsley (1893: 41), Thackeray (42) and Tennyson (48).

Tagore in *Letters from a Sojourner in Europe*, while refusing the enchantment offered by Europe and England, also showcases, with one stroke, his informed cosmopolitanism and the ignorance and insularity of the English. Close upon the heels of declaring that 'they [the English] are unable to imagine that any country could be in any way different from England', Tagore writes:

> This gentleman is only aware of the fact that a poet named Shelley was once born in his country, but not that he had written a play called *Cenci* or that there exists a poem by him called 'Epipsychidion', all of which he heard the first time from me! (2008: 40)

Informed enchantment allows the Indian traveller to present himself as a cultivated gentleman in the imperial centre. Writing about African American travellers in England, Tim Youngs notes that tourism and the arts enabled the former slave William Wells Brown to create a persona (2006: 175–176). For Pillai, Doss, and others, it is travel and travel writing that empowers them, and allows them to present their persona as cultivated individuals and therefore as cultured tourists rather than simply as culture tourists. Thus, the conventions of travel writing—references to earlier texts, literary history—are empowering for the Indian traveller. Doss, for example, when describing the Tower of London, refers to its bloody history not via a guidebook purchased on the spot, but through what Pratt calls *antecedent literarios*, or prior literary productions (2007: 228). These *antecedent literarios* and events from English history, which the traveller can 'perform' as memory acts when writing his memoirs of the journey, constitute his memory citizenship. Doss writes, 'It was through this gate that the seven Bishops were taken into the tower, as Macaulay describes it' (1893: 58). Baijnath, when viewing the Tower of London, quotes Macaulay's account of it (1893: 24). Baijnath also speaks familiarly of Hogarth, Reynolds, Gainsborough and other English painters when he describes his visit to the National Gallery (26).

One acquires a sense of this empowered role early in Pillai's narrative. Pillai seeks to convey the native subject's ability to absorb English customs and not be daunted by the task. The native subject is open to new cultural practices but is also able to adapt himself to these new practices because he has some textual knowledge of this 'other' culture. Pillai describes the voyage out to England:

> It is a great advantage that you are compelled to go to England by sea. On board the steamer, you begin to eat English dinners, you dress like English gentlemen, you learn English manners and become accustomed to English ways ... so that when you land, you feel quite at home, whether in the bath room, or at the dinner table, or in the public streets. (2006: 13)

Pillai is underscoring his ability to use the space of the voyage to acquire a sense of English culture and also its cultural practices of dining, socialization and personal deportment. A short while later, Pillai describes how one deals with the menu in restaurants, especially when the items are listed in French:

> At any of these places you may have your *table d'hote* or you may dine *a la carte* giving the finish with a dip of your hands in rose water. You see how easily one becomes accustomed to French expressions here. This is inevitable as long as you dine in restaurants. Your menu is often written in French and your waiters are generally foreigners, mostly Italians. Fancy your being asked whether you wish to begin with *hors' d'ouvre*, have any *poisson*, pass on to *entrée*, and wind up with *fromage* by Gati, Obertti, Frascarti or Lombardo! (15)

Pillai here presents himself not as an 'innocent abroad', but as an informed traveller quite at ease with cultural differences, a person who is able to slide into another cultural practice without much trouble. Pillai also seems to present the native not as an awe-struck, ignorant subject but as a culturally adaptable one, familiar with croquet, fine wines, dance forms and music.

Arguably, England represents the high point of the traveller's itinerary (which, as noted before, often also includes Europe), functioning as the symbolic and literal destination of their journey. To adapt Carole Fabricant's argument about 'domestic tourism' in eighteenth-century England, in which English lands, owned by the upper classes, became accessible and even 'possessable' by their often middle-class audiences (1987: 259), I propose that a similar 'possession', however partial it may be, within the narrative of recognition by the Indian traveller, is generated by acts of memory, and provides the traveller with a cultural insiderness through 'memory citizenship'.

Michael Rothberg and Yasemin Yildiz (2011) argue for a 'memory citizenship', wherein 'memory-work' or 'performances' of memory, regardless of citizenship status, situate the individual within the past, and within the histories of nations, races and ethnicities. Migrant archives of memory, they argue, constitute a new engagement, multidirectional and transnational, with historical pasts. The recall of English poetry or English historical events, the genealogy of monarchs, and the ability to visually locate and identify antiquarian buildings and places suggest that the English identity and its cultural forms are preserved in more than English memories and circulate through multidirectional memories within the 'migrant archives' of Indian travellers. This memory citizenship of the Indian traveller does, admittedly, situate him within an English identity as a colonial subject with English poetry as *his* legacy as well. But in conjunction with the discursive, 'recognitive' possession enabled by tourism, the memory citizenship marks him out as a colonial subject. He is a subject whose knowledge and textual 'memories' of England generate not open-mouthed awe, but showcase, alongside his cultural malleability ('how easily', he says in the earlier quote, one adapts to cultural difference), a rather nonchalant approach to the Western cultures he encounters. Rather than shock or awe, he seems to display a certain informed detachment and minimal amusement.

Understandably, Pillai is impressed and marvels at each of these moments, practices and events. The Rajah of Kolhapur takes dancing classes and records how he 'danced the Lancers with Miss S-' (1872: 32). He also learns to play croquet (40–41). Baijnath notes that he had 'read so much' about the Tower of London at school (1893: 23). All this points to informed enchantment. Thus, on the one hand, his memory citizenship marks him as a colonial subject whose aesthetics derive from his English education and access to English literature and history, but on the other hand, it also bestows upon him a certain agency of positioning himself as a knowledgeable aesthetic agent.

What we see here is an Indian's self-making through the acquisition of cultural insiderness and familiarity, immersing himself in the cultural practices of England, and of Europe in general, but with a sense of knowing them all. While not strictly 'passing', it is empowering in the sense that the acquisition of these practices and social skills help the Indian 'feel quite at home'. To transform a strange land into something akin to home is an empowering act of agency, made possible through an aesthetic and cultural understanding.

Antoinette Burton proposes that the documentation of their enjoyment of English theatre indicates the 'identification' of the Indian eye with the English 'optic' (1996: 138). It is also possible, however, to see these as instances in which the Indian sets himself up as a cultural insider who, having trained himself—perhaps through English education—to understand the plays or the museums, has insinuated himself into English tastes. Again, this is indicative of the agency of the imperial-subject traveller who, by virtue of acquiring a taste for things English, demonstrates his adaptability. He becomes an aesthetic subject in England. However, it must be added that this 'becoming' is not one that originates in England: the colonial subject is already prepared for England through the *prior* knowledge acquired and employed/deployed when they 'see' England. In other words, the self-fashioning of the aesthetic subject is one marked by a dynamic engagement with both, the prior knowledge gleaned through books and conversations (in a textual witnessing of England), and the immediate cognitive appraisals and re-evaluation of the sights eyewitnessed on the experiential journey.

This aesthetic subject, on the one hand, expresses his learned fascination (originating in the textual witnessing of England and the prior knowledge I mentioned earlier) for England, but on the other hand, he is intensely aware that as he observes England, he is also being observed. That is, we see in these narratives the emergence not only of the aesthetic subject, with his memory citizenship, making authoritative comments about English culture, and thereby positioning himself as a spectator and observer, but also of the self-aware subject who presents himself as an object of admiration and exotic difference. He recognizes that he is a source of enchantment to the English because he embodies difference. Most of the travellers in these narratives, therefore, mention, with not inconsiderable pride, the emblazoning of their Indian presence in London. Even as they marvel at the crowds in London, Baijnath, Pillai and Doss are aware of their being part of the spectacle, being marvelled at. The spectator here is no more the passive viewer, but one who is aware of the politics of looking (indeed one could study the entire oeuvre for the Indian travellers' alertness to being stared at, of himself as a spectacle, but one who also, often, reverses this scrutiny). He attests to the wonder of the English spectator, acknowledging that he *is* himself a strange spectacle as an Indian in London. Rather than anxiety at being watched, one gets the feeling from these travellers that they were eager for such an audience in such moments of auto-exoticization.

Lala Baijnath recounts how the Englishwomen in London 'now and then stared at my Indian dress' (1893: 39). Baijnath, like Pillai, discovers an advantage to his native costume when in London. When the crowds throng the street during the Jubilee celebrations and have to be managed by policemen, he alone is left untouched. Baijnath insisted on wearing his full native costume to the celebrations, an act that locates him as a culturally distinct individual in a very English scene. Baijnath writes:

> No carriages were allowed in any of the principal streets ... Here, as on other occasions, my Indian dress proved to me of some advantage. But for that dress and the kind care of certain friends who accompanied me, I would not have been able to enjoy the sight and return home unmolested by the immense crowd in the streets. (82)

Baijnath discovers that his cultural distinctiveness did not simply draw attention: his path was smoothened even in the crowds. Baijnath is speaking of an ease of mobility in an alien/English space due to his cultural difference. Doss notes that the English, though curious about him, were never rude. Doss writes:

> I need not mention that I was noticed by almost everyone in the streets. My dark complexion ... attracted every body's notice. They looked at me, and it was quite natural for them to do so; but none ever rudely stared. (1893: 37)

The Rajah of Kolhapur who was surely more aware of his social class and the need to be impressive in his appearance also seems to expect such attention from the English audiences. He records that when he entered the theatre at Oxford University for the convocation, 'the graduates and undergraduates ... who were assembled in the gallery, made a great noise—I don't know if it was in my favour' (1872: 5–6). The Raja's ego, the product, undoubtedly, of years of such splendorous public outings and adoring attention from his subjects back in India, causes him to assume that the English audience at Oxford was clamouring to see him. Pillai, like Baijnath, 'covets' (his word) this kind of attention, but also acknowledges that it can be overwhelming. Pillai writes:

> The worst of it [the turban] is that you are the object of too much attention in the streets when you walk about with a turban on. Who will not covet to be the cynosure of all eyes in London?—and such pretty eyes too? (2006: 14)

The aesthetics of wonder here is turned around when the Indian, in an auto-exoticizing act, watches himself being watched by 'pretty eyes'. The wonder is here the spectacle of *English* wonder, as the Rajah of Kolhapur notes: 'The people who were walking in the park [Victoria Park] were astonished to see us natives, and used to make a great noise whenever they saw us' (14). In all these cases it is also important to note that the native subject revels in the ease with which his cultural distinctiveness smoothens his interaction with the curious English onlookers: the exotic appeal produces a cultural passage for the Indians into the consciousness of the English who wish to see him and know him better.

*

The Indian traveller is transfixed by the exotic diversity of England. He records his awe at the wonders he sees, in landscapes, city life and industry. This same traveller, however, is alert to the nature of the diversity within England and Europe: the foreign and the alien, who is embedded in English culture and landscape in interesting ways, creolizing this space. In the process of recording these wonders, diversity and exotic, the Indian traveller positions himself as knowledgeable, appreciative and above all, agential. The ability to comprehend, provide a literary geography of the country *and* locate the foreign at the heart of the imperial nation, which then refuses a single, dominant narrative of 'Englishness' or 'Europeanness', contribute to this sense of agency even as it generates an Occidental exotic in the narrative.

If, as Benjamin Schmidt proposes in the case of early modern Europe, 'Europe gains its identity *through* the exotic world; in both, global exotica and their pleasures coalesce around a freshly constituted idea of "Europe"' (2015: 5), the Indian traveller achieves two significant effects: he destabilizes the idea of an essentialist or cohesive England/Europe by pointing to its reliance on xeno-figures at its very heart and, more importantly, becomes the instrument of this instability. The Indian traveller reorients European identity itself, by observing and documenting the Other at its heart. The imperial-subject traveller has now fashioned himself as a connoisseur of the exotic, but one attentive to an exoticism that significantly multiculturalizes and creolizes English and European identity. Rejecting, as an imperial subject, any possibility of the hegemonic exoticism of the foreign defined as simply 'English', the Indian traveller as he emerges with this documentation of the xeno-figure in Europe is a globally informed traveller.

Notes

1. The Panorama was, originally, a vast canvas painting stretching from floor to ceiling, to be viewed from a viewing platform. Created by Robert Barker in London in the 1780s, it was a huge innovation in visual spectacles. City landscapes and battle scenes were common panoramas.
2. The Crystal Palace Exhibition first opened in 1851, and was originally meant to showcase Britain's manufacturing industry, including new mechanical inventions. It was also designed as a massive spectacle and consumer paradise. This exhibition would be the first of a series

of similar international fairs and expos across Europe and the United States. However, the 1851 Exhibition was also seen by some as a symbol of divine support of England's (and the world's) human endeavours. *A Moral and Religious Guide to the Great Exhibition* put it this way:

> It would surely be no inappropriate means towards this end to dedicate the Industrial Exhibition, at its opening, to the Great Disposer of all events, and for the whole assembled multitude to unite in one song of praise and thanksgiving to Him, that he has put it into the mind of Royalty to conceive, and the wealth, the enterprize, and the industry of the world to carry out a plan so calculated to promote universal peace, and cement the union and brotherhood of man … (Anon 1851a: 12)

For many Englishmen and women, it was an astounding experience of variety. The artist Henrietta Mary Ward would write:

> From every part of the globe came representatives, many gorgeous in oriental robes. Dusky Indian Princes with turbans and jewels on their foreheads; sallow-faced Chinese Mandarins in silken embroidered dress; sedate little Japanese potentates with inscrutable faces; broad-faced, woolly-headed African Chiefs wearing bright colours; travellers from America, Australia, Canada ... mingling with Russians, Poles, Frenchmen, Italians and Austrians. (cited in Cantor 2011: 21)

For a collection of source materials on the 1851 Exhibition, see Jonathon Shears' invaluable *The Great Exhibition, 1851: A Source Book* (2017).

3. For a history of exotic animals in England, see Grigson (2016). For a fascinating account of an Indian rhino's peregrinations across Europe (including England) see Ridley (2004).
4. In other cases, the pedagogic purpose fails for other reasons. Tagore, for instance, simply admits: 'Quite like garnering an education at Calcutta University, I looked at everything at the Paris Exhibition but failed to see anything properly' (2008: 34).

4

Vernacular Cosmopolitanism in the Age of Empire

> *The chief value of travel in foreign countries ... is to enlarge one's ideas, to make them broad enough for approximation with the ideas of other nations—to make one* cosmopolitan, *in a word; cosmopolitan, not necessarily in habits and manners, but in sentiments, sympathies and aspirations.*
>
> —A.L. Roy, *Reminiscences English and American* (1888, emphasis added)

Like aesthetics and Occidental exoticism, cosmopolitanism reconfigures the imperial-subject traveller, and the components of this cosmopolitanism is the subject of this chapter. In reframing the view of the imperial subject as not entirely subject to the Empire due to his attitude of, if nascent, cosmopolitanism, I draw upon Babacar M'Baye's reading of W.E.B. Du Bois's cosmopolitanism:

> Du Bois's trips to France produced the two major patterns of his cosmopolitanism in which he attempted to balance his romanticization of the métropole as a symbol of freedom with his de-idealization of this nation as an emblem of colonial subjugation. (2017: 61)

M'Baye continues:

> [Du Bois's] statements convey his attraction to a charming France which he regards as stretching beyond the nation's relics, landscape, geography, and material culture. The assertions show that Du Bois also romanticizes France as an idyllic land of cosmopolitan possibilities ... cosmopolitanism as long as it could bring universal acquisition of equality and rights. (62–63)

But Du Bois also 'envisioned a transnational and cross-racial unity in which Western powers and formerly colonized people would work in harmony toward the betterment of the world' (74). In similar fashion, the Indian traveller who is impressed by England's cosmopolitan possibilities is at once aware of the colonial roots of this cosmopolitanism *and* the necessity of expanding these possibilities to the colonies under England's rule.

The Indian traveller's cosmopolitanism has many layers and nuances—not to mention ambivalences—that may be productively read as part of the process of reconfiguring the so-called 'imperial subjectivity' of the traveller. The Indian traveller's cosmopolitanism is double-edged, looking towards and outwards at England/Europe and the West but also towards and within India.[1] An additional layer to this double-edged perspective is made of the affective and ethical perspective that many (but not all) travellers bring to their gaze when observing the working-class poor in Europe. There is a sliding between and folding of the 'international or transnational dimension [as] … a continuance of the nationalist struggle', to adopt Homi Bhabha's phrasing (2001: 40).

In other words, there is the romanticized view of the economic and political power of England, its hoary history and vibrant culture, but this is tempered by the quiet reflection on the nature and source of England's power: colonialism and exploitative racisms. The first drives a romantic cosmopolitanism, albeit an informed one (as argued in the preceding chapter), where the Indian traveller equipped with considerable knowledge responds enthusiastically to the imperial country. The second, which causes the traveller to look *back* at his own country *and* at working classes, refugees or the urban poor in London, informs a different form of cosmopolitanism, one which I term, following Pnina Werbner, Homi Bhabha and others, a vernacular cosmopolitanism. Werbner defines it as 'an oxymoron that joins contradictory notions of local specificity and universal enlightenment' (2006: 496). Werbner continues:

> the local, parochial, rooted, culturally specific and demotic may co-exist with the translocal, transnational, transcendent, elitist, enlightened, universalist and modernist—whether boundary-crossing demotic migrations may be compared to the globe trotting ... (496)

Werbner links the idea/attitude/concept of vernacular cosmopolitanism with travel when she writes:

> Vernacular cosmopolitanism is perhaps the most ambiguous of these conjunctural terms: are we talking about *non-elite* forms of travel and trade in a postcolonial world, as in the case of the Senegalese Mourides described by Diouf (2000) and others, or of *non-European* but nevertheless *high* cultures produced and consumed by non-western elites, such as those of the Sanskritic, Urdu, Persian or Ottoman worlds. (497, emphasis in original)

Now, the tension between the romantic and vernacular forms of cosmopolitanism is a productive one for it resists the imperial subject traveller's complete assimilation as a subject but also as just a cynical cosmopolitan. This folding of the romantic with the nationalist, the transnational with the national and the political with the affective constitutes the vernacular cosmopolitanism of Lala Baijnath, Behramji Malabari, Romesh Dutt, and other late nineteenth- and early twentieth-century travellers.

Indian travellers like Jagatjit Singh or Lala Baijnath (king and an officer in the judicial services) occupy a strangely liminal space, being both 'migrant elites' (Werbner 2006) and imperial subjects. When they dine with the European ambassadors and royalty they appear to socialize globally as equals. When they turn their attention to the laws of England, they recognize that they in India are treated unequally, as *subjects*. They admire England's progress and social mores, mourning that such was not the case in England's colony (India), and wish these were also made available in India and to Indians. It is this liminal state that layers their vernacular cosmopolitanism.

Vernacular cosmopolitanism is a strange admixture. Werbner calls attention to some of its complications:

> Vernacular cosmopolitanism is perhaps the most ambiguous of these conjunctural terms: are we talking about *non-elite* forms of travel and trade in a postcolonial world, as in the case of the Senegalese Mourides described by Diouf (2000) and others, or of *non-European* but nevertheless *high* cultures produced and consumed by non-western elites, such as those of the Sanskritic, Urdu, Persian or Ottoman worlds. (496, emphasis in original)

Adapting Kwame Appiah she says:

> cosmopolitans begin from membership in morally and emotionally significant communities (families, ethnic groups) while espousing notions of toleration and openness to the world, the transcendence of ethnic difference and the moral responsibility for and incorporation of the other. Postcolonial migrant elites may and do feel sentimentally attached to several homes in several different countries. (496)

It is made up of the 'cosmopolitan nationalism' that Sheshalatha Reddy (2010) identifies in Sarojini Naidu, where cosmopolitanism is not incompatible with nationalism. Vernacular cosmopolitan subjectivity is imbued with a 'cultivated partiality', embodied in 'a reflective return to the cultural origins that one can no longer return to in any unthinking manner (Small 2012: 87). Such cosmopolitans often, like Tagore in Poulomi Saha's reading, contradict their rootedness in their local cultures with their 'worldliness' (2013). But it is also a cosmopolitanism wherein the locals gain cosmopolitan knowledge in order to maintain the integrity of their communities (Murphy 2013) or, as in the case of Malabari, hope to revitalize their communities with ideas learnt from their wanderings outside India. There is a clear affective and moral, empathetic and sympathetic, response that the Indian travellers record when they see poverty, difference and the helpless in Europe. They are also aware of their marginality as imperial subjects, and their membership in 'communities of interest', producing what Bhabha terms a 'cosmopolitan community envisaged in a marginality' (2002: 42–43). Suggestive of both a subaltern cosmopolitanism (Balachandran 2014, Zeng 2014) and a moral-sentimental one (Long 2009), vernacular cosmopolitanism is a complicated perspective and attitude.

Vernacular cosmopolitanism does not abandon one (the native/local) in favour of the other (the global and universal) but engages in a dynamic that complicates the relations between the two, a dynamic embodied in the traveller. Further, the cosmopolitan stance and critique, it may be argued, targets an audience that is made of both British and Indian readers. N.N. Ghose summarizes this aspect of the Indian travelogue when he writes in his Preface to T.N. Mukharji's *A Visit to Europe*:

> The observations, and reflections of such a traveller ought to be of interest alike to the Hindu and the European. The Hindu cannot fail to regard the account as something like a revelation and the European will learn to see himself as others see him. (1902: xiii)

Vernacular cosmopolitanism that foregrounds the traveller's national identity and nationalism is layered with an interest in the subalterns of other countries, the cultures of poverty in Europe and the fragile social ontologies of the underprivileged. These moments and layers, which are not always discrete, are on many occasions infused with a deep moral stance and sentimentality which, this chapter argues, is also a constituent of the vernacular cosmopolitan, which I term 'moral and sentimental cosmopolitanism'.

The chapter moves from the 'mediating cosmopolitanism' of the Indian traveller to his encounter with the lower classes and the underprivileged and the making of a subaltern cosmopolitanism within subaltern contact zones. It then moves on to discussing the specific moral and sentimental responses of the Indian travellers towards the proletarian and the plebeian Europeans they encounter. Finally, it turns to the self-fashioning of the Indian traveller as a cosmopolitan nationalist.

Mediating Cosmopolitanism

John McBratney in his reading of Dickens's *Great Expectations* proposes a 'mediating cosmopolitanism' that leads to a 'partial universalism' (he is following Kwame Appiah here). He suggests that Victorians typically looked outward to enlarge the Empire and also toward rural England, and were not entirely comfortable with the fluid national identities of the age (2010: 541). For the Indian traveller in England, we can make a case for a similar mediating cosmopolitanism.

The aesthetic produced by the simultaneity of two geographical locations (England and India) and two subjectivities (colonial subject, informed/competent ethnographer-traveller) is a cosmopolitan aesthetic. It is also a geopolitical aesthetic in which many of the travellers are conscious of England's global position. Further, each one of these travellers visits several European nations, Australia, the U.S. and very different parts of England, such as Scotland and Wales. Thus, the visit to England is part of a larger itinerary (the 'West'). Rather than a destination, England was a stopover, a median point, and thus quietly erodes the uniqueness of England as a destination. Pillai refers to Parisian beauties and charms in his Letters X and XI. Jagatjit Singh's travel narrative charts an exhaustive journey through Egypt, Italy, the Alps, Belgium, Switzerland, Austria, Paris, England and New York, covering all the major cities and cultural capitals of these countries. Jhinda Ram travels to Paris, Turin, Florence, Rome and Milan. Baijnath's narrative has a chapter devoted to his travels in Switzerland, Egypt and Italy, and another on his Sri Lankan sojourn. Doss's travels take him through England, Sri Lanka, Tasmania, New Zealand and Australia, clearly signalling what Tabish Khair presciently identified as a third axis beyond the colonial periphery/centre: the 'play of difference and similarity between the so-called colonial periphery and colonial centre [is] nuanced by the third axis of continental cities like Paris or Rome' (2008: 9).

Antoinette Burton notes a 'distinctively Indian eye' in these travellers, where London became the subject of scrutiny and which was created to demonstrate the Indians' ability to produce an urbane, national vision (1996: 143). This vision is always double—the informed enchantment with things English, and perceiving England through its poetry, history, and the arts in general, and subjecting it to comparison and contrasts with things Indian.

Thus far I have suggested that travellers like Pillai sought to acquire a cultural insiderness, facilitated by a memory citizenship of the Empire, through an informed enchantment with things English. This informed enchantment was consistently underwritten by the double vision of looking at England and India and seeing in England points of comparison and contrast with India. What I see as the Indian traveller's mediating cosmopolitanism is the availability of a cosmopolitan sensibility that accrues through both the acquisition of cultural insiderness and the ability to use this sensibility to offer comparisons of the two cultures. Here I differ from Codell's assessment that the wonder at England in these narratives turns to 'cynicism' (2007: 178). It is not cynicism as much as irony that one detects in these texts, when the Indians, through their informed enchantment, delve deeper into English culture. Wonder here leads to inquiry, and not necessarily disenchantment: the Indian travellers are then able to temper their previous amazement with authoritative interpretations of the lacunae in England's life.[2]

Writing about London at night, G.P. Pillai describes the scene as 'an enchanting sight' (2006: 32). He has also just quoted Wordsworth's 'Westminster Abbey': 'earth has not anything to show more fair!' (32). Pillai thus not only appreciates the sights and beauties of England, he even describes them in English terms and a language directly borrowed from English poetry. However, this appreciation is not untempered. Indeed Pillai, like other travellers, is also quick to point out to his readers the problems and less appealing aspects of English life and culture. Pillai writes:

> But stay, here is a mass of human flesh animate or inanimate you don't know, which on nearer examination resolves itself into half a dozen individuals, sleeping in the most fantastic positions ... pinched cheeks and ragged limbs, hatless, shoeless, bearing unmistakable marks of misery! ... The sight of men of hungry and hunted look, women

> bonnetless and with dishevelled hair and children extremely dirty and shoeless ... (33)

Mediating cosmopolitanism is what enables the Indian traveller to tone down his appreciation of England by comparing it to other parts of the world, with India, or by criticizing what he saw as the problems of English culture. Thus, N.L. Doss is disappointed when he sees St Paul's Cathedral as grimy and sooty, saying, 'the walls of St. Pauls in Calcutta look far cleaner and nicer' (1893: 50). He makes a similar comment about the Bank of England as well: 'it has not that imposing look from outside which the Bank of Bengal in Calcutta presents in its frontage' (54). Durgabati Ghose speaking of Venice—where they are visiting Sigmund Freud—after passing through London writes:

> People in these countries lived in such sparse settings. All their showing off is when they visit a poor country like ours. On seeing the Buckingham Palace from outside in London I had realised that our Governor's House and the Mullick Palace at Chorbagan were much larger. (2010: 72)

Baijnath compares St Paul's with French and Italian churches and finds it 'much inferior' (1893: 23); performing the same with English castles vis-à-vis French castles (76). The Indian King's jewel room is 'far richer' than the jewel room of the Tower of London, he notes (24). The East End of London, writes Baijnath, with its 'by-lanes and its lifeless streets ... its insalubrity and drunkenness are not seen even in the smallest town in India' (30). Pandian, an indefatigable explorer of English housing, notes the appalling conditions of London's poor (1897: 17–18). Pandian is also disappointed by the Houses of Parliament, whose 'interior does not impress the visitor with the notion that he is standing in the national council halls of an imperial people' (28–29). He goes on to make similar comments about Whitehall, the India and Foreign Offices, the Home Department, the Colonial Office and other public meeting places (29). Pandian seems to suggest that the buildings are not worthy of an imperial people. This might be read as an act of demystifying the wonder of imperial London that simultaneously underscores the encomium of a colonial subject and the fragility implicit in the edifice. Baijnath, who comes to the Houses of Parliament 'with feelings of awe and reverence' (1893: 56), admits that 'there is not ordinarily much eloquence in the House' and that he was 'somewhat disappointed with the way in which business was transacted here' (58). At one point, he notes that English society is 'too great a worshipper of nobility', before going on to add:

> The Englishman is as great a supporter of caste as the Hindu; and even the most radical peer in England would indignantly scout all ideas of fraternity and equality ... English society though it professes to be democratic, is really a very aristocratic society ... (61)

Baijnath is also categorical in his criticism of the British government in India. He describes it as follows: 'a despotic government, conducted by means of a close bureaucracy, but which, unlike eastern despotism, is a benevolent despotism, ruling after civilized methods and guided by public opinion' (64). He then embarks on fulsome praise for the material progress India has attained under the Raj (65–68), even as he points out that this connection (with India) has 'vastly benefited England' (69) and is a 'valuable acquisition' and thus exhorts its subjects to 'take that interest in its [India's] affairs which in its own interest is required' (69).

Expectedly, many things English are rated higher than their counterparts in India. The British domestic servant, writes Pandian, is much better than the Indian one, since in India 'integrity and efficiency cannot be said to be commonly characteristic of the domestics' (1897: 14–15). Pillai speaks of the incorruptibility of the English policemen (2006: 30), and Pandian of the railway porters (36). This could either be read as a simplistic binary or as a version of internal criticism integral to mediating cosmopolitanism through a moral geography. When Pandian ponders, 'what might India not become, if my countrymen could only be roused from their national condition of suicidal lethargy?' (47), he is offering not a simplistic binary as much as an internal criticism.

Mediating cosmopolitanism is also characterized by considerable self-reflection. The Indian 'observer' of England is also an observer of India when he travels abroad. I have already proposed that the Indian traveller engages in self-making through the aesthetics of recognition. Seeing things as an Indian, Doss, for instance, is able to criticize the aesthetics of Greek and Roman statues in the Crystal Palace. Instead of a blind acceptance of English aesthetics, Doss actually points to its inferiority. Doss writes:

> Much may be said of the artistic beauty of several of these figures ... but tastes differ. The place is so full of naked female figures in the shape of the graces, nymphs, venuses and other mythological characters, that it almost impossible for a person of delicate sensibilities to walk there in the company of ladies. Perhaps an Englishman with all his refined sense of decency will not feel any hesitation in doing so, but we orientals do. (1893: 61)

Doss here contrasts not only aesthetics but also aesthetic sensibilities, categorizing them along racial-national lines. While not entirely critical of the aesthetics here, and admitting to his own discomfiture, Doss extends the benefit of the doubt to the Englishman in what sounds suspiciously like a tongue-in-cheek comment. Baijnath, while praising the English, also refuses to reject his own traditions. Considerable space is therefore spent on the merits of the Upanishads and the Hindu traditions (Baijnath 112–117), thus suggesting a self-reflexivity alongside the 'looking outward' stance of the traveller. This is an instance of the 'overlapping allegiances' of the traveller's cosmopolitanism: the memory citizenship that enables a certain cultural insiderness that causes a shift from a narrative of (cognitive) awe to a more muted—informed—enchantment with things English, and the double vision that derives from a self-reflection.

The cosmopolitanism of the colonial subject in England also embodies a tangential but related moment. We have already noted that the aesthetics of wonder was articulated as an interest in England and English culture's antiquity. It is possible to read this interest as a romantic historicism where, as James Chandler has argued, the emphasis is on the dating of cultural place and the locality of cultural moments. What the Indian traveller does is to focus on the distance in time of England's buildings and seek to locate a cultural moment in its place. Akin to modernism's dynamization of temporality, the mediating cosmopolitanism of the Indian traveller constantly moves between present and past, even as, on many occasions, they use these 'models' of modernity to reflect upon India's future.

When Pandian rejects India Office and the Houses of Parliament as unworthy of an imperial people, he has effectively located a cultural moment (imperialism, overseas expansion and, most importantly, England's internationalism) within a space. Doss, for instance, recognizes England's internationalism in the British Museum with its collections from Egypt, Greece and other countries (56). He also notes the supply of fruit from countries like Australia and Tasmania, which are 'separated from England by half the globe' (65).

This form of cosmopolitanism where the Indian not only admires England but also critiques it even as he reflects on comparable examples from India is not a 'top-down' abstract cosmopolitanism of the Kantian kind. Rather, it is a cosmopolitanism that is born of very particular transnational experiences: the Indian is embedded in (*a*) his Indian ethos, and (*b*) his English learning. He is able to situate himself at a 'reflective distance', as Amanda Anderson puts it, from both India and England as he navigates the cultural topoi of England. And this, in Lauren Goodlad's account, is no 'mere endorsement of multiplicity or hybridity' (2010: 401).

I have argued elsewhere that the Victorian age sought to define Englishness as cosmopolitanism, whereby the ability to adapt to, appropriate and assimilate other cultures was treated as a sign of English identity—in contrast, of course, with cultures like India's, which remained determinedly stuck in tradition (Nayar 2012). The pageants and exhibitions in London from the 1870s to the 1920s were, I argued, a showcasing of their cosmopolitan tastes and sensibility.

The Indian traveller is partaking in this. Even as he responds to the English aesthetic as an Indian (see Doss's self-reflexive comments earlier), he is able to position himself as a connoisseur of English sensibility as well. Mediating cosmopolitanism is the calculated detachment from both domains in these narratives. The traveller's memory citizenship offers multiple allegiances where both histories—Indian and English—work in conjunction.

The cosmopolitanism of these travelogues is restitutive; it restores to the colonial subject (who is otherwise just a subject) a sense of moral and social authority, commenting confidently about English culture, being self-reflective about his identity as an (informed) Indian in England and offering internal criticism of India as well. The aesthetic engagement does not allow a simple sense of enchantment to operate, even though this engagement might be worked through as a part of the memory citizenship emerging from the authors' *antecedent literarios*. Ethnography demystifies the wonder of England, and fulsome praise simultaneously retains it. This simultaneity of a knowledge-driven demystification *and* the retention of wonder for the colonial master's culture is the mediating cosmopolitanism of the Indian travellers.

The cosmopolitanism of these travel texts showcases a modernity that is transnational and global while being embedded in the local. Thus, we cannot see the learned Baijnath (he was a judge in the judicial services), the evangelist Doss, the Rajah of Kolhapur (who was introduced to the Queen of England), Jagatjit Singh (who dined with royalty across Europe) as embodying a simplistic nationalist-racialist binary of native versus foreigner, Indian versus English. The modernity embodied in these works is cosmopolitan in which the first signs of a global Indian are visible in their easy mobility across England's *cultural* geography recorded in these texts. The cosmopolitan colonial subject whose origins and characteristics I have traced here is a cosmopolitan whose aesthetic engagement with England, derived from very real historical and geographical contexts—colonialism—ensured a complication of the racial and national binary. The aesthetic subject who emerges in these travel texts embodies the 'reflective distance' Amanda Anderson identifies as 'cosmopolitanism'. It is precisely this 'distance' and its attendant mobility away from India, through England but ultimately also away from imperial as well as racial-national formations, that produces the freedom of the Indian at the heart of the Empire.

Polyrhythmia and the Cosmopolitan *Flâneur*

When the Indian traveller walks through London we see two spatial practices: that of the imperial subject citizen's own *flânerie* in the heart of the Empire and that of the London working class. The result is a polyrhythmia,

> where diverse rhythms coexist side-by-side, without producing an 'arrhythmia', a dissonant conflict between the rhythms of the different spatial practices which make up the city (Rhythmanalysis 77). Such a polyrhythmia is characteristic of Wilde's London and offers precisely a theory of 'cosmopolitanism'. (Whiteley 2017: 131)

There are aspects of this *flânerie* that, in conjunction with the theme of polyrhythmia, contribute to the self-fashioning of the imperial subject traveller as cosmopolitan.

The imperial subject citizen traveller during his *flânerie* documents the polyrhythmia of London, serving as the witness to the multiple and uneven rhythms of the city, with all the dynamics of class and political affiliation of the people. The recording of his own and others' rhythms, where the former, as in the case of Baijnath or Jagatjit Singh, is informed by class privileges, is itself an act of self-fashioning: the Indian *flâneur* in the Western metropolis. If, as Keith Tester suggests, '*flânerie* can be understood as the observation of the fleeting and the transitory which is the other half of modernity to the permanent and central sense of self' (2006: 7). Tester elaborates:

> In these terms, the figure, and the activity, of the *flâneur* is essentially about freedom, the meaning of existence (or the lack of a meaning

> of existence) and being-with-others in the modern urban spaces of the city. Freedom because the figure revolves around the dialectic of self-definition and definition from outside (although this freedom is perhaps something more by way of a curse than a promise); the meaning (or lack of meaning) of existence because the figure is about the flux of life and the requirement to make its meaning for one's self … (8)

It is also connected to the 'empire of the gaze and the spectacle' (18). More importantly, as Mona El-Sherif has proposed,

> in a cultural milieu that privileged visual semiotics of identity, the literary productions of the nineteenth-century Arab writers represent a crucial intervention as they engage with the European gaze and grant their narrator, the shaykh, authorial command over the new urban experiences. (2018: 30)

When Pillai wanders through London, Paris and Edinburgh, he documents the people he meets. He refers to the 'strange characters in a strange land' (2006: 8), after listing the policeman, the newsboys and the postman. London, he says in the same paragraph, is 'a land of strange people and strange sights' (8). In London, he writes, 'Lord, Commoner and the working man may be seen commingling together on the pavements of any street on any day' (19). It is a 'million-voiced city', he says (27), and lists the variety of people:

> The crisp clean businessman, the prosperous, heavy-cheeked tradesman, the dapper little clerk, the hard, coarse-visaged costermonger, the pale and serious artisan, the shop-girl of ample chignon and prodigal of all colour … all tossed in the thick of the battle of life. (27)

Then, as noted in the section on the subaltern picturesque in the preceding chapter, Pillai documents the homeless and the unemployed, especially of London's East End. But, writes Pillai, 'strange cries you begin to hear from all sides. You cannot make out a single word. You do not know whether they are English or Tamil …' (34). There are 'numerous, able-bodied men browned by the sun and burdened by never-ending labour' (34). Examples of a similar kind, documenting his encounter with the various working classes are scattered throughout the text (44–46, 56–57, 70–72).

Lala Baijnath, in like fashion, notes his fellow-walkers in London:

> In the streets you see people walking like infatuated beings … An English porter carries a heavy box upon his shoulders which it would take three Indian coolies to carry … an English groom does the work of three Indians … (1893: 22–23)

While Baijnath does admit that 'both men and women, except the very poorest, look well-fed and well-made' (23), he spends considerable narrative space on the working-classes he encounters in his London stroll. For instance, about Hyde Park, he is quick to record that 'it is full of people … after dusk socialist preachers, psalm-singers, women of easy virtue, etc' (36).

I propose that the spaces of London or Paris in these texts is Lefebvre's representational space, 'space which the imagination seeks to change and appropriate. It overlays physical space, making symbolic use of its objects' (Lefebvre 1991: 39). Pillai's or Baijnath's referencing of the social space of London as 'strange' with unrecognizable sounds and sights approximates, in Giles Whiteley's reading, to the *unheimlich*, or uncanny (2017: 128). To adopt Whiteley's phrasing for my purposes, 'London is no utopian cosmopolis in practice. What is allegorised is not simply the internal psychological drama, but social relations themselves, hence Lord Arthur's 'strange pity', his pathetic identification with these figures' (128). The physical space is overlaid with the symbolic and the affective here: working-class London and the businessman's or statesman's London. Baijnath or Pillai encounter William Gladstone and the monumental dimensions of London, even as they are accosted by working-class people or at least witness them in their habitats. Jhinda Ram is the subject of opprobrious remarks about his 'colour, nose, teeth' (1893: 62), making him feel 'disagreeable' in that setting.

An attention to the semiotic markers—such as clothing, headgear—of identity, is now an established feature of the *flâneur*. In his very first pages, Pillai notes the 'fantastic head-dress' of the 'Lords and ladies gay' of London (2006: 8). Later, Pillai would write:

> The top-hat of course is the most important. It looks as if the basis of the British Empire rests on the top-hat. The Indian student is seldom seen without a top-hat. The City clerk never leaves his top-hat behind. It often adorns the head of a cabby as well as the busman. But there is a way of wearing the top-hat … (48)

In his own case, Pillai notes the attention his headdress receives:

> Fondly attached as you are to your orthodox turban, you and your turban become gradually estranged in London. The occasions when you don it become few and far between. Unless your genial host or more often hostess, insists upon your appearance at the dinner table in your oriental costume or you feel that you can make up for your want of eloquence at a public meeting by the attractions of your head dress, you don't wear it … The worst of it is that the you are the object of too much attention in the streets when you walk about with a turban. Who will not covet to be the cynosure of all eyes in London? … If you don't walk home directly and say farewell, a long farewell to your bright little, nice little turban, you deserve to be congratulated on your pluck. (14)

Lala Baijnath records how his turban is treated as a hat (1893: 143).

The Indian *flâneur* is caught between his being objectified as a spectacle in the places he travels in (as exemplified by the earlier excerpts from Pillai, Baijnath and others) and his own self-definition determined by his conscious spectacularization of London, Paris and the Western world at large. Mona El-Sherif, acknowledging this tension, proposes that the Arab traveller (her case study):

> experiences modernity as novelty, but also as an anxiety-provoking experience because of the objectification he encounters on the streets of the metropolis. Only through writing does the *shaykh* gain authority and command over the new metropolitan experiences as he negotiates a place for himself amidst the new forms of life that sprang up in the modern city. (2018: 36)

The imperial subject traveller's *flânerie*, then, is the beginning of a self-fashioning process out of the dual and conflicted experiences of being objectified *and* authorial command.

The latter is made possible by the aesthetic studied in the earlier chapter, but is also helped by the kinds of perspective the Indian *flâneur* adopts and adapts when travelling through the modern spaces of London, New York or Paris: a perspective that arguably pays as much, if not more, attention to the lower classes and the poor as it does to the upper echelons of the social order. Such a move not only establishes his more democratic 'connection' across the various members of the diverse social orders (not limited to specific classes) but also a greater empathetic connection that marks the moral cosmopolitan (to which I shall turn in a subsequent section).

I build here on the work of Tuire Valkeakari who has proposed that black *flânerie* does suggest such a wider human connection, as compared to the European *flânerie* (2019). While the Indian *flâneur* continues to pay attention to the usual constituents of modern urban life—advertising, transport and consumer products in every single travelogue of the period—he is also alert to the class and economic status of the people he observes and documents. If the white man's *flâneur* narrative traditionally sought a form of authorial control, in the case of the Indian traveller, any potential authority he sought was always under threat due to his own subject position as an imperial subject and a spectacle. It is by paying attention to the underbelly or the subordinated classes of the urban space rather than just its consumer-spaces, arcades and monuments that the Indian *flâneur* frees himself from the burden of being just an imperial subject.

By creating a narrative of working-class distress, discrimination and suffering, the Indian *flâneur* effectively rewrites, as Tyrone Simpson II (2012) has argued about black *flânerie*, the very idea of the perceptive white *flâneur*. Just as Giles Whiteley has argued a case for the polyrhythmia of urban life in specific *flâneur* narratives, the Indian *flâneur* shows us the Others within the urban spaces of modernity.

It is from such a position of being an Indian *flâneur* setting out to document the pleasures of Paris and London but also their social inequalities that the Indian traveller designs his moral and subaltern cosmopolitanism.

Subaltern and Moral Cosmopolitanisms

Debbie Lisle in her study of contemporary Western travel writing argues that 'travel writers seek to jettison their colonial heritage by focusing on the harmonising effects of globalization, they employ what I call a *cosmopolitan vision*' (2006: 4, emphasis in original). These authors 'frame encounters with others in positive ways—they reveal moments of empathy, recognitions of difference, realizations of equality and insights into shared values' (4). While Lisle is keen on establishing the empathetic imagination as a feature of the contemporary travelogue, signs of this imagination are already visible in the nineteenth-century travel account—even by non-Europeans.

Empathetic perceptions of the East emerged in European texts through the nineteenth century but were essentially focused on specific classes of natives when the Europeans observed, interacted with them, and documented these interactions. David Cannadine has proposed that after the 1857 'Mutiny', the British view of India's 'basic structures … caste-ridden, village-living and princely-led' hardened, and became central to the 'conventional British wisdom' through which the social order was viewed and commented upon (2001: 45). They began to pay greater attention to the princes, who came to be seen as essential structures for the stability of the Empire (46). Caste and social hierarchy became, for the British, a key form of knowledge of India. The creation of imperial orders and ranks, complete with gun salutes and honours, was a central feature of this phase of the Empire. It brought together, writes Cannadine, 'the British proconsular elite and the indigenous colonial elites into a unified, ranked, honorific body' (89), not only in India but in Britain's other colonies as well. Britons, as a consequence,

> saw their empire as an extension of their own social world rather than in contradistinction to it. They exported social perceptions on the presumption of sameness as much as they imported social perceptions on the presumption of difference. They were as eager to make it seem familiar as they were to recognize that it was unfamiliar, to see it as a social hierarchy rather than as a racial hierarchy. (134–135)

Moral cosmopolitanism is a mode, perception and perspective cultivated by the elite Indian travellers that enables them to make simultaneous and dialectical moves. First, it inserts them into a social hierarchy of compassionate, concerned and well-meaning *elites* across the European empires. Second, and in contrast, it caused them to engage with *Europe's subalterns*, a move that was, implicitly, a process of fashioning solidarity with similar others who have been subject to Europe's exploitative and unjust economic, social and political systems.

G. Balachandran, writing about subaltern cosmopolitanism, argues:

> the arenas of subaltern cosmopolitanism are not purely discursive. They are also generative of norms and practices rather than discourses … Subaltern sociality is 'cosmopolitan' for its seeming capacity to accommodate the working poor from all parts of the world, irrespective, though not heedless, of race, faith, nation or gender and to translate and mediate habits, attitudes and meanings to affirm and sustain such sociality. (2014: 529)

This subaltern cosmopolitanism is, for Balachandran, a form of *sociality*. He continues:

> Prone to viewing 'minorities' only as victims of racial and other forms of discrimination, multiculturalist histories largely neglect the resistant lives of cosmopolitan sociality that mixed communities on the margins of state and society improvised. Attending to these lives, their stories and the deep anxieties they provoked among the dominant classes and social groups may point us beyond currently authorized tropes of difference and genealogies of multiculturalism. (546)

It is within and through these apparently contradictory moves, of alignment with both ends of the European social spectrum, that the

Indian fashions a self different from that assigned him by virtue of being an imperial subject. He is at once ensconced within the top ranks of the English social hierarchy and connects with, at least morally, the dregs of its social order.

N.N. Ghose summarizes this dual movement in his Preface to Mukharji's work when he writes:

> In Europe too, in consequence of his official position, he found easy introductions to the highest classes of society and learnt more in nine months than could be learnt in a much longer period by one not so favourably situated. He saw a good deal of humbler life also. (1902: xiii)

Here is an interesting example of the subaltern contact zone, where the elite-yet-imperial subject encounters the European subaltern classes at close quarters:

> On seeing a number of beautiful girls alight from every omnibus that I saw, I asked them if they were all coming from school, when they replied that they were shop-girls. In the large shops hundreds of girls are employed as saleswomen and seamstresses. To see these girls was to love them, so beautifully fair and young were they. I was forcible reminded of those tales in which even kings were willing enough to be led in silken chains by girls of plebeian birth, and what to me at once time only fiction seemed now very likely to be the truth. (Jessawalla 1911: 282)

Following Mary Louise Pratt writing in the context of colonial travel writing, I suggest that for the traveller, this encounter enables a specific move: '"embracing" such groups into the political and social imaginary—as subalterns' (Pratt 2007: 99). Pratt argues that in sentimental fiction, 'political uncertainties [are resolved] in the sphere of family and reproduction' (99). For the Indian traveller, it becomes, I suggest, a solidarity with the lower classes of Europe that carves out an entirely different kind of contact zone. Such a subaltern zone in *England* is different from the one in India (their homeland) where, even with the illusory coevalness of rank between English and native elites (as David Cannadine argues), the zone underscored the racial hierarchy between the two. In England, Jessawalla's text suggests the appropriation of the shop-girls into her sentimentalized social imaginary, which has a multicultural slant as well. The imperial-subject subaltern in England forms a social cosmopolis—structured around the emotion of 'love' in Jessawalla's passage—with the white shop-girls, however ephemeral it may be.

Shop-girls come in for Behramji Malabari's attention too.

> My impressions of London shop-girls in this respect are more favourable. Whether at the shop, the open stall or booth, or in the restaurant, they have, as a rule, dealt fairly with the stranger, sometimes generously. Poor little things!—hungering for a kind look, a kind word, which they seldom get. How they hover about you, clearing the tables, holding up the things you want, explaining the difference between them, sometimes venturing upon a bit of advice! Poor, weary, ill-paid drudges! What a mistake you are! What a freak of fortune! I almost wish at times the law allowed infanticide at the birth of girls like you. (1895: 199)

Malabari's focus, one notes, is not on the girls alone but on the social order that pays them low wages. Thus, identifying the poor as victims is accompanied by the finger of accusation pointing to the socio-economic contexts of poverty. Malabari also offers a fuller picture of England's poorer classes in his chapter 'Life as Seen in Public Affairs':

> Poor as India is, I thank God she knows not much of the poverty to which parts of Great Britain have been accustomed—the East End of London, for instance, parts of Glasgow, and other congested centres of life. Men and women living in a chronic state of emaciation, till they can hardly be recognized as human …
>
> In London itself there are hundreds of thousands who have a daily, almost hourly struggle of it, to keep body and soul together. So fierce is this struggle for existence that the victims can hardly find time to emerge from their work-holes for a whiff of fresh air …
>
> Hundreds of them may be found every month on the pavements, on the roadside, on house steps, starved, cramped, or frozen to death. Hundreds die every month for sheer want of means to keep alive.

> Thousands drag on a miserable existence, embittered by disease, from which death, too long delayed, is the only relief …
>
> Though suffering in all cases is infinitely more keen than it would be in similar cases in India, though the extent of it is smaller.
>
> And side by side with such heart-rending scenes of misery, one sees gorgeously dressed luxury flaunting it in the streets, dragged along by horses, better fed and better looked after than many a human … (85–87)

Tagore offers a detailed account of how he saw England's poor:

> I have never seen anywhere such a constant struggle for livelihood as in this country. The people of this country are not Nature's pampered children—no one has the opportunity to sit back idly, reclining on a cushion. Not only does the soil of this country not yield fruit as it does in our country by merely scratching at its surface; it also has to fight the winter's chill … Only the fittest survive in his land, and only those who have the ability may raise their heads high; there is no consolation for the weak—not only does one have to fight Nature, one must also deal with much competition in the workplace.
>
> The working classes of this country do not seem to have any trace of humanity left in them—they seem to be placed only a step above animals. When I see their faces—or, perforce, some of their faces—I shudder at the sight; none can call them the 'human face divine'; those reddened faces with replete with bestiality are somehow repulsive. And it is difficult to describe how filthy they are … (2008: 39)

This subaltern cosmopolitanism, I now propose, is a variant of Mary Pratt's idea of the anti-conquest. Pratt defines the anti-conquest as a system of representation that eschews the general trend in travel writing of emphasizing an imperial authority—ocular, discursive—over what the traveller observes:

> [The anti-conquest] differed sharply from overtly imperial articulations of conquest, conversion, territorial appropriation, and enslavement. The system created, as I suggested above, a Utopian, innocent vision of European global authority, which I refer to as an *anti-conquest* … In travel literature … science and sentiment code the imperial frontier in the two eternally clashing and complementary languages of bourgeois subjectivity and sentimental travel writing represents a form of 'anti-conquest'. (38, emphasis in original)

Pratt admits: 'so does the anti-conquest "underwrite" colonial appropriation, even as it rejects the rhetoric, and probably the practice, of conquest and subjugation' (52). I expand the term's semantic scope here to signal the imperial subject's rejection of imperial authority and conquistadorial rhetoric, replacing it with a moral connection and appropriation of difference into a multicultural, sentimentalized social imaginary. The imperial-subject traveller does not seek to conquer England or Europe as a colonial, but a form of appropriation does take place in the form of moral, sentimental and subalternized connection, solidarity and authority over the world they traverse.

In some cases, this moral connection and sentimentalized imaginary has very definite political overtones. For instance, Kshitish Banerjee encounters a friendly young woman in London, who directs him to his residence when he is lost. He then narrates:

> She is a German Jew. It was very painful to learn that she was one of the many who fell victims to Herr Hitler's wrath. I was greatly moved when she related in reply to a query of mine how she was forced to leave Germany with a paltry sum of only eighteen shillings and how she had to struggle hard for maintenance for months and months together in a foreign land. (1938: 124)

She also tells him how she had to leave her siblings behind in Germany, 'leaving them to be subjected to more humiliation' (124).

Immediately after this incident, Banerjee meets some Chinese students who were 'talking about the war going on in their country' (125). Banerjee continues:

> At that time the Sino-Japanese war was an important topic of discussion everywhere—in the parks and streets, hotels and restaurants and offices. And the sympathy of the average people always went with the ill-fated Chinese. At a time when the public were much perturbed over the massacre of the unarmed civil population of China by the invaders, news of some provocative nature about the war often found extra-ordinary prominence in the London press. (125)

On the very next page, he reports the victory in boxing of the American Joe Louis over the British Tommy Farr: 'Far from according congratulations to Mr. Louis, the champion, they all became one to find fault with him. It was probably his dark complexion that made them so' (126).

Banerjee's attention across these three pages is entirely consumed by examples of people belonging to races and nationality who were, at that moment in history, persecuted: German Jews, Chinese civilians and African Americans. That the Banerjee text foregrounds these populations and individuals points to Balachandran's idea of a 'subaltern sociality' at the heart of London.

S. Natarajan discovers that in Germany, 'nobody wanted to discuss' the 'Jewish question' and 'chang[ed] the subject rapidly' (1938: 34). In England when he, Natarajan, speaks to an Englishman, he recognizes that as an Indian and an imperial subject 'it is a deep feeling of humiliation that I cannot speak as a representative of one free country to another' (107). Natarajan states that, like in Hamburg, 'no one in England talks of subject peoples' (107). The fact that Natarajan observes the silence around the oppressed Jews and the subject peoples of India is a form of subaltern solidarity and a cosmopolitanism generated from compassion and a recognition of suffering and subjugation.

In some cases, the Indian traveller points to English colonial rule and 'civilization' as creating conditions of poverty and destitution in many parts of the world. Sullaiman Mahomed writing in 1895 about his travels in New Zealand says of the Maoris:

> It is a thousand pities that contact with the west has not conferred upon them an unmixed blessing. They are extremely addicted to drink which threatens to work their ruin. It seems alcohol dogs the footsteps of European civilization, wherever it goes. It has done so in India, and indeed, wherever Europeans have planted their rule. (1895: 68)

Mahomed's critique of European colonialism brings together Maoris and Indians and other parts of the world, 'wherever Europeans have planted their rule'. This is an excellent instance of the transnational subaltern linkage in the discourse of Mahomed.

The obverse of this social imaginary of multicultural suffering and injustice occurs in some cases where the Indian is aligned with the suffering races. For example, Cornelia Sorabji narrates an account of meeting an English cleric who greeted her with, 'It's so good to see you … so like Home'. Sorabji, since she has 'never seen this man before' asks 'Do you know India' or Indians, and he says 'no'. And then he explains: 'But it's *so* like Home to see you. I've been working among the Coolies in South Africa!' (1934: 53, emphasis in original).

There is also, evidently, a sense of the 'portability of race' (Nussbaum 2009) in the Englishman's observations where India and South Africa, Indian and African races become nearly the same in his perceptions.

Even where there is no distinctive alignment of the Indian traveller with the injured or dead European Other, the detailing of European suffering constitutes, I suggest, a form of subaltern cosmopolitanism driven by a moral outlook on events such as war and its attendant suffering. For instance, Durgabati Ghose travelling through Lucerne visits a war museum. She observes there a painting of the 'war between France and Prussia from 1870 to 1871'. She writes: 'There were several ambulances all round. Dead and mutilated soldiers and horses lay scattered here and there …' (2010: 33).

Subaltern cosmopolitanism is a form of anti-conquest and moral affiliation of the Indian traveller with subordinated populations and their memories—Nazi Germany's onslaught on their Jews, the memories of the Japanese atrocities on the Chinese during the Sino-Japanese war, and of course the racism of the United States and Europe that denied the blacks both citizenship and personhood. Further, the insulting 'portability of races' that Sorabji faces when the English cleric assigns her the same class and racial category as the 'coolies' in South Africa implies a solidarity, however unwanted and unwarranted, across oppressed peoples.

Adapting the work of Michael Rothberg on multidirectional memory (2011), I suggest that when the Indian traveller brings together images, events and memories of diverse but similar subaltern populations and states-of-being, s/he is constructing an alternative history of the colonies and of Europe. Thus, it is not possible to separate the troubles visited upon the Maoris due to the European colonial project from the subjugation of Indians and the oppression of the blacks in America and the extermination of the Jews in Nazi Germany.

The larger point I wish to make is that each individual history, whether of poverty in England's streets or India's, of Maori alcoholism or American racism, is read in terms of *other* such histories. When Malabari witnesses hungry boys and girls on the streets of London, he pauses to reflect on the famine in India:

> Practically, hunger in England is as keen as thirst in India. It is in London that I can realize the havoc of famine in my own country, the semi-starvation of 40,000,000 in India year-after year. There must be thousands upon thousands in England, too, whose pangs of hunger I can well imagine, who suffer more keenly, though by no means so largely, as my own people. (1895: 90)

The observation and citation of one incident/condition in the light of others is an 'archive of multidirectional memory' (Rothberg 2011: 524) in the Indian traveller. Such an archive is the very foundation of the traveller's self-fashioning. S/he is the *moral* subject of the Empire, whose moral response towards suffering in any part of the world and the discursive inventorying of this suffering, is the basis for subjectivity within the confines of the imperial-subject position s/he occupies. The memory of slavery in America or the memory of Indian servitude thus enables the Indian traveller to provide an alternative history of the world from the perspective of a *disenfranchised* subject.

The Sentimental Response

In his account of Paris, Pillai focuses on the working classes. In the course of an extended paragraph, he surveys a variety of members of this group.

> Long before the grey hours of the morning, you find a woman picking her weary way along the gutters of the roads, lantern in hand, bending

> under the heavy burden of her huge basket of rags and refuse. That is the poor rag-picker dependent on the rag and refuse of her town for her living. She is indifferent alike to wind and weather. With the morning there appears the Flower-dealer with her little cart full of flowers picked from the nearest flower garden, inviting her customers to relieve her of the load … The female crossing sweeper is more common in Paris than the male. Old and decrepit, she sweeps the streets early till she is relieved by the Street-waterer armed with his water tubes … Here and there, at street corners, you see the Boot-black standing in expectation of custom … Here goes the Laundress-girl, basket in hand, lean and lank, very much like a scarecrow … (2006: 75–76)

Pillai draws our attention to the scrawny physiques, the weariness and the general air of decrepitude that marks the working classes. While carefully avoiding any overt statement of his sentiments at the sight of these workers, Pillai's inventory, by focusing on the broken body, implicitly enunciates a particular subject position for himself as a man who records (not unlike the observer-surveiller of Blake's celebrated poem, 'London') suffering but also labour.

The focus on vulnerable bodies captures, in terms developed by Judith Butler and recent critics (Butler 2004, 2009; Murphy 2011), the universal injurability of *all* humans, even in distant Paris. Then, by underscoring the various professions to which these specimens of vulnerable bodies/persons belong, Pillai points to their 'social ontologies' (Turner 2006). That is, while vulnerability is common to all humans, in these cases, Pillai implies that it is the social setting of these persons that induces injurability and vulnerability. In other words, even when he restrains himself from any overt expression of sympathy with the suffering Parisian workers, the focus on their bodily conditions *in* context (class, profession) clearly are statements of empathy and focused attention doubling as criticism of the social inequality of the city.

Graham Long in his study of moral and sentimental cosmopolitanism writes:

> Moral cosmopolitanism emphasizes our duties to other human beings, regardless of nation or state. The key claim of moral cosmopolitanism

> is that 'every human being has a global stature as an ultimate unit of moral concern.' In the particular context I want to discuss here, this involves duties to the world's poor. Moral cosmopolitanism challenges us to extend our concern for justice globally, and not view borders as morally relevant boundaries. For most moral cosmopolitans this means ending or ameliorating global poverty. Sentimental cosmopolitanism is focused not on our duties, but our emotional attachment to others. It goes deeper in emphasizing the kind of person we are and how we feel about others. It demands that we become, in Nussbaum's phrase, a 'man or woman of humanity.' On my interpretation here, this involves encouraging empathy with, and sympathy and compassion (in the sense of sharing the suffering of others) for, all human beings ... moral cosmopolitanism, to be truly effective as an argument for the realization of our global duties, requires support from a more sentimental approach. (2009: 317)

Sentiment, then, is central to the generation of moral cosmopolitanism. Others, too, have pointed to the centrality of sentiment in the engagements with distant Others. Critics have argued that 'the sentimental novel's "repetition and rehearsal of emotions" [Lynn Festa] for the disenfranchized contributed to the broad reimagination of a more inclusive human community' (Dawes 2009: 397). But Pillai's strategy, rather than state his sentiments clearly, chooses to provide a catalogue of disenfranchised people. If statistical discourse, as Poovey argues, is meant to be objective and scientific, then Pillai disguises his sentimental responses in the form of a list. Yet, it is the unrelenting and incessant documentation that alerts us to the disguised rhetoric. In other words, what Pillai does is a self-reflexive move, of burying his emotions in the unceasing march of the catalogue.

When Romesh Chunder Dutt says of the Irish farmer, 'this is not the only fertile country in which the cultivators are exceedingly poor' (1896: 78), he is making a larger case for global poverty and concomitant ethical responses that then constitutes his own moral cosmopolitanism.

Other moments of moral cosmopolitanism are to be found in the travellers.

Here is N.L. Doss on his Paris trip, where, for reasons unclear to anybody, his friend takes him to visit the morgue.

> I passed through the vestibule and was all at once ushered into the presence of four dead bodies—three males and one female—which were exposed there, behind a glass screen, for identification. You can imagine what my feelings were then. All cases of suicide, murder, or accidental death are exposed there, for identification by the friends of the deceased. I was told that there was one case on the average per day of deaths in Paris, and that house is never without one or more bodies on view. Besides these bodies, I saw several hundred photos of men and women who had died thus in the two previous years, and had not been identified before. Their photos were still hung up on the walls for identification. These facts do not speak much to the credit of the morality of the Parisians. (1893: 134)

My argument is related but not identical: it is the repetition of the figures of dispossession and disenfranchised, rather than any one character, that constitutes the moral dimension in people like Pillai and Doss. I suggest that the emphasis on poverty—the feature of much 'poverty-porn' in the contemporary as well—by the Indian traveller is directed towards two ends. First, it points to the frayed *social* ontologies even in cities like Paris and London. Second, it is part of a cosmopolitan project in that it seeks to mobilize sentiment about the distant others. (That it already inverts the picturesque into a subaltern picturesque has been argued in the early chapter.)

When Doss focuses on the photographs of the unidentified dead in the Paris morgue, he is, in fact, addressing (and directing us to) melancholy objects: objects that are linked to the dead and are metonyms for mourning and memory (Gibson 2004). But what about the photographs of those we never knew, such as the ones Doss views? Doss is not exactly indulging in acts of personal grief, although he does enunciate his shock at the numbers of dead and what he terms the 'morality of the Parisians'. He is first offended by the display, then by the numbers and finally by the social context that allows bodies to remain unclaimed and unidentified. The logic of the visual image of suffering and broken bodies, writes Elizabeth Dauphinee, 'risks the final obliteration of the human subject whose world is already undone by the experience of pain' (2007: 140). Refusing—in contrast to purveyors of torture- or death-porn—Doss expresses his shock by asking us, the readers, to imagine his 'feelings'. With this, Doss has rejected any alignment with the camera that captures the suffering (which would make him complicit with the image). Further, he positions himself as an ethical witness when he comments, critically, on the morality of the Parisians. He also puts pressure on us to imagine his suffering, thereby aligning us and him. Adapting the words of Sue Tait writing on 'body horror', Doss sets out, I suggest, to 'politicize the immorality of suffering' (Tait 2008: 92). Given the violent nature of their deaths, the images that Doss observes and inventories for us work to 'extend … an imagined right to see to a host of contexts through which the body is rendered monstrous by violence' (108). The fact that he does so for a foreign context and in a foreign setting renders Doss's narrative amplified power, for he is positioning himself not only as a moral cosmopolitan witness to the Parisian 'immorality of suffering' but also as a historian of such a suffering for readers globally.

Having discussed poverty in England and India, and the problems that may accrue to India should England lose its status as an economic power to the United States and the rest of Europe (165–166), T.N. Mukharji (1902) proceeds to make a set of interesting observations about India's potential contributions to the English people. He begins with this:

> We can help the people of England materially by cheapening the cost of living in that country. In this vast continent of India we have numerous food-substances on which the poor of England can live as well as the Hunias in the high altitudes of the Humallays, the Badagars among the forests of the Xilgiri hills, and the Kurumbas in the Mysore plateau. (172)

He then adds, expanding the geographical range:

> We have millets and seeds which yield as nutritious a food as wheat, rice, the pulses, and the potato. Create a demand for these, and the vast expanse of land now hung fallow in Chota Nagpur, the Central Provinces, Central India, Mysore, Assam, and Burma will smile with a verdure through which will peep the white bunches of *Sorghum vulgare* (Joar) the golden spikes of *Paspalum scrobulatum* (kodo), the red heads of *Amarantus Blitum* (Chua), and the brown claws of *Elcusine coracana* (Ragi), and its kindred ... He who has seen with his own eyes the sufferings of the needy when famine raged in India, or the chronic hunger that prevails among the: poor classes in Europe has no room in his mind for another feeling than the ardent wish to alleviate human misery ... What I mean to say is that the distress prevailing in this country in ordinary times is not so excruciating painful as what prevails among the poor in Europe. (173)

Mukharji then sets out to prove his aforementioned claim:

> The utter helplessness in which a man without means of living finds himself in England makes his situation doubly insupportable. No river has been left for him where he can try to catch a fish, there is no jungle where he can dig' for a root or pluck the tender leaves of a tree, he has no neighbours who would share with him their scant meal, and he has no home where he can lay himself down and die. The land in that country belongs only to a few individuals and they have all enclosed it with hedges and wire fences, so that he has no place like our mango groves where he can lie down and rest his weary body. And consider what his misery would be if he had little ones depending for their food upon the fruits of his labour! Do you ever hear in this country of people drowning themselves to save themselves from such misery? Such things happen in England. (173–174)

Mukharji's moral cosmopolitanism, imbued with sentiment in the form of shock and sadness, leads him to reverse the colonial-imperial philanthropic mission when he claims Indian grains and pulses can alleviate the situation of the hungry poor in England. Then he proceeds to demonstrate that being poor in England is infinitely worse than being poor in India. Romesh Chunder Dutt (1896) makes a similar point when he writes: 'a sight of misery compared to which the poorest classes of people in our own country are well off'.

Like Doss's opinions about Parisian morals, Mukharji attributes the abject state of the working classes in England to its social structures. Like Mukharji, here is Romesh Dutt documenting the poverty and unemployment in England:

> There is capital in the country which can find no investment, there are goods produced year after year which find no market, there are millions of English labourers in the towns and in the country willing to work for their bread, but who can find no work and are on the brink of starvation. This is a real and a serious evil, and it seems to be a growing one also. (1896)

In Europe, too, Durgabati Ghose discovers, that there are jobless people, but in countries such as Germany, schemes such as large parks were initiated 'to support jobless people after the war' (2010: 64).

That is, the vulnerability of the poor in England is the result of a failure of social systems (the land being privatized, poor employment potential). It is the social ontology of the English poor that attracts Mukharji's attention and constitutes his moral cosmopolitanism as an imperial subject in the heart of Empire.

In Pillai, Doss, Dutt and Mukharji, the moral cosmopolitanism is an offshoot of their social and cultural cosmopolitanism. Robin Vandevoordt, situating the former in the latter, writes:

> *a sense of responsibility for or between distant others.* The main advantage of this notion is that it helps us to examine under which conditions *social and cultural cosmopolitans*—people who, respectively, have regular contacts with individuals from across the globe, whether because of the neighbourhood they live in or because of travelling and, people who have an open disposition towards unknown beliefs and customs (Vertovec and Cohen, 2002; Hannerz, 1990; Skrbis and Woodward, 2007)—also become *moral cosmopolitans*—people who experience a sense of responsibility towards distant others. (2018: 196, emphasis in original)

The Indian traveller, even of elite class, possessing less social and cultural power in the context of the Empire, acquires a subjectivity through this moral cosmopolitanism that enables him to erode the corrosive identity of an imperial subject. The moral cosmopolitan, as is evident from the tone adopted by the travellers, positions himself in the role of the compassionate, pitying and critical traveller, not one who sees himself as lesser than the English or Parisian populace.

The expression of sentiment towards the subjugated, oppressed and destitute classes of people across the globe may be seen as not only the enunciation of political affect but also as the mobilization of public sentiment around a range of structural and other inequalities in the world. Such a discourse, Michael Rothberg rightly argues, 'would risk downplaying historical heterogeneity, with uncertain effects for political mobilization and moral vision' (2011: 537). Rothberg's caution is directed at the effects of such memory-work, but my point is slightly different here. I suggest that the insistence on moral and sentimental responses in the traveller is primarily a mode of constructing her/his subjectivity. This is not to say such discourses of moral sentiment do not have a dimension beyond the personal and the individual, but rather to point to the exercise of affective subjectivity in the face of diminished political subjectivity by virtue of their being imperial citizens.

National Cosmopolitans/Cosmopolitan Nationalists

When one reads Behramji Malabari's *The Indian Eye on English Life* we encounter a double vision in the way he perceives himself, England and India. Despite his imperial subject position, he gains access to people, places and events through his education, networks and relative privilege. Acutely aware of this, he fashions his cosmopolitan stance around England as the pedagogic locus of his political aspirations, and India as the performative site where these aspirations *need* to be played out. I invoke here Bhabha's distinction of the pedagogic and the performative. For Bhabha the 'performative' is aligned with instability, a 'practice that destroys the constant principles of the national culture' (2001: 303). Where the pedagogic produces a rigid set of codes and homogenizing identities, the performative unsettles them. Bhabha argues that the performative destabilizes the stereotypes on which the nation depends, and which miss 'the zone of occult instability where the people dwell' (2001: 303). Bhabha elaborates:

> We then have a contested conceptual territory where the nation's people must be thought in double-time; the people are the historical 'objects' of a nationalist pedagogy, giving the discourse an authority that is based on the pre-given or constituted historical origin in the past; the people are also the 'subjects' of a process of signification that must erase any prior or originary presence of the nation-people to demonstrate the prodigious, living principles of the People as contemporaneity: as that sign of the present through which national life is redeemed and iterated as a reproductive process. (297)

The cosmopolitan nationalist, I suggest, folds the pedagogic and the performative in interesting ways. First, he recognizes the colonial pedagogy—of the Empire constituting the people of India as subjects within a particular historical past. Second—and herein lies the layering of the traveller's complex cosmopolitan nationalism—figures like Malabari, Dutt, Doss and Baijnath also treat England's political structures, rules and laws and social mores as pedagogic in an entirely *literal* sense, as offering lessons and solutions for Indian society and politics. Third, the traveller takes this pedagogic *value* gleaned from England as a *potential* performative for India. That is, the Indian traveller draws the lessons for a performative *for* the colonized race—Indians—in terms of reforms (political and social) and rights *from* the imperial culture he is travelling through. The performative is not necessarily one that India needs England to bestow (as legislation, for instance), but one that the traveller's internal critique of his culture suggests Indians undertake for themselves.

The first and third mark his nationalist, native and localized position, while the second signals his cosmopolitanism.

Take, for instance, G.P. Pillai's point about the operations of gender roles in England and India. He observes that increased interactions with women when travelling through England means that 'you cease to be nervous in the society of women: you are not shy ...' (2006: 55). He continues: 'You meet with women of different intellectual calibre. You begin to admire their mental culture and to like their company charmed by their manners and easy conversation' (55).

He then moves on to make this comparison:

> While in India, you found it so difficult to separate real, genuine affection for a woman from passion and love; and you sought the company of only one woman—your wife. That was due to your training and to the sort of society that exists there. But society as it exists in England makes you admire women, free altogether from the grosser form of love. The more you move in the company of English women, the more you are convinced that it is possible for you to admire the intellectual culture of your friend's sister or even her personal charms without harbouring any unholy thought in your breast. Society as constituted in India does not recognise this distinction; in fact, people who have known no higher forms of life think it impossible to separate the two ... (55)

Pillai's comparison foregrounds several aspects of the social that arrests our attention. He shifts between a 'you', which references himself, the Indian traveller in England (who is implicitly 'here' contrasted with the 'there' in line three), in the third person *and* the implied reader in India, addressed in the form of a second-person narrative. In the process, he makes his second move, from the stereotypical views of man–woman relations in Indian society to the *possibilities* of a different kind of those relations, resulting in a reform of this society.

I see this as an instantiation of a vernacular cosmopolitanism in Bhabha's sense of the term. Pillai engages in what Bhabha characterizes as '*a parallaxal shift in the subject of the event as the enunciating I shifts its geopolitical location and rhetorical locution*' (2002: 44, emphasis in original). Bhabha's key point here is that it is in the very ordinariness of the everyday, that 'we become unrecognizable strangers to ourselves in the very act of assuming a more worldly, or what is now termed "global," responsibility' (44). For Bhabha, this parallaxal shift is not the 'instantiation of the commonality of history and culture' but the 're-visioning, so that the process of being subjected to, or the subject of, a particular historicity or system of cultural difference and discrimination has to be … "recounted"' (45). Pillai, I propose, uses the scene of everyday interactions in England to speculate on the socializing of genders in India, even as he shifts the rhetoric from the 'you' that refers to himself, to the 'you' which refers to any Indian male. He *retains* the specificity of historical context, as Bhabha would insist when he speaks of 're-visioning, in two clear paired and mirroring sentences: 'society as it exists in England', 'society as constituted in India'. Yet, it is in this parallaxal shift, from England to India, from one addressee 'you' to another 'you', that the cosmopolitan nationalism emerges.

The cosmopolitanism that enables Pillai to assimilate England's modernity of gender roles is not just imbued with the sense of wonder at cultural difference but has a clear nationalist agenda of reforms in India. Yet, it is not enough to conclude with this extract that appears to fit so well with the 'global responsibility' that Bhabha attributes to vernacular cosmopolitanism. When the earlier passage concludes, Pillai admits that 'there must be a limit to all kinds of liberties and the tendency of the age is to increase and unfortunately to abuse the liberty of women' (55). At this point, Pillai once again shifts the focus from the necessary freedoms to women and gendered social interactions to the possible abuse of the same. Given that he has expressed implicit support for more equalized and open gender relations in India, the previous statement with which he concludes this chapter appears strange. Yet, we also know from Reddy, Saha and Patrick Murphy that the cosmopolitan nationalist is alert to the possible loss of their home culture's uniqueness. Murphy writes:

> Cosmopolitanism is not defined in terms of individuals bringing their global knowledge to bear on a particular location but rather in terms of locals gaining cosmopolitan knowledge in order to maintain the cultural integrity of their communities. (2013: 156)

One can see that Pillai seeks precisely this. He would like the freedoms from England to be the norm in Indian social interactions. But this knowledge of Western mores is accompanied by the alertness to the possible unravelling of the (rigid) social order in India. Mimetic transplantation of the Western mores runs the risk of causing the Indian social order to lose its 'Indianness', so to speak. Hence, Pillai's cosmopolitanism does not seek a dismantling of the home country—and in this, he asserts a nationalism that appears to directly conflict with his cosmopolitan worldview.

Behramji Malabari, writing a few decades before Pillai, records his views of London, England and Europe. He foregrounds his own subjective viewing position and often makes pronouncements that, as Antoinette Burton puts it, construct 'his position as the authoritative, manly voice of Indian reform' (1998: 165; also see Siganporia 2018: 206). When examining the 'woman question', Malabari first rejects the idea of two distinct sexes, noting that such a binary 'is being eliminated in sciences, art and literature' (1895: 154–155). He is clear that 'the time seems to have come for a moderate instalment of Women's Suffrage in England' (155). One notes Malabari's cautious 'seems' when stating his opinion, moderating it in the process. He admits that the 'excesses' of 'balls, dances, and other exciting amusements' (163) 'is apt to be carried too far' (163). He then turns to the 'Eastern' situation in terms of gender roles.

Malabari suspects that 'the proud, Parda-ridden Oriental should misunderstand the scope and importance of the social amenities' (dances, balls) that he has described. He claims that all that he has said is 'not in a doubting but in an inquiring spirit' (164). He proceeds:

> It will be a long time before the Eastern mind can distinguish between courtesy and familiarity, as exchanged between the sexes in Europe ... Where men and women are allowed to meet openly, on terms of equality, the glamour of sex is bound to disappear ... What this glamour of sex is, and what a fatal fascination it exercises on those who are doomed 'to burn from within', is best known to the heart and mind of the East. It permeates the whole texture of our existence and our national literature, corrupts the morals of our youth, and tends powerfully to keep up the artificial barriers that divides the children of God. It is sad to see some of our best Indian thinkers generalising, at times, from instances of those miscarriage of affections. (164–165)

He then berates those who view any companionship or socializing between the sexes through a prism clouded by what he terms a 'lack of clarity':

> It shows a sad lack of charity to rush to a conclusion against a man and woman talking, sitting, or taking a walk together. A little reflection will show the harmlessness, even the usefulness, of the thing. If either of the parties happens to be married, so much the worse for him or her, in the eyes of the Indian critic. (165)

He then proceeds to criticize the 'jaundiced eye of the zenana' that causes the Indians to view such social gatherings as immoral (166).

Having made these comparisons, wherein the East is indicted for its narrow-minded attitude to gender relations, Malabari, like Pillai, sets out to modify his views:

> Long courtships and flirtations are certainly not to be defended. But though flirtation is to be reprobated in all eases, there are many cases in which courtship is permissible as a prelude to wedded happiness. We are not likely to have much of courtship and the whole gamut of love-making in India, so long as we keep out the system of late marriages. Early marriages are best suited to our *present* requirements, though there is no excuse at all for infant marriages. (165, emphasis added)

This is the 'cultivated partiality, a reflective return to the cultural origins that one can no longer inhabit in any unthinking manner' (Amanda Anderson cited in Small 2011: 87) of the Indian traveller. Malabari, impressed by the advances he sees England having made in terms of gender equity, recommends these same reforms for India. Once exposed to the merits of the gender parity social orders of England, Malabari can no longer desist from seeing the flaws of the 'jaundiced eye of the zenana' that informs the Indian attitudes towards women. This is the cosmopolitan gaze that slides from an admiring look at the cultural Other (England) to a critical observation of the home (India). This is the double-consciousness that marks the cosmopolitan nationalist. Malabari's quick tempering of the criticism of Indian social mores may be read less as ambivalence than as a vernacular cosmopolitanism that serves to illuminate both the cultures he traverses.

Even as he crafts his subjectivity in terms of the observer-traveller-commentator on English life and culture, he also distances himself from it by pointing out the potential perils of courtship and socializing between genders. Thus, in M'Baye's terms, there is a romanticization of English social norms that is then quietly eroded by Malabari's distancing from them. The subjectivity of the traveller is precisely this productive 'cultivated partiality' which leads Pillai and Malabari to constantly renegotiate their terms of engagement with the foreign culture *and* their own. Keeping the best interests of the Indian women at heart, and thereby situating themselves as reformer-nationalists, they appropriate the Western norms as cosmopolitans, yet both nationalism and cosmopolitanism are shot through with cautious scepticism.

When Malabari claims that 'early marriages are best suited to our *present* requirements', he states that he does not seek immediate and drastic change: he sees change as a future-prospect, as potential. Malabari, diplomatically, sees/states gender equality as a yet-to-come event. This temporal distancing (India's future social order of gender equity) of a culturally different present (England's social norms) is a vernacular cosmopolitanism imbued with what Bhabha termed the 'temporality of continuance' (2002: 40). Malabari sees India's society continuing England's mores into the future, even as his discursive strategy enables him to present change as *potential*. Malabari, in other words, relocates (unsettling) social change into a temporally different and distant place, an imperial subject's equivalent of the Renaissance storyteller's situating troubling, and politically dangerous, themes of monarchy and religion in distant/other lands (Nelson 1973).

Occasionally, the Indian traveller exhibits the tensions of the contesting pulls of individualism and communitarianism. Lala Baijnath is commenting on the nature of committees constituted to enquire 'India affairs.' He writes:

> Lord Randolph Churchill's earnest interest in the subject [Indian affairs], though not the same, did not seem to me to have quite died out. Lord Northbrook's committee appointed in 1886 was too heterogeneous a body to be of much use. A smaller and more compact body would do better. Such a committee, if appointed, might either summon leading committees from each presidency in India to give evidence before it, or depute some of its members to take evidence, like the late Famine Commission. The staunchest advocate of the Indian Government needs take no objection to the inquiry. If his own countrymen find the native view of the question right, he ought not to complain. Indians, on the other hand, have too great a faith in British justice to be afraid of their affairs being discussed by impartial judges; and I hope they may yet see their way towards giving India such an inquiry. (1893: 72)

Baijnath here first foregrounds his personal subject position ('seem to *me*') and is thus self-reflexive about his 'observations'. In the same breath, he assumes the role of a spokesperson for his community as a whole when he enunciates the views, opinions and general feelings about the British government in the subsequent lines. Baijnath thus claims to speak on behalf of himself and his countrymen, signalling a sense of community and national identity. As Sheshalatha Reddy reading Sarojini Naidu points out, the individual resists any signs of her/his opinion being entirely private ones. Just as 'Naidu desires to be seen as an Indian-English poet working within English literary traditions, even as she sees herself as an Indian poet of an Indian nation writing for the Indian "people"' (2010: 577), Baijnath ensures that his opinions are seen as metonymic of the Indian people as a whole.

Baijnath's account here ends with the ironic comment he makes about the Indians' trust in British institutions. He suggests that there is 'too great a faith' that the Indians lay in British systems of governance and jurisprudence. When he syntactically places this in conjunction with the expression of hope that England would indeed create an impartial inquiry commission for India, he implicitly criticizes the Indians' trust in England. Thus, Baijnath first endorses the British interest in India and is mostly accepting of the committees put in place by the British government. Then he ponders over the best possible composition of a committee for India. Finally, he is uncertain that Indians can place so much trust in the British systems. He does not wish Britain to dismantle its structures, nor does he believe the Indians' trust in British governance is entirely legitimate. Taken together, these three moves Baijnath makes signal a cosmopolitan nationalist where he wishes to take British systems of inquiry, legislation and governance and vernacularize it for India. To vernacularize, writes Bhabha, 'is not simply *to be* in a dialogic relation with the native or the domestic, but it is to be on the border, *in between*, introducing the global-cosmopolitan "action at a distance" into the very grounds—now displaced—of the domestic' (2002: 48, emphasis in original). Baijnath's suggestion that (*a*) the British government ought to take Indians on board when discussing Indian affairs and (*b*) Indians accept British systems of inquiry and systems (like he does as an individual) but not trust them implicitly signals, I propose, a cosmopolitanism imbued with a clear nationalist sensibility. He positions himself at a complicated intersection: he is a native speaking on behalf of other natives, concedes that his countrymen's faith in England is a bit naïve, endorses the British interest in India *and* believes that England should do more with the natives.

That is, Baijnath wishes the British system to continue but vernacularized with native members and opinions integrated into the system. Now, it can be argued that Baijnath *is* speaking of the British government in India, and hence the latter is already, in one sense, a local government. But Baijnath's quibble over the composition of the committee suggests something more. It is not enough, Baijnath implies to have an interest in India's welfare: this interest must emerge from opinions and expertise framed within the 'native view of the question', a view shared by many natives. Thus, the idea of an 'interest' in India affairs is more than vernacularization. It is tantamount to what Emily Johansen describes as 'a *territorialized cosmopolitanism*—cosmopolitanism located in specific, though often multiple, places' (2008: 2, emphasis in original).

Baijnath's cosmopolitan nationalism also emerges in another section of the travelogue, just preceding the excerpt cited earlier. Baijnath sets out to compare the British government in India with other colonial and non-colonial governments.

> No well-wisher of India would desire to have introduced into it the unstable democratic Government of France ... or the party Government of Great Britain whose promises often last till the elections, or the democracy of the United States, which those best likely to know think fails to represent the intellect, the culture and the moral sentiment of the people. In France the error has been committed by breaking entirely with the past ... Speaking of the United States on the other hand, Mr Fisher says: 'The Government is below the mental and moral level even of the masses. Go among them. Talk to the farmer in his field; the blacksmith at his anvil; the carpenter at his bench—even the American labouring man who works for hire in the Northern States—and compare their conversation, so full of good sense and sound feeling, with the ignorance, vulgarity, personality, and narrow partizan spirit of an ordinary Congressional debate, and with the disclosures made by investigating committees. Evidently the mind and moral sentiment of the people are not represented.'

> These pitfalls cannot be too carefully avoided in India; and all that the most ardent well-wisher of this country can legitimately demand of its Government is, more sympathy with its people, greater readiness to adapt their policy to their growing needs and aspirations and to look upon its measures not only from its own but from their eyes also, speedier fulfilment of past promises and greater consideration for their opinions. (67–68)

Baijnath here demonstrates a characteristic feature of the cosmopolitan nationalist. He first references the sentiments and thoughts of strangers—from the French to the American working classes. Then he turns to the requirements of India in particular, situating these in the context of how these other governments have reneged on their promises to their people: the British party system of government, the French and the American. Baijnath uses this comparative history of political systems not to instantiate a commonality of history but to posit a 'similar but not identical' subjecthood of India with strangers and foreigners. That is, in order to assert the national demands of Indians, he develops a framework akin to Michael Rothberg's 'multidirectional memory' (2011: 528): to show how various governments in different parts of the world have failed their people, before expressing the hope that England would not treat India and Indian views this way (in the second paragraph of the previous excerpt). Nationalist aspirations in Baijnath's discourse, then, are embedded in a transnational framework where people's aspirations in France, England and the United States have been thwarted. Arriving at his national/ist aspirations through a detour of other nations and their peoples is a cosmopolitanization, and a discursive strategy that folds various ethnic, class and racial identities into a large category of subalterns: citizen-subjects whose governments have failed to respect their opinions.

A variation of the cosmopolitan nationalist may be seen in G.P. Pillai's concluding paragraphs:

> India must stand or fall with Britain. And the only way in which this fact can be made real is by unifying the interests of India and

> Great Britain, by removing the gap which unfortunately separates the British and the Indians in India: in fact, by obliterating all distinctions of colour. No such distinctions are observed in Great Britain; why should they be in India? Colour is certainly an object of curiosity in Great Britain. In the streets of London, I have been stared at; in Edinburgh, little boys and girls running about, have suddenly stopped to look at me; in Dublin, fair women found it impossible to suppress their laughter on seeing me; and in Chester, on the borders of Wales, I have been pointed at as a black man, by fond mothers to their little children. Nevertheless, neither in England, Scotland, Ireland nor Wales, have I heard a single unkindly word used with reference to me by anybody. The people have been uniformly courteous and even anxious to please. (2006: 81)

Even as he underscores that he was an object of curiosity to various people, from England to Wales, Pillai records the experience of always being treated well by the people. On the one hand, admitting the exoticism of colour that he experiences, Pillai is quick to localize this exoticism: it is *within* the geopolitical territory of the English nation. Pillai's nationalism here involves seeking to at least discursively limit the practice of racialized exoticism to the British Isles.

Pillai here also effectively reverses the 'geographical morality' that Edmund Burke bemoaned and criticized in English attitudes as far back as the 1780s. Pillai proposes that what is minimally acceptable within the boundaries of the English nation is not acceptable, and in fact is downright reprehensible, in the context of the subcontinent. Pillai projects race-based exoticism (but shies away from identifying any race-based *exploitation*) as a spatially *restricted* phenomenon even though, within the countries of Ireland, England and Scotland, it is widespread. Racial inequality and exoticism, he implies, is not portable across the seas into the colony. Discovering the 'problem' of race, for Pillai, involves a transnational engagement and exposure, from the subcontinent to England. Pillai also implies that this spectacularization of difference is a universal phenomenon, but he also employs this to speak of his own cosmopolitan peregrinations across England (and later, Europe). Yet his concern, he notes, is *not* this spectacularization and exoticization founded on race, when he is travelling across Europe, but with the same objectification and spectacularization back in India.

Finally, Pillai's concluding remarks indicate that his exoticism was a part of his own cosmopolitan adaptation to various places and cultures. Retaining his spectacular difference across various cultures is an exploration of the 'cosmopolitan possibilities' that Laura Rosenthal claims is integral to European exoticism. The fact that he elicits courtesy and cooperation from various places and cultures is not simply a sign of their social etiquette but also of his own cosmopolitan adaptability *in the face of his objectified exotic difference*.

Cosmopolitan nationalism also appears in these texts as an insistence on social reforms in India, founded on cultural codes and literacy gleaned not just from England but from other countries as well. That is, the Indian traveller develops a set of ideas and opinions about, say, social reforms from multiple genealogies. While *one* of their primary sources may be Indian/Hindu/Christian, as we see in the case of Lala Baijnath for example, they also cite examples from other cultural practices and texts.

Baijnath visits two societies in London: the Vegetarian Society and the Society for the Prevention of Blindness. The former, he discovers, 'is making some headway amongst the working classes' (1893: 97). He then mentions the tensions between Hindus and Muslims in India over the practice of eating beef. He expresses the hope that if Indian 'youngsters … adhered to their old habits, they would enjoy better health [and] more than half solve the caste question on return from Europe' (98). That is, Baijnath hopes the Indians studying in England would abandon the practice of eating beef in England, and therefore on returning to India, would change the social equations in India. In the case of the Society for the Prevention of Blindness, Baijnath hopes, given the 'number of blind in India … alarmingly on the rise', such a society 'is badly wanted here as in England' (98). In both these cases, Baijnath seeks the reform and modification of Indian conditions—of diet or of health—to originate somewhere in the West.

Baijnath also finds equivalence, interpretations and parallels for Hindu thought and ideas in sources that are from elsewhere. For instance, he argues that 'God of the Hindu ... is also the God of Hegel ... the Idee of Hegel, which is unconditioned abstraction, is the Brahma of the Hindu' (173). In his conclusion, he declares that 'Kant, Hegel, Schopenhauer are nothing more than Western Vedantists' (233). Later, exhorting India to work harder, Baijnath would offer this:

> It is now the struggle between the productive powers of the West and the West; and Indians ought to realize the ideal of appearing as Englishmen's competitors, not only as farm labourers and mill hands but also as capitalists. (207)

Baijnath would, in the course of his travels through Sri Lanka, claim that 'Buddhism in Ceylon, like Hinduism in India, had become a religion of forms and dogma' (224). Baijnath hopes Indians would acquire 'intellectual emancipation', and he cites Goethe's definition of the same (232).

Jhinda Ram praises the 'forfeit game [where] male members can kiss fair members of the family, and vice versa' (1893: 88). Ram goes on:

> Why should we not do away with the nasty purdah system, which is injurious to society no less than it is ridiculous? Why our ladies should not walk in streets without covering their faces? What is the harm if their faces are seen by men? ... Rise up India, rise. Before clamouring to get political rights you must improve your society and your social manners and customs. If once you prove to the British Government that you are nearly equal to the civilized countries in social reformation they will be compelled to give you the political rights of these civilized countries ... Look at Japan how far ahead they have gone of you in a short period in social transformation. (88–89)

Ram's source for this plea of 'modernizing' Indian gender roles and relations draws upon not just England, but the world, especially East Asia (Japan).

T.N. Mukharji, who spends a considerable amount of time extolling Western modernity, writes about religion:

> On the easternmost limits of the East, Confucius, on being asked by a disciple to include in a single word, the sum of human duty, said, 'Does not Retribution do this? Thou shalt not do unto others that which thou wilt not that they should do unto you'. Five hundred and thirty years later, another great oriental said the very same thing on the westernmost limit of the East. In the middle, I mean India, not only did our sages give expression to similar sentiments long before the birth of Confucius and Jesus Christ, they also asked us to consider this golden maxim binding on us not only in our dealings with brothermen, but also in our dealings with all things that have life … (1902: 337)

While there is some jingoistic nationalism at work in Mukharji's rhetoric, mainly in terms of claiming a certain antiquity to Hinduism in comparison with Confucianism or Christianity, he also points to a cosmopolitanism of a certain belief system and moral code. Even with the historical differences between the regions and the religions originating therein, thereby invoking plural genealogies, Mukharji gestures at an ethical universalism of the ideas that he *now* espouses.[3]

The global register of progress is not always, however, enunciated in the 'report', so to speak, on India. Travellers like Syed Ahmed Khan were also thinking in terms of other identities. For instance, Khan writes about the Muslims elsewhere:

> I am really pleased to see that, though our Hindustani Muslim brethren are bogged down by utter ignorance, our Muslim brethren in other countries have started making progress in culture and refinement. Muslims of Turkey and Egypt under the Sultanate of Rum are progressing steadily in this regard. It is indeed a matter of great pleasure that the Muslims of Turkey are increasingly leaving behind or rather getting rid of the prejudices usually based on foolishness and ignorance that lead to their disgrace and humiliation. (2011: 182)

Khan praises the education of women in Rum [Arab names for the Christian and Greek Orthodox regions around Syria, Lebanon, Israel, but also Turkey] and in Egypt (183), the Egyptian visitors in the metropolises of England and France (182–183) and concludes with:

'It is a matter of great pleasure to see the increased mutual love and diminishing hatred and savagery of human beings, which is also the true purpose of Nature' (183).

Khan fits into the 'Muslim cosmopolitanism' argument persuasively offered by Seema Alavi (2017). Alavi examining Muslim fugitives and emigres in post-'Mutiny' India demonstrates how these individuals found the space between the British and Ottoman empires as conducive to remaking the global 'as something that was non-British or non-Eurocentric' (23). The idea of the global and the cosmopolitan, writes Alavi, were part of 'the Islam-driven modern imperial vision of the late nineteenth century that appropriated moral and political reform and attributed it to Islamic origins and history' (29). Alavi is pointing to *other* cosmopolitanisms that were not organized along the lines of European/Indian colonialism which this book proffers, but finds distinctive cosmopolitanism emerging from territories and cultures that are not part of this (Europe/subcontinent) geocultural grouping.

*

In these cases, what is evident is that social transformation or moral advancement at the level of the local (India, or Muslim, in the case of Khan) is cast in a global register of improvement, equality and modernity, whether it is in the domain of gender, capitalist production or diet. This constitutes a case of vernacular cosmopolitanism for, as Debjani Ganguly has demonstrated in her work on Ambedkar and Gandhi, 'the vernacular cosmopolitics of a Gandhi or an Ambedkar is about generating transformation in the assured global registers of the political through their translations into and from myriad petit registers' (2007: 259–260). Even when these thinkers draw upon an ancient lexicon such as Hinduism or Buddhist terminology, it is shot through with 'modern hybrid genealogies that bespeak the historical and cultural permeability of modernity's multiple practices' (259). As a result, she proposes, the easy 'dichotomy of a modernizing cosmopolitanism and a vernacular traditionalism' is untenable (259). The nationalist cosmopolitan or cosmopolitan nationalist attains the 'reflective distance' from his home and from the world. This distance enables a certain kind of 'reflection' which, in many cases, focuses on subalterns in various parts of the world. It is a vernacular cosmopolitanism that seeks to turn their learning from foreign shores into an advantage for India, and this positions the traveller as a pivotal figure in nation-building.

Notes

1. Harmony Siganporia, writing about Behramji Malabari, uses the term 'dual lenses' to describe his mode of addressing 'Indian and English readers in different capacities: as an Indian imperial subject, and as a flâneur laying claim to the privileged position inherent to the act of observing life in the metropolis' (2018: 217).
2. On irony in T.N. Mukharji, see Childers (2004).
3. Interestingly, Mukharji cautions the Europeans about assuming homogeneity across all non-European cultures:

   > The separate standard of civility and morality that Europeans evolve in non-European countries, as differing from that prevailing among themselves, for application to the people among whom they sojourn, is a mistake in India. (1902: 350)

   This, he says, is because Indians are 'not like Africans and Aboriginals' (350). G.P. Pillai makes a similar comparison when he writes: 'as the Indian feels when in contact with a Negro, so the Englishman feels when he comes across an Indian that he is decidedly superior ...' (2006: 84).

5

The Globalectic Imagination and Connected Histories

Travelling on the Indian equivalent of the Grand Tour, Romesh Chunder Dutt documents the ports in Sweden and Norway:

> When the seaports of Europe were closed to English trade in 1806 under the orders of the great Napoleon then supreme in Europe, Gottenburg formed the great depot of English trade in the north and received a fresh impulse in trade. (1896: 196)

Later he would describe Paris as a war zone among European powers striving to cut up the area for their own imperial ends (215). N.L. Doss mentions the 'cooly labour from India' introduced into South Australia 'under English capitalists', exactly 'as it had been done in the West Indies and Mauritius' (1893: 213). Where Dutt observes the interconnected nature of ports, shipping, trade and national identity besides, of course, European imperialism's militarisms, Doss recognizes the globalizing power—and modes of operation—of slavery and Empires. Both document the similar but not identical movements of European imperialism, and the apparatuses and structural processes—ports, shipping, wars, slavery—that map, shape and dominate, materially, the entire surface of the earth, from Norway to Ceylon, Australia to the Caribbean. Land and sea, port and hinterland are parts of the same process—an imperial 'terraqueous history' (Bashford 2017) of Europe. Slavery, capital and imperialism are common to the history of the world, too—and the imperial subject traveller recognizes this, intensely aware that India's colonization finds resonances across the world.

As they journey across Europe, Australia and often, the United States, many Indian travellers such as Doss and Dutt draw attention to these connected histories across geocultural zones in the heyday of European empires. This chapter examines the Indian's travels beyond and outside England: those sections of his narrative that document the peregrinations through the European continent (approximating, often very closely, to the traditional Grand Tour), Australia, New Zealand and, sometimes, America. Reinforcing the subaltern and vernacular cosmopolitanism, studied earlier, the Indian traveller's 'globalectic imagination', as I term it, and its two key constituents—connected histories and ekphrasis—generate a tension between national identity and global citizenship.

The Grand Tour was an integral part of the European elite youth's education. While England's youth dominated the Grand Tour, the German and French were not far behind. Italy, Switzerland, Sweden, France and the Riviera were fixtures on the Grand Tour through the eighteenth century (Black 2011). Cities integral to the itinerary included Rome, Paris, Athens, Constantinople, in the main. The British tourist visited museums, viewed antiquarian ruins—Rome being the prominent destination for this—and often had portraits commissioned by well-known painters. They purchased paintings and souvenirs. Many of the tourists, Stiliana Milkova points out, were already familiar with the landscape and antiquities through the paintings of artists like Claude Lorrain (2015: 497–498). Those who could not travel to these places found 'travel replacements'—grand panoramas consisting of sweeping views of these cities that were exhibited across European and American cities (Neumann 2008).

The conventions of Grand Tour writing, critics note, included the documentation of the picturesque and the experience of pleasure at the views, the rhetorical strategy of ekphrasis, the account of antiquity, among others (Chard, Milkova). In the nineteenth century, Karin Baumgartner notes, there is a perceptible shift from edification and education to pleasure in the traveller's focus when speaking of the Grand Tour (2015: 2). These conventions of the Grand Tour and its narratives were not unknown to Indian travellers.

Numerous accounts of picturesque European, New Zealand and Australian landscapes occur in the Indian traveller. The term itself is employed frequently by Baijnath, Dutt and Doss. Dunedin, writes N.L. Doss, 'seen from the bay or any of the hills that surround it, it presents a picturesque sight' (1893: 165). Jhinda Ram would exclaim that 'for picturesqueness and grandeur no sight in all the world can well surpass Venice as seen from the Canal Grande' (1893: 114). Baijnath in Lucerne, Switzerland, says the town, 'attracts lovers of the picturesque from all parts of Europe'. He continues: 'Its lovely mountains, its fine landscapes, the air of quietness that prevails all round, its numerous walks shaded with lovely trees on the shores of the lake, that have made it the mecca of all lovers of the picturesque' (1893: 209).

As set out in the Introduction but worth citing again, the Indian traveller reverses the Grand Tour's generic conventions:

> Western travel narrative naturalized 'ideal' travelers—male, privileged, and autonomous agents, possessing leisure and means to satisfy their wanderlust. Indian travelers fit this profile but were not on quests for self-discovery, which occupied Western authors. They wanted to see Britain and Europe firsthand, judge what their colonizers told them, discover what colonizers did not say, and transmit information to other Indians. They negotiated conventions of travel literature in resistance to *and* in compliance with generic expectations, creating hybrids that drew on guidebooks (in an age of guidebooks), local histories, autobiography, and ethnography.
>
> Hybridity fit their reversed Grand Tour throughout Great Britain, one of their many reversals of generic features, such as the Western smorgasbord descriptions of sights, tastes, and sounds. Most Western travelers explored the 'unexplored'—places Europeans had not been before, which they tried to dominate through heroic claims and notions of the 'other' as exotic, inferior, quaint, erotic, and picturesque. Indian travelers played with these conventions by applying them to the over-explored, over-discovered Western metropole, reversing the hierarchy of periphery and center, and recalling the aristocratic eighteenth-century Grand Tour of Europe. (Codell 174, emphasis in original)

Jayati Gupta sees domestic tourism narratives set in India, such as Bholanauth Chunder's, as embodying an interesting tension and vision: 'of burgeoning nationhood as well as the potential of global expansion' (2008: 65). It was a cosmopolitan rather than a 'Hindoo' vision, argues Gupta (65). More importantly, travel, including travel through Europe, was an exploration of the interiority of the colonial subject, and Gupta finds an intense self-awareness in these Indian narratives. That this 'awareness of the self is problematized by the plurality of selves' (67) is a part of the cosmopolitanization of the Indian and colonial subject.

This self-awareness of the colonial subject through travel was enabled by the appropriation of the picturesque aesthetic and the vernacular cosmopolitanism of the traveller, as argued in the preceding chapters. In addition, as this chapter will argue, the imperial subject-traveller is also possessed of a globalectic imagination, marked by an alertness to *connected* histories and concurrences: of trade, travel, capitalism, slavery, wars, and imperialism. The idea of the globalectic imagination draws on Ngũgĩ's 'globalectics'. Ngũgĩ wa Thiong'o's definition of 'globalectics' is worth citing in full:

> Globalectics combines the global and the dialectical to describe a mutually affecting dialogue, or multi-logue, in the phenomena of nature and nurture in a global space that's rapidly transcending that of the artificially bounded, as nation and region. The global is that which humans in spaceships or on the international space station see: the dialectical is the internal dynamics that they do not see. Globalectics embraces wholeness, interconnectedness, equality of potentiality of parts, tension, and motion. It is a way of thinking and relating to the world, particularly in the era of globalism and globalization. (2012: 36)

Travel literature, for Nicklas Hållén, embodies this globalectics:

> It is a literary form that facilitates articulations of global sameness—the present that is shared across cultures, nations, regions, ethnicities—as well as local difference—the spatial distribution of concurrent world-views, interests, claims, beliefs, and conditions. Because of its focus on mobility and subjective impressions, travel writing in general and the

> book-length, novel-like travelogue in particular, thus carries within it the components of a globalectic literary imagination. (2017: 74)

Resonating with the globalectics of Ngũgĩ, but speaking from a different vantage point, the historian Alison Bashford calls for a new view of geographical and cultural spaces and processes. Bashford writes:

> I collapse the enduring couplets—land and sea, earth and ocean, imperial and naval—into a new historiographical and conceptual formation, 'terraqueous history'. The term terraqueous serves world historians well in several ways. It comes to us directly from the history of globes, a reminder of the genealogy of 'global' history. In that context, 'terraqueous' had an expansive early modern meaning, signalling not just land and sea, but the transforming matter that constantly connected them: atmospheres, vapours, airs, and waters. This is useful for current historical conversation that has a renewed interest in the relationship between climates and humans in the past … (2017: 255)

She calls for 'the comprehension of globalization (and counterforces to globalization) that for centuries took terraqueous form' (255).

Bashford is attending here to linkages rather than discrete processes or entities—from climate to territory, global flows of water and air, carceral spaces and trade routes, to which we can add capital and people as well. If Bashford is primarily interested in ports, islands, and the oceanic, we can perceive in her moves the globalectic tensions that determine and mark the fates and futures, like the pasts, of diverse regions of the world.

In line with the globalectics of Ngũgĩ and terraqueous histories of Bashford, Brydon et al. call for concurrences as a methodological approach to history. Concurrences are 'understood as located within specific times and places at scales below that of the global' (2017: 4). They are 'points of convergence or confluence where there may be gaps in communication, failures to connect, or forms of coming together where friction predominates' (4). It requires 'a concurrent examination of the truth-claims to be found in assorted archives, performances, and artistic texts' (5). Concurrences in 'lived lives', writes Gunlög Fur in the Brydon volume, 'lead to concurrent histories that lay claim to territorial and temporal landscapes of the past' (2017: 40). When the Indian traveller exhibits an intense awareness of and pays intensive attention to, say, slavery in ancient Rome, the early moments of European Christianity, botanical transplantation across the world or processes such as slavery and capitalistic conquests, he is not engaging in concurrences as methodology for reading the world:

> It is not a multiplicity of histories per se that interests me but the way in which they become entangled, ensnared by their competing jurisdictions. *Concurrences* points to those zones of entanglement where simultaneous presence in time and space reveals not only separate claims on jurisdiction but also how people deal with difference and similarity, closeness and distance, in ways that belie simplistic categorizations and predetermined hierarchies. (Fur 46, emphasis in original)

Harnessing the idea of globalectics to travel writing (as Hållén does) and studying the genre's methodology of concurrences, with due attention to historical entanglements, enables us to see how the Indian traveller brings together processes and structures as diverse as seaports, voyages, botanical populations, slavery and Empire, *from the standpoint of the imperial subject.*

The Indian traveller, even when engaging upon pleasurable pursuits such as landscape viewing and museum visits, was aware of the geographically wide-ranging transformative effects of imperialism and the interconnected nature of global movements of capital, material objects and people. The emphasis on connected histories in these travelogues shows a clear awareness of the tension between national identities—of the travellers' *but also of the peoples of other nations*—and the global forces in play in the nineteenth and early twentieth century. Second, the Indian traveller is able to effectively use the conventions of Grand Tour writing to characterize a wide range of material objects such as buildings, monuments, cities *across* Europe as ekphrastic prompts. That is, ekphrasis, suitably modified, I shall argue, was integral to the globalectic imagination of the Indian traveller.

These dual foci, connected histories and ekphrasis, positioned the Indian traveller as a self-aware cosmopolitan negotiating the diverse worlds of Europe, Australia and other places armed with the conventions of European writing, but subtly altering it to suit his needs.

Connected Histories and Entanglements

In the process of documenting connected histories, historians ought to note how different knowledge systems evolved in different quarters of the globe, independently but concurrently. These indigenous knowledges and epistemic communities contest the jurisdictions of imposed and dominating imperial knowledge forms. Fur refers to 'contesting jurisdictions':

> they signal the existence of competing jurisdictions, of concurrent worlds colliding, rather than (only) being examples of European translations of other people's self-understanding. Invoking such examples is not to suggest that one side is right or better equipped to respect concurrences than others, or that these statements are untarnished renderings of indigenous truths; rather, they are suggested as methodological windows. (43)

Travel writing offers us an opportunity to see these contestations of interpretation and the competing jurisdiction in action. Concurrences point us to what Fur terms 'areas of contested jurisdiction' (41), and therefore of frames of meaning-making where 'indigenous, non-European modes contest the dominance of European modes'.

'Areas of Contested Jurisdiction'

Fur cites the Native Americans disputing the Englishman's law, attitude and approach to 'their', that is, Native American land as an illustration of contested jurisdiction (41–45). For Fur,

> these statements [by the natives and non-Europeans] were prompted by demands that European agents made, and in this way they signal the existence of competing jurisdictions, of concurrent worlds colliding,

> rather than (only) being examples of European translations of other people's self-understanding. (43)

But such an account of the Native Americans' statements, that contest European attitudes and enunciations, are also found in Indian travellers. For instance, P.C. Mozoomdar travelling through America pays some attention to the Native Americans. He writes:

> The Indians complain bitterly of the approach and aggressions of the white man. He has shot them and they have scalped him. Wherever the Indians are, robbery, fighting, and mutual extermination are going on. Some of them, have been converted to Christianity, but most are not. Yet some of them are not wanting in fine sentiment and heroic impulse. The Sacs, and the Foxes, the Cherookees, Dacotas, and Sieux have some fine men among them. One of these tribes was, many years ago pushed back from province to province, and their chief had occasion to speak of the American war. He said:
>
> That land was ours. But the white people began to want it for their cotton and their slaves. We said, "No; this is our hunting-ground. The bones of our fathers lie here ... We will not part with it". They said they must have it, one way or another. We held a council, but it broke up; nothing could be done. Then the white people passed laws over our heads, that broke our government all to pieces. They took us prisoners for every little debt, and they made debts in order to take us prisoners. In every way they rode over us roughshod. We appealed to the Great Father at Washington. He said, "I cannot protect you where you are. But you have lands west of the Mississippi, I will remove you there." This was what they wanted—to get us away, and take our land. We held another council.—It lasted four days. I was a young man then, but I was one of the council. We said, "This land is ours. Let us live and die here." The Secretary of War was there, and his mouth was full of promises. But we said, "The Secretary of War will die, the Great Father at Washington will die; and all this will be repudiated." The Secretary had bribed one of our chiefs—a half-white and half-Indian—to sign the treaty; and soon as he got it signed he went away, the traitor also fled, for he knew that we would kill him. Order came for us now to move. We said, 'No, we have been betrayed." Then came General Scott, with 6000 men, to drive us off at the point of the bayonet. We fought, but the white man was too strong for us. Then we said; "We will go." It took three years to move the nation across

> the Mississippi. On our way the cholera took us, and swept off our people by thousands. (1884: 70–72)

Mozoomdar's account gives a voice to the Native American, offers us the Chief's view of the events and processes that caused the displacement and death of many Native Americans. In doing so, the Indian traveller's text offers a counterpoint to the European view of American history. Mozoomdar is not, however, glorifying the victimhood of the natives, for he admits they are prone to drink and wasted lives: 'The fatal vice of the Red man is his craving for drink. He will sell his house and home, his gun and wigwam, desert his wife and children to obtain rum' (72–73). Later, N.L. Doss will have almost the same things to say about the English destruction of the Australian Aborigines, and like Mozoomdar, will mention the Aborigines' predilection for drink and ruin.

Interpretations offered by Indian travellers of institutions like the law and religion further illustrate Fur's concept of competing jurisdictions. When, for instance, Doss visits the famed cathedral of Notre Dame, he spends some time on the architecture. After describing the exterior and interiors of the building, he writes:

> With all its grandeur and ornament, the interior looked very gloomy, and the gloominess within the walls was quite emblematic of how popery has shut out the true light of heaven, from those who meet there to worship Him who is the light of the world. (1893: 33)

A few lines later, he records:

> As we neared this spot [a figure of the Madonna], a man came up to us, and offered wax tapers for sale, thinking we had come there to pay our devotions in the catholic way. Here too the house of God was turned into a place of merchandise. (34)

And in the very next paragraph:

> In front of this building [the Paris Town Hall] is an open space, which, I was told, had been stained in days gone by with much Protestant

> blood, when popery was powerful in France, and her sovereigns were bigots of the catholic creed. (35)

Doss is clearly invoking a specific history of Europe here: the Catholic–Protestant conflict spread over centuries. He transforms the architectural and structural darkness of the cathedral into a metaphor for the darkness of Catholicism itself, much as the English treated the dark interiors of Hindu temples in India as a sign of the religion's dark beliefs. When travelling through Europe, Doss invokes the cultural memory of Europe's bloody religious wars, and consequently reads the architecture differently. Rather than simply see the edifice as an architectural marvel, Doss chooses to metaphorize it for events in Europe's conflicted past. A relatively different frame of interpretation, and new ways of looking, I suggest, are evidenced in Doss's text. Doss invokes, in the process, not only a specifically European history and memory *not* materially evidenced in the concrete structures, but a metaphor. Doss's reading alters, at least within the frames of the text, the 'meaning' of the Notre Dame structure. When he mourns the commercializing of prayer in the cathedral and the 'stain' on the streets of Paris, he is, likewise, imposing a parallel reading on the structures. Doss's reading, then, in Fur's words, suggest 'other ways of looking, searching for new angles that reveal different ranges of illumination' (2017: 45). Doss's annoyance at what he perceives as the commercialization of devotion is only matched by his sad memory of the Catholic triumphs over Protestantism and the latter's martyrs.

Re-reading architectural and spatial history in terms of an imperial subject's perspectives and memories of European and Christian history offers a non-European 'angle' of viewing but also demonstrates the existence of an epistemic community outside the map of Europe (even if that community has been exposed, like Doss, to Western education). In short, the architectural history of Notre Dame serves as a space of competing jurisdictions of meaning when the Indian traveller invokes a specific historical moment when describing it.

Lala Baijnath witnesses the Volunteer March Past at Buckingham Palace. He notes there were 20,000 men, of the total 2,20,000 enrolled. He writes:

> To me the get-up of the corps, their arms and their equipments as well as their movements, appeared to be equal to that of any company of regulars. Foreign critics think that as a body British volunteers do not form an effective force. But England is not a military power and her regular force, though a good force for action on the defensive, is not sufficient for offensive purposes. Her volunteers are thus a good supplement to it; and I think them to be a body of whom their country may be reasonably proud. (1893: 84)

What is important in terms of contested jurisdiction is the meaning Baijnath brings to his reading of first the Corps, and then of British military prowess itself. Baijnath believes the Volunteer Corps are indeed an effective force. Then he proceeds to claim that Britain was not a 'military power'. Even its regular army can only be useful as a defensive army, not an offensive one. For such a defensive armed force, the Volunteer Corps are adequate. Treating Britain as less than a military power ensures that Baijnath contests not only the role of its armies and Volunteer Corps but also its very national identity. Given that Britain was pre-eminently an imperial nation at the time of Baijnath's travels and writings, the opinions and comments seem decidedly ironic. Yet, it is also possible to see Baijnath as undertaking an inversion of the global image of Britain, from the *position of an imperial subject*. Refusing to treat and describe Britain as a military power enables the construction of, first, a more 'mellow' imperial England. Second, it erodes, in my view, the possible image of England as a ruthless colonizer of India, and conversely reinforces the image of a benevolent Empire. Using the foreign critics' views of England in order to forward his own 'softer' vision of England—as having just a defensive armed force!—Baijnath imposes an entirely different meaning upon the iconography of an imperial power. Where the foreign critics supposedly see an ineffective force, Baijnath believes that a more effective force is not essential to Britain at all, since she is hardly an offensive power. He, therefore, reworks the very idea of the ineffective force as a virtuous condition of England's being. As a member of the colonized race, Baijnath's eagerness to present a non-militarized, non-threatening ('not offensive') England indicates a contested jurisdiction of the very nature of imperial power and process.

I suggest that, like in Doss's treatment of the spaces of Notre Dame, Baijnath's account is embedded in the social world he occupies when he views the Corps: the world of metropolitan London, the imperial centre of the world, where he is an imperial subject traveller. He seeks to define English identity *within* this context, using the parade as a site. The English parade is a space where concurrent voices—the 'foreign critics', as reported by Baijnath *and* his own, as an imperial subject—are heard. That is, Baijnath agentially appropriates the English space of the parade in order to impose a specific meaning upon English history, politics and imperial project.

Elsewhere Baijnath invokes, akin to Doss in the Notre Dame cathedral, a social history of England to generate a different frame in which to read the sermons he attends at churches. Baijnath begins by stating 'the ordinary Englishman goes to church because it is a part of good breeding to do so. He leaves his religion behind him when he leaves his church' (166). He continues: 'the church is, moreover, the church of the rich, and not of the poor' (166). Having prepared the grounds for a re-reading of the role of religion and religious discourse in English life, Baijnath proceeds to give an account of the service and sermon he attended:

> I once happened to be present at the sermon preached by one of the most eloquent preachers of his time ... It was his Jubilee sermon, delivered in his most impressive and eloquent style to a crowded congregation in St. Margaret's Church, Westminster. Yet, I thought the sermon fell short of arousing in the minds of his hearers feelings of gratefulness for the many favours which the Almighty had bestowed upon the English nation during the fifty years of the Queen's reign. The learned divine's pictures of the progress and prosperity of his country

> during that period, though extremely flattering to his audience, were to me a little too rose-colored in the face of the great misery and squalid poverty of one-tenth of the population of London. These conditions require greatly to be ameliorated before the English nation can be complimented upon its progress during the Queen's reign. (166)

Here Baijnath makes two moves: first, to press upon us the fact that the sermon fails in achieving a serious impact on the audience, and second, that the sermon cannot be effective because the material reality of England—its poverty and squalor—defies and defeats any high-valency praise of the nation. Baijnath again transforms the public space of the church and the discourse of prosperity into the site of his alternative meanings for England. But this is not all.

Soon after this and another paragraph on churches, Baijnath expounds on comparative religion in two semantically rich passages.

He first records the question raised by Indians: 'why does the British Government not patronize their religion ...[?]' (167). He then declares that the Europeans are adopting a variety of religions, including 'Christianity without Christ' (168). Then he writes:

> The Baptist, the Church, the London [the Church of London], the Methodist and other Missionary Societies with incomes of hundreds of thousands of pounds per annum carry on their operations in India, China, Japan, Africa, Ceylon, the West Indies, New Zealand, etc. and though it is very doubtful if their conversions are in any proportion to the money they spend ...
>
> The Christianity of to-day is, moreover, not the Christianity of Christ. As taught by him it was the religion of loving God with our hearts, all our souls, all our might ... It was not the profit-and-loss philosophy of modern Europe ... Fetish worship, caste or other eastern customs which are the subject of much criticism by foreigners, are now-a-days not confined to the East. In England also they appear to flourish with full force though under different aspects. For instance, their fetish is money instead of gods and goddesses; and instead of hereditary castes they have even more rigid social distinctions, based on wealth ... in England distinctions based upon money give rise to much anxiety among people of one class to mix or get into another and of the other to keep them down ... In short, while Christianity did

> much in the past for the human race, it can scarcely be called a force in modern Europe. (168–169)

Baijnath here places a wholly different reading of Christian, imperial England and sets about dismantling not just the notion of a Christian England but also the link between Christianity and Empire.[1] He moves between centrifugal and centripetal rhetorics to show this collapsing link.

He begins by rejecting the power of conversion, questioning whether the amount of money invested in these Missionary Societies ever produced adequate numbers of converts to Christianity. Baijnath thus offers an entirely different view of both, the civilizational mission and the proselytising component of Empire. I suggest that what Baijnath is undertaking is the exploration of the *limits* of Empire. By identifying far-flung and peripheral territories, such as the Caribbean and Japan, through his centrifugal move, as spaces where Christian missionary work *failed*, he is, in fact, drawing a map of regions where imperial influence and reach had *waned*. In other words, Baijnath's rhetoric shows an imperial project that is no longer imperious, whose power of conversion no longer has a role to play in those geographically distant shores. This is the imperial subject traveller disowning the power of the Empire, bringing together the far reaches of the imperium only to prove that the centre no longer has that degree of control over the periphery. The imposition of this meaning on imperial geography illuminates the Empire differently.

Then he shifts focus, and opts for the centripetal, moving inward from the distant colonies to England. He claims that England's Christianity is not what it used to be. Moreover, he says, it has given itself over to various other religious beliefs. Thus, there is no link, in Baijnath's opinion, between national identity and religious identity. This shift, following close on the heels of the previous comments on England's evangelical mission, achieves some truly interesting results. Having dismissed the role of Christianity in the imperial process of converting the distant people, Baijnath now literally *shrinks* the geographical reach of Christianity. Even within England, Christianity is not a powerful social adhesive. As noted earlier, he has already proposed that Christianity cannot make sense in England as long as there are so many suffering poor. Now he proposes that what passes for Christianity, even within the geocultural space of the British Isles, is hardly Christianity as originally formulated. Thus, Baijnath literally and metaphorically erases, or at least minimizes, the spaces of Christian influence: it has no power over the distant peripheries, and it has no role within England either. The geographical shrinkage in Baijnath's rhetoric, narrated from the perspective of a devout Hindu (he expounds on Hinduism immediately after these sections on England and Christianity), offers a whole new perspective on imperial Christianity.

Baijnath (1893) also overturns a key stereotype of colonial discourse when he claims that 'while Christianity did much in the past for the human race, it can scarcely be called a force in modern Europe'. As numerous postcolonial readings, from Edward Said onwards, have demonstrated, imperial discourse needed to situate the colonized's culture in the distant past. Arguing that places, like culture, may have been glorious, all this glory was somewhere in the distant past. India, as Said notes, was frozen in time and had not progressed since then. Any progress would require, so argued imperial discourse, English intervention and cultural renovation of the colony through Western education, Christianity and imperial administration. Baijnath inverts this discourse to claim Christianity was undeniably a power to reckon with—but this was in the past. Thus, Baijnath calls into question the idea that a Christian Britain can be an ameliorative influence on the colonies since its own Christian powers lie only in the past. The static, frozen nature of the Orient, the staple of imperial discourse, is now the descriptor for Europe itself: Europe has stagnated and therefore can hardly expect to lead the world to modernity.

One notes that Baijnath says 'modern Europe' and not just England/ Britain. With this expansion of the geopolitical terrain of discourse,

Baijnath points the finger at the entire colonial project, cutting across all the imperial powers among European nations. Where homogenization was a key mode of representing the 'East' or 'Asia', worked through a portability of race (Nussbaum 2009), Baijnath aligns French, British, Dutch, Belgian, Portuguese empires. The portability of these racial and cultural identities implicit in Baijnath's centrifugalizing rhetoric merges different forms of colonization in Africa, South East Asia, South Asia—and claims that they all suffer from the same lacuna, that they are no longer Christian.

Finally, he believes the belief systems of the East and its caste system are replicated in England and its class-based social order. Baijnath here is dismantling the very vocabularies of Empire. The language of caste and religious superstition, long the hallmark of imperial discourse, Baijnath suggests, find their semantic, structural and social equivalents in England's *class*. The so-called Eastern obsession with gods and goddesses that the imperial discourse found fault with for centuries, is replicated, argues Baijnath, in the English worship of money ('their fetish is money instead of god and goddesses'). Through this employment of the rhetoric of similarity, Baijnath imposes a new frame over the idea of enlightened Britain. Even if we admit that Baijnath's descriptions are laden with irony (especially the comments about England's fetishes around wealth), the discourse captures the imperial subject's quite mocking, and undermining, of the stereotypical binaries: of the 'superstitious East versus the rational West', the 'modern West versus the orthodox East'. Writing from within the heart of Empire, then, Baijnath refuses to endorse such binaries and frames, choosing instead to question, overturn and reject them outright.

Thus, Baijnath not only undermines the Christian imperial discourse that are prevalent during the era. He also refutes the very image of England as a Christian nation. With this, he effectively takes apart a central element of British colonial rule: its moral imperialism. In other words, he reframes England by disputing the power of its moral imperialism *and* its national identity as a Christian nation. Its Christianity is no longer Christian, the progress of the nation reported in sermons (such as the one he attends in St Margaret's Church) is given the lie by the visible poverty all round, the proselytization in the colonies has never been as effective as expected from the investment made. Finally, the moral imperialism that England prided itself on has also collapsed, in Baijnath's reading. This is not just a reversal of the imperial gaze by the colonized; rather, it draws attention to the constructed nature of cultural binaries and the glossing over of material conditions (poverty) within nationalist sermons and discourses.

Behramji Malabari concedes that England is a place of great significance:

> With all its unattractiveness, London is still a Mecca for the traveller in search of truth, a Medina of rest for the persecuted or the perplexed in spirit ... to the searcher after enlightenment it is a Buddha-Gaya; a Benares for the sinner in search of emancipation. (1895: 2)

Malabari reads London's significance in terms of *non-European* places of enormous religious and cultural significance: Mecca, Medina, Benares, Bodh Gaya. Making a case for concurrent histories, Malabari situates England, Arab and subcontinental places on a continuum. He is, in the guise of praising England, writing a *global* history of learning and cultural capitals in different parts of the world. The cosmopolitan Indian traveller is one who is alert to this global history and sees mirror images of these when he observes London.

Reading these texts, one notes that the famed imperial ethnographic and 'scientific' observations made on the colonized by the colonizer finds its unexpected double in the Indian travel account. Julie Codell has spoken of the 'reversal' of the ethnographic and scientific gaze of the Europeans on India when the traveller institutes his inquiries into England's social life or economy (2007: 178). Codell is right in her reading, and we can see instances of such a reversal in a figure like Malabari. Appropriating a discourse between the scientific and the ethnographic, Malabari makes a connection between English weather and the English character. (The English traveller since the seventeenth century had linked Indian indolence to its climate. See, for instance, John Ovington's *A Voyage to Surat*, 1696.) Malabari writes:

> The climate of a country reflects itself pretty clearly in the temper, habits and general surroundings of the people. This is a scientific truth, the force of which is brought home to my rude intelligence most vividly in England. The people seem to be as changeable and restless as the weather. They are always on the move. Watch them where you like, at home or abroad, they seem to be full of the question—what next? No amount of walking, riding, sight-seeing satiates them—they will have something more, something, if possible, in another line. This is perhaps best seen during the holidays, when the Londoner strikes you most as an abandoned, unscrupulous holiday-maker. I know not if many parents will be deterred from enjoying their holidays by illness at home amongst their children; the majority of children are not so deterred by the illness of their parents. This may look unnatural, but is not so in reality. It is mainly the climate, and the peculiar mode of life the people have to live in obedience to climatic influences, that make them so keen about everything. (40)

Malabari does not end with this correlation of climate and character. He proceeds to then dissect English character by imposing an entirely different meaning on the English lifestyle. Opening up the space to multiple interpretations, as Fur has proposed, implies not just agency but an entirely different meaning system as well. Malabari follows up the previous passage with the following comments:

> It is inevitable, under these circumstances, that life should be a mad scramble, and that keen enjoyment and keen suffering should exist side by side in most places … That a life so artificial blunts human instincts, and lowers the standard of public morality, goes without saying; but it is equally certain that the mode of life is forced upon the people. It is bound to be a life of extremes, with the happiness of the family and of the community often sacrificed at the altar of individual interest. Nowhere could the law of the survival of the fittest be more inexorable in its working than in this vortex of high-pressure civilization. People live in a whirlwind of excitement, making and unmaking their idols

> almost every day. They seem to be consumed by a mania for novelty; everything new serves to keep up the fever of excitement. To-day they will set up a fetish—anything absurd, fantastic, grotesque—and worship it with breathless enthusiasm. It matters little what the fetish represents to the moral sense of the worshippers. (41)

Malabari moves from the scientific (including citing Darwin's theory of natural selection) to the moral explanation for the English's interest in novelty. He then posits a binary, so common to colonial discourse, of the life of the instinct and the modern (English) way of life, with the interpretation that the latter is 'artificial' and 'lowers the standard of public morality'. Critiquing (Western) individualism and the pursuit of novelty, Malabari uses the term 'worship' to indict the English. Like Baijnath, the use of such descriptors quietly undermines the stereotype and binary of the superstitious East versus rational west when Malabari shows the English as equally prone to belief systems and worship—albeit for different gods.

Generating moral readings rooted in their own contexts of beliefs and faith, the Indian traveller (such as Malabari and Baijnath) refutes and rejects the accepted, circulating discourses and stereotypes of England/Europe and India.

In a different mode of offering evidence of contested jurisdiction, T.N. Mukharji comments on the political scene in England. He writes of the tensions between two candidates for Chelsea, Sir Charlies Dilke and Charles Whitmore:

> If an outsider were to believe what, roughly speaking, one half of the English people said of the other half, he could not help taking both the halves as extremely selfish and immoderate lovers of office and power. Leaders of both parties fought as desperately as the gladiators of old fought in the arena of a Roman amphitheatre. (1902: 139–140)

Notice here Mukharji's rhetoric. First, he refuses to rate one side's views over the other's. Second, his analogy, drawing from Roman history, positions the English politicians as gladiators. The analogy is interesting for the parallels it sets up. The British Empire was seen and believed to be the inheritor of the legacy of the Roman Empire (see, for instance, Rudyard Kipling's poem 'A British-Roman Song')—and this may or may not be Mukharji's context, but is an important *subtext* to what Mukharji has to say. The bloodletting, he implies, marks the gladiatorial fights in the ancient world and political contests in the present one. Like Kipling, Mukharji, too, perhaps unconsciously situates the English as a successor to the Romans when he depicts the English as gladiators. Whether this reframes the spectacle of Empire as a spectacle of degradation and violence is a moot point, of course, but that he does see a bloodlust common to both cultures and Empires is a point to consider. But when he draws our attention to this analogy, he is also pointing to another aspect: the gladiators fought for their life whereas these leaders fight for love of office and power, thereby slotting the British politician far lower than the gladiators in their violence.

Later, Mukharji would be all praise for the British sense of fair play and sportsmanship:

> In all the fights that I witnessed in that country I never saw two or more men combining to waylay and strike at one. It is often done in this country by my countrymen who as often or not call themselves 'gentlemen.' (148)

He then proceeds to make a pointed observation about such sporting Englishmen when they are in India. He writes:

> I would have given the British very great praise for their mode of fighting, but for the cases that happened in this country of late years in which certain individuals maltreated and beat to death feeble and weak-bodied Indians, who would not for their very life return the blow, and who, if I have heard aright, were often kicked when they were down, and that in a bad place of the body. I have heard that in England too people of certain counties end a combat in this dastardly fashion. But I must say that such conduct is considered by the Britishers in general as cowardly, as well as the act. (148)

The Indian is feeble and weak-bodied, and the Englishman has no compunctions about beating him, writes Mukharji. Mukharji has already emphasized the unequal, because racialized, power relations between the Indian and the Englishman beating him. These power relations, he argues, ensures that the Indian will not be able to retaliate: the Indians 'would not for their very life return the blow'. That is, he castigates the English for not recognizing, or caring about, the sheer inequality between combatants.

Mukharji is, in fact, invoking the idea of 'geographical morality'—a charge levelled by Edmund Burke in his famous impeachment speech against Warren Hastings where he observed that what would be morally unacceptable in Englishmen and women in England seemed to be more than tolerated south of the Equator, in India.[2] Recasting the idea of English courage when they face Indians *outside* England, he notes with despair that they are not above beating an unarmed Indian. In the process of calling into question the issue of English courage, Mukharji also alerts us to the double standards and geographical morality that informs the so-called brave, or virtuous, English.[3]

The Indian traveller demarcates areas of contested meanings within English and European culture. One needs to see such a demarcation of competing jurisdiction over meanings as an instantiation of the agency of the imperial subject traveller in imposing new ways of seeing the English, to generate alternative meanings of England and the English. Contested jurisdiction and the making of new/different frames of reading are one part of the connected histories one perceives in these texts. A second part is the emphasis, often implicit, on entangled histories across the world, an emphasis that clearly signals the globalectic imagination of the Indian traveller in Europe and the world.

Entanglements

T.N. Mukharji praises England for being a freedom-loving nation and waxes eloquent as to how fortunate India was to be ruled by England. He then proceeds to set up a comparative history of empires:

> Thus we see the hand of Spain deeply dyed with American blood, but yet the transatlantic history of Spain has no case comparable

> in iniquity to the act of the Portuguese in Brazil, who deposited the clothes of scarlet-fever or small-pox patients on the hunting grounds of the natives, in order to spread the pestilence among them; and of the Europeans in North America who used strychnine to poison the wells the Redskins were in the habit of visiting in the deserts of Etah; of the wives of Australian settlers, who, in time of famine, mixed arsenic with the meal which they gave to starving natives; or, finally, of the English colonists in Tasmania, who shot the natives when they had not better food for their dog. (1902: 170–171)

In the process of praising English rule, Mukharji ironically points to the global role of Europeans in the oppression of native peoples, from India to America to Tasmania. That is, a comparative history of European empires is also a *connected history of dispossessed natives* in various parts of the world.

At one point in his narrative, N.L. Doss would record his happier experiences in Paris as follows:

> My friend then took me to the Maison des Missions, or the Mission House of the above Society [Paris Evangelical Missionary Society] ... Although I was a perfect stranger and an alien to them by nationality and language, yet the all-powerful bond of our common Protestant Christianity drew us nearer together, and we never felt as aliens and strangers, but as brothers and sisters ... They did all in their power to make me feel happy, and I thoroughly enjoyed my stay of two days there. (1893: 129–130)

Doss here is documenting entangled histories of a particular kind. Cutting across the racial and 'national' divide between Europeans and their imperial subjects, Doss discovers solidarity and community through a religious identity, which is his inheritance from European missionaries in India. Thus, when visiting France, without the language of the country at his disposal and requiring translation throughout (as he notes, 130), Doss does not feel like an 'alien' or a 'stranger'. This sense of belonging is the product of entangled histories embodied in Doss's very mobility: from Calcutta through Christianity into Europe and then Paris. His experience of Paris, smoothed through the camaraderie of Protestantism, implies that the Indian traveller's regimes of mobility itself are the product of such entangled histories. Such entangled histories are also part of his sightseeing expedition elsewhere. In Christchurch, New Zealand, Doss walking through the streets records: 'I was not a little amused to find, that two of the streets were called Madras Street and Colombo Street respectively, perhaps after the names of those two old Indian bishoprics' (169).

Doss is clearly elated at the entangled and creolized histories of European settlements in parts of the world like New Zealand and their Asian (Indian and Sri Lankan) connections.

Many of the travellers dwell, explicitly or implicitly, on such entangled histories. These histories are of a diverse variety, from horticulture to religion, slavery to capitalism, and geographically range from Europe to Tasmania.

N.L. Doss's awareness of the botanical colonization of Australia and other places signals connected and imperial histories. He states:

> Since the discovery of New South Wales, the colonization of Australia was commenced by the English, and settlements began to be formed in different localities, a few penal settlements at first, and others for purely *agricultural* and pastoral work. (176, emphasis added)

He later visits a garden in Wellington, New Zealand:

> However, I met here with an agreeable surprise. I found our old familiar friend the *Batabi Nebu* (shaddock) of Bengal growing on some trees. I do not know where they have been originally brought from. In the town I met with a few other familiar friends. They were a number of *Maina* birds, the ordinary *Shalik* of Bengal. They have been introduced from India, and seem to have taken well to their new place of abode. Every morning I used to be aroused from sleep, by the chattering of these old familiar friends, a lot of which had taken shelter on the trees of an adjoining garden. (171)

Continuing his interest in entangled botanical histories, Doss in Sydney encounters numerous plants native to India and Bengal: the bamboo and the banyan trees. He observes: 'All these trees and plants must have been originally introduced into the country. But there they were when I visited it' (193).

Transplanted species, whether achieved intentionally or unwittingly, were instruments of ecological imperialism (Crosby 1995). The import of exotic plants and the building of collections in hothouses in Kew and other places, the work of botanists like Joseph Banks and Joseph Hooker were a part of the imperial project (Brockway 1979, Arnold 2005). We now know that bioprospecting was central to the imperial project as well, and botanists, collectors and scientists capitalized on indigenous knowledges of plants and natural resources (Drayton 2000, Schiebinger et al. 2007).

Doss's inventory of animal and plant species recalls both, the link between botanical settlement of distant lands and the 'creation of identities for individual plants [that] allowed naturalists to undertake a variety of operations with the species while maintaining authority over it as a single, historically continuous entity' (Spary 2007: 379). The construction of definite species identity and the transplanting of commercially viable or scientifically useful plants were constitutive of imperial expansion:

> Colonial botany—the study, naming, cultivation, and marketing of plants in colonial contexts—was born of and supported European voyages, conquests, global trade, and scientific exploration. The expanding science of plants depended on access to ever farther-flung regions of the globe; at the same time, colonial profits depended largely on natural historical exploration and the precise identification and effective cultivation of profitable plants. (Schiebinger and Swan 2007: 14)

Thus, Doss implicitly points to the entanglements of science, trade and colonial expansion as manifest in the plant and animal life in distant Australia. Aware of the provenance of the species and the species identity, which he connects to *his* homeland, Doss takes on the role of the scientist even as he alerts us to the colonial expansion of animal and plant geographies. He writes:

> In travelling through the land one comes across immense corn fields, and at the railway stations and other places which have communication

> with the sea, especially in South Australia, one sees heaps of sacks of corn for exportation to Britain, or transmission to other parts of the colony. Fruit growing is another occupation, and the grape, the apple, the peach, the apricot, the orange and other fruits, all introduced by the settlers, either from Europe or Asia, flourish well. Some of the prettiest sights I have ever seen, were the orange gardens of South Australia. (1893: 178)

The commercial and the scientific are all woven together, just as Europe, Asia, Australia are part of Doss's connected histories narrative. Plants are a part of the imperial network, and the produce from them feed the various corners of the network. From Doss's narrative, it becomes clear that it is not possible to separate either geographical territories from each other or instruments of empire and imperial trade (such as fruits and plants).

Like Doss, Lala Baijnath also documents plant life in the colonies. Travelling through Sri Lanka he notes: 'Thence the coach takes you to the sanitarium of Ceylon in about one hour through tea gardens and Indian forest trees intermixed with those of European countries' (1893: 226).

Soon after, Baijnath visits the Peradeniya Botanical Gardens and writes:

> Here you see not only India-rubber trees as large as our Indian banian trees, nut-megs hanging like apples upon trees, pepper creepers. Cocoa-nut trees in great variety, ebony and other trees peculiar to Ceylon, but also a large collection of trees from South America, Islands of the Indian Ocean, the Malay Peninsula, etc., etc. (227)

Like Doss, Baijnath is paying attention to the cash crops and the commercially useful plants that populate the garden, and is aware of the global provenance and distribution of the products from these gardens in Sri Lanka, directly signalling both transnational (connected) histories and colonial trade.

Botany and lifeforms are not the only foci of Doss's or Baijnath's explication of connected histories.

Doss recognizes the global flows of labour, people, capital and material products when he travels through Europe and Australia–New Zealand–Sri Lanka. Writing about Tasmania, Doss records:

> The aborigines did not cultivate the land, but seemed to have lived on the wild berries and mushrooms of their native forests … These aborigines have died out with the progress of the English, and not a single individual of the race now exists. I am told that the only trace that is now found of them, is to be seen in a few inhabitants, living in the northern part of the island, who are of mixed origin, i.e. born of native mothers by European fathers, the unfortunate relics of the vice of some of the early settlers. The wild animals have also greatly decreased with the advance of the English settler. The few that are left, have receded to the mountain fastnesses which the settler has not yet invaded … I hoped to meet some of these [the 'Tasmanian Devil'] or their fellow denizens of the woods, but unfortunately I came across none. To my disappointment the Englishmen's gun, I found, has done as much havock [sic] on them, as his axe has done on the few giant trees of the island. (1893: 147–148)

Doss maps English presence in terms of losses and a history of destruction: of aboriginal lives lands and the plant and animal life on the island. Offering us evidence of the European conquest of distant nature studied by scholars such as Richard Drayton (2000), Doss in fact documents various dimensions of colonialism. Calling our attention to the sheer quantum of destruction perpetrated by the European settlers, Doss's accounts of Tasmania, Australia and their townships, suburbs and outback are in fact accounts of colonial deforestation and displacement. The link of this process—the campaign against nature and native, so to speak—with English/European concepts of private property and ownership is also something Doss is very aware of. The shrinking of spaces for the aborigines is noted as well.

A few pages following the earlier description Doss writes in a detailed chronicle of how the Englishman builds a home in Tasmania:

> Wherever the Englishman settles down, he first of all encloses his land, which is very often a large area, with a rude fence of boughs of trees with which his new home abounds. He is sure to mark his property, and settle in this way the boundary of his little domain. Although it may enclose several square miles. He lets his sheep and cattle graze on the land, while he builds for himself a small cottage of plants or what I called a weather board house … He then begins to clear the

> ground, first of all by setting fire to the scrub or the underwood, which also burns and kills many of the larger trees. The next process is 'ring barking' the trees, i.e., cutting a notch around the tree, at a height of about two feet from the ground, through the bark and into the sap-wood, to prevent the sap from rising and nourishing the tree. This kills the trees. He lets them stand until they decay down or a second or a third fire destroys them altogether; for to fell them down with the axe would require a great deal of labor and expense. He then cultivates the ground as he goes on clearing it, or lets the grass grow freely for his sheep and cattle to graze on it. You see numberless decaying or charred stumps of trees in every field under cultivation. Those that have been brought long under cultivation, you can make out from the paucity of these stumps.
>
> Even in the midst of these bushes the Englishman's home, though it may be a solitary cottage standing in a lonely wild, is not without those conveniences and comforts which it has in the more civilized abodes of men. (152)

Doss is, in fact, writing the environmental history of Tasmania here and the processes that produce large-scale changes in the land wherever the Englishman settles down. The periphery, Tasmania, is subject to the same kind of approaches to land as England: enclosures and privatization of lands. Doss's focus is on the control and destruction of natural resources that the English undertake anywhere they go.

The sense of property and possession, of entitlement and rights, observes Doss, informs the Englishman's attitudes towards other immigrants who may, like him, stake claims to the land. Many English, he notes, came 'either as capitalists or labourers' (182). He praises the English for their hard work, so that 'the labourer of today [in Australia] is the employer of tomorrow' (182). Doss notes, later, the 'problem' of immigration in Australia:

> The wages of tradesmen and mechanics are proportionately higher, and they are over-jealously guarded against all competition and the intrusion of foreign and cheap labour in the market. The teeming hives of China are always ready to send in their swarms, wherever they can make a living and turn an honest penny … But the English Australian is jealous of the Chinaman, and looks upon him as a formidable rival

> ... Of late there has been a great deal of heart-burning at the influx of Chinamen into Australia, and there have been many instances of cruel unkindness shown to them there ... The English Australian will not tolerate any encroachment by the Chinaman upon his favourite preserves, and in a land where democratic principles are on the ascendant, it is no wonder that measures are being adopted, which will eventually oust the Chinaman altogether from Australia. (182–183)

A few pages later, Doss would return to this theme, and use the same tropes to describe the Chinese immigrants to Australia. Doss writes:

> Of recent years there has been a great agitation among the people of all classes in Australia, as in America, on account of the influx of the Chinese into the island. They come into all the Australia colonies, in order to earn an honest livelihood by the hard labour of their hands. They generally work as market gardeners or mine labourers, and a few of them become cabinet makers and general traders ... Thus there is always a large number of Chinamen present in the island ...
>
> The number of these intruders was constantly on the increase, and every steamer that came from China brought some Chinamen for the colonies. This excited the fear and jealousy of the colonists ... An English gentleman of Sydney told me, that not only was there fear of the labouring classes being ousted from the labour market, but that there was political danger to the whole colony ... The Chinese swarm their own country in such vast numbers, that if ten or twelve millions of them came to Australia ... the Chinese would be strong enough ... to swamp the two or three millions of Englishmen, inclusive of women and children who occupied it ... There is, no doubt, some truth in this ... The Chinamen had no fault except that they were Chinese, and not English or Scotch ... (195–196)

Doss recognizes the exclusionary operations of the European settlers in Australia here. But he also observes that the labouring classes now contain a large number of Chinese, implying that the latter are integral to the economy of the island. He also describes them as 'honest'. The rhetoric Doss employs appears to participate in this exclusionary mode of perceiving and thinking about the Chinese: intruders, swarm, swamp, all suggestive of alien invasion and invasion by lower forms of life. When the passage concludes he admits that the only flaw the Chinese can be accused of is that they are not English or Scot. The not-so-subtle expression of sexual anxiety discernible in the reference to 'women and children', in the Englishman's comments to Doss, coheres around the racial identity (Chinese) of newer immigrants arriving in Australia.

He also records how, even as the English refuse Chinese presence, they have evicted the aborigines from Australian land.

> So far I was disappointed; and it is not to be wondered at, since the aborigines do not live in the southern parts of the island, which I visited. These are now almost entirely inhabited by Englishmen. The aborigines have receded with the advance of the English, and now occupy only the out of the way places, mostly in the northern part of the island, where they live undisturbed in their native wildness. (186)

While exhibiting some ambivalence in his own attitudes towards Chinese immigration, Doss acknowledges both racism and connected histories. The losses to the white labouring class due to the immigration, Doss admits as a likely consequence of immigration. But the politics of exclusion wherein settler-migrant populations from Europe being opposed to other immigrants, entirely based on racial difference, is also highlighted. Rather than offer an account of white-settled Australia, Doss opts to show the various racialized networks, including the labour market, shipping and legislation, that brought certain people in and kept others out.

Doss's account of the Australian settler's racial politics may be read in the light of his comments elsewhere too. When in Sri Lanka he observes: the 'English capitalist [who] has also made his way into these hilly regions [of Sri Lanka] and taken up more space than the native farmer' (222). The colonies are, as Doss documents, raced capitalist spaces. By pointing to the Englishman's objection to the Chinese in Australia following so soon after his documentation of the Englishman's displacement of the Sri Lankan farmer, Doss forces us to see the iniquity of imperial expansion across *all* colonies.

Just as Doss notes (cited earlier) the displacement of the aborigines of Australia and New Zealand due to encroaching English settlements in those regions, P.C. Mozoomdar would also reference the loss of Native American territory. Mozoomdar writes:

> It is supposed by some that the American Indian is dying out before a superior civilization. Others maintain that he is prospering and multiplying as ever. In any case the fact is undoubted that the Red man is seldom met with. In the Eastern States you don't see him at all. In the far Western regions he now and then emerges into view. He lives in the territories known as Indian Reservations. There are about 300,000 of American Indians divided into many tribes, the wildest of which are said have died out. (1884: 193)

Romesh Dutt notes of Norway:

> We were now in Norwegian Lapland, the region which was at one time almost entirely populated by the Lapps. The number of this strange people has however now gone down to only 30,000, i.e., about 18,000 in Norway and 12,000 in Sweden and Russia. (1896: 169)

The Indian traveller has documented, then, the displacement of natives by the colonizing Europeans the world over, from America to Australia to Norway. Connecting the histories of these countries are the concurrent European approaches to the land that reject any native rights over it.

That imperialism connected various parts of the globe is documented by many Indian travellers, who thereby communicate the global expansion of Europe into distant places and affect the lives and lands in those places. Their accounts of connected histories will pay attention to the history of transnational trade, the role of ports and land routes linking Europe with the other parts of the world and the movement of products and people.

Transnational trade, notes Dutt, is a part of much European history:

> Early in the 13th century Bruges was the centre of the famous Hanseatic League. Venetian and Lombard merchants exposed here to the gaze of astonished and rude barons the famed manufactures of India, and the carpets and silk of Persia; and rich argosies from Genoa and Constantinople were unladen at this place. (236)

Exploring the history of European cities, Dutt maps their transnational connections and the role their ports and shipping lines played in the global traffic of materials:

> Antwerp rose in importance as a place of commerce as Bruges fell in the 15th century, and in the 16th century Antwerp is said to have been the most prosperous and wealthy place in Europe, surpassing Venice itself! Thousands of vessels are said to have lain in the Schelde at one time, while a hundred or more arrived and departed daily. The great fairs held here attracted merchants from all parts of the civilized world ... Thousands of industrious manufacturers left their home and fled to England where they established factories and stimulated the trade of England. (256)

Holland's prosperity in the sixteenth and seventeenth centuries, Dutt notes, was contingent upon its trade. Ports, therefore, played an important role, he observes in the passage already cited earlier and in other descriptions of Dutch cities: 'These towns do not pretend to the beauty of Paris or of Brussels, but are merely systems of canals,—successions of quays, wharves and jetties, with hundreds of vessels and ships eternally unloading their cargoes from the far Indies!' (260).

From trade to imperialism, Dutt notes how the colonies were integral to Dutch identity and prospects:

> The foreign colonies and possessions of the Dutch multiplied every year,—and at the present date they are, next to the English, the greatest colonists in the world. Sumatra, Java, a part of Borneo, and the whole of Celebes and Mollucca islands in Asia own the Dutch rule and have a population of over twenty millions! (262)

He is also aware of the interconnected histories of Holland and England: 'Hanover is closely connected with English history and has given England her present reigning dynasty;— George I. and his successors were electors of Hanover as well as kings of England' (280).

Moving into Italy from Holland, Dutt again documents such connected histories: this time, of early Christianity, Europe and the rest of the modern world:

> In the early dawn of modern civilization, Pisa took the lead of the Italian commercial republics in the tenth century of the Christian era. In the eleventh century, the fleet of Pisa was supreme in the Mediterranean, commanded the coasts of Corsica and Sardinia, Sicily and Africa, and helped the early crusaders in their memorable expeditions to the East. (348)

War, notes Dutt, was also a component of connected histories because the fate of European nations and cultures were intertwined in the outcomes of the war and the alliances forged in the process. Thus, when describing the battle for supremacy between England and France in Napoleon's time, Dutt records the 'nationalist' responses to the English victory:

> Such was the battle of 'Waterloo' which popular English writers of the day described as exclusively their victory, which the Prussians mainly attribute to their desperate and heroic fighting, which the Germans claim as their victory as well as that of the English and the Prussians, and which the Netherlanders have celebrated by building a huge mound or hill on the battle-field with the Belgian lion on the top of it, looking towards France! (254)

Dutt records these as indicative of how the resources and fortunes of *many* nations—he has preceded the preceding passage with an account of the movements, on the battlefield, of the various troops from Prussia, Germany and England—were linked to the defeat (or not) of Napoleon. The subsequent *nationalisms* of the countries—allies—who participated in the battle emerge from the connected history—when they had come together for a common cause, against a common enemy. The shaping of Europe's geopolitical and national contours, implies Dutt, was the *effect* of entangled histories—of trade, wars and peoples.

After the chronicles of colonial conquest, the appropriation of lands and the displacement of the native inhabitants, trade and wars, that signal the connected histories of the colonies and of Europe, there is another key focus in the Indian travel narrative of the period:

the aspiration for freedom and the battles, resistance movements and campaigns for cultural and national identity in various parts of the world.

Jhinda Ram travelling through Turin has this to say about the city:

> Turin had always been the focus of national struggles for unity, and at last succeeded … in giving to United Italy its reigning prince. The noble poet Byron scarcely knew when, his heat throbbing with sympathy towards Italy … that so soon after his death, Italia would fling away her fiddle and shoulder her gun and throwing off the foreign yoke, be independent. (1893: 107)

Jhinda Ram quotes Byron's praise of Italy in *Childe Harold* (Canto IV). Visiting Scotland and the exhibition of the country's regalia, Lala Baijnath would argue that Walter Scott was not averse to the union of England and Scotland, and cites the novelist's criticism of the 'generous boast of a precarious national independence subject to all the evils of domestic faction and delegated oppression' (1893: 204). However, other writers disagreed and people like 'Burns and Smollet [sic] did not think in this way. They liked independence', writes Baijnath, and quotes the following lines from Smollett:

> Thy towering spirit is now broke,
> Thy neck is bended to the yoke.
> What foreign arms could never quell
> By civil rage and rancour fell.
>
> (Baijnath 204)

Soon after, in Switzerland, Baijnath records:

> At Rutle Schwur [sic] are figures of three Swiss who are swearing to free their country from the Austrian yoke. Foreign nations, much wealthier and more refined, truly envy the love of liberty of this simple people; their moderate wealth, moderate taxation, moderate revenue, and military conscriptions of a nature that turns people to serve their country in times of need. (211)

He cites a section of Scott's comment from the pamphlet, *Description of the Regalia of Scotland* (1819), in which he supposedly does not endorse Scottish independence from England. The passage from which Baijnath cites is this:

> We, who now reap the slow but well-ripened fruits of the painful sacrifice made at the union can compare with calmer judgment, the certain blessings of equality of laws and rights, extended commerce, improved agriculture, individual safety and domestic peace, with the vain though generous boast of a precarious national independence subject to all the evils of domestic faction and delegated oppression. With such feelings we look upon the Regalia of Scotland, venerating at once the gallantry of our forefathers, who, with unequal means, but with subdued courage, maintained the liberties and independence of Scotland with ten centuries of almost ceaseless war … (34)

Commentators have noted that Scott, and the exhibition of Regalia, were seeking to appeal affectively to Scottish national feeling and 'to accept its evolution into a pride in Scotland's Britishness' (Burgess 2007: 116). It is where the past and the present meet. He sees the participation as equals within Britain as the 'endpoint and fulfilment of Scotland's independent development as a nation' (Burgess 115). The Rütli statue Baijnath cites refers to the 'Three Confederates', which in turn is a monumentalizaton of the Rütli oath dated to AD 1307 that signifies the union of the three cantons of the Old Swiss Confederacy. Taken together these citations alert us to the elements of Baijnath's discourse.

First, the intertextuality of Baijnath's discourse, from Scotland to Switzerland, generates a focal discourse of national identity. Thus, Baijnath aligns the histories of freedom movements and campaigns for national identity across the world. Indeed, the world is mapped in terms of the discourse of national identity, even with the variations within specific cultures. Second, Baijnath is aware of the contradictory impulses of complete freedom and unification with the larger entity. The references to the Scottish union with England and the union of Swiss Cantons signal a political unconscious *for India*, informed by this contradictory impulse. Instead of directly commenting on India's possible independence and burgeoning national identity, Baijnath opts to cite instances of similar national histories elsewhere. That is, Baijnath's referencing of the freedom versus merger dialectic in various European histories are instantiations of a political unconscious of the imperial subject unable to decide whether he should opt for one or the other: freedom from Britain or freedom (such as it was) within the British Empire. Third, the invocation of textual and material symbols from around the European continent are signs of an entangled history of similar campaigns and resistance movements for national identity.

This sense of national identity and national pride manifests in another fashion in Romesh Dutt. After cresting a hill in a company of German, French, English and American people, Dutt records their celebrations:

> Groups of Germans sang their national songs until the midnight air re-echoed their voice, and Americans hoisted their national flag,—stripes and stars,—over a stick, and drank to the formation of a universal Republic of Peace! I will not conceal the pain and humiliation which I felt in my inmost soul as I stood on that memorable night among representatives of the free and advancing nations of the earth rejoicing in their national greatness. Champagne was drunk on the top of the hill, and Germans and Frenchmen, Englishmen and Americans, pressed us to share their hospitality. I accepted their offer with thanks on my lips, but I felt within me that I had no place beside them. May we in the course of years progress in civilization and in self-government, in mercantile enterprise and in representative institutions, even as the young English Colonies in Australia are doing year by year. And may our sons' sons when they come to Europe *feel* that India can take her place among the great advancing countries of the earth. Let us trust to the future, but trust still more to our own honest work and hard endeavour. There is not a race in Europe or in the whole world but has gained its place by hard, severe, unremitted struggle and toil. And if we too, each individual among us, learn to work honestly and truly for our country, we cannot fail. (1896: 173–174, emphasis in original)

When in Bruges, Dutt comments:

> The story of the battle for popular freedom is an old one;- in the middle ages it was first fought by the free towns of Italy and the free towns of

> Flanders. And though after a severe struggle of centuries the people succumbed under the growing power of Feudalism and of Royalty, still this was for a time only, and the battle has been recommenced and won all over civilized Europe within the last two hundred years. (239–240)

Later, Dutt would describe the European cathedrals as 'witnesses of the progress of nations from feudal barbarism to modern culture and freedom!' (363).

In the face of a triumphant (racialized) nationalism that Dutt encounters, he recognizes not only his imperial subject position but also the necessity of, at some point, possessing a national subject identity—like the Swiss, the English, the Americans and others. Dutt is mapping a history of freedom movements *across* subjugated peoples and cultures. Expressing his aspirations for the future of India, he positions India within the comity of nations that have, by dint of hard work and determination, acquired a place in the world. Not only does Dutt present a *model* of national identity—fought for, acquired sometimes through battle—for India, he sees India as carrying within it the same potential as these other nations. Admittedly, he observes that the European nations had acquired their freedoms well in the *past*—a move that situates India as a latecomer to the idea and condition of freedom, but carrying within it the aspirations of freedom nevertheless. If, as Mary Louise Pratt argued, travel and exploration writing has 'produced Europe's differentiated conceptions of itself in relation to something it became possible to call the rest of the world', the Indian traveller also discovered something similar. An emergent nationalism, reinforced by transnational histories of nationalism and national identity, is clearly visible in these texts.

Transnational Ekphrasis

Entering the Church of St Louis, Paris, Jhinda Ram offers us this:

> My eyes were drawn to the flags suspended from the roof … In the other part … beneath the beautiful gilded dome, 340 feet high, an

> excavation 19 feet deep, in the centre of which stands the beautiful sarcophagus containing the ashes of Napoleon the Great, is surrounded by a circular marble balustrade. (1893: 99)

Soon after, he visits the Arc de Triomphe:

> It is situated in the centre of the city on a height whence radiate twelve five [sic] avenues, nearly all of them sloping upward to the arch ... It is 160 feet high, 116 broad and 72 feet deep and cost £ 400,000. On it you see the groups of statuary, carved in high relief and gigantic proportions representing the victories of the Great Napoleon. Vendome Column is another monument of Napoleon the Great. It was erected by his order to commemorate his grand victory over the Russians and Austrians in 1805. It was begun in 1806 and finished in 1810, in imitation of the column of Trajan at Rome. The shaft of the column is of stone, cased on the outside with bronze from the metal of 1200 guns taken from the Russians and Austrians, in a series of brass reliefs representing the battles and victories of the French during the campaign in question. It is 142 feet height, and 13 feet in diameter. (100–101)

Ram combines a statistical and artistic account of the monument with a historical one, dwelling upon each of these aspects for some time before moving on to the next monument, building or museum. The object here serves to *slow* down the narrative, as in classic ekphrasis, except that instead of a painting or image, it is a material artefact that achieves this effect in the Indian traveller.

Ekphrasis was a key rhetorical feature of the European Grand Tour narrative (Milkova 2015), serving to position and fashion the traveller as a connoisseur of the arts and as a careful observer. The accepted definition of ekphrasis is: 'a verbal representation of visual representation' (James Heffernan cited in Wagner 1996: 10). Recent studies, however, point out that ekphrastic descriptions were not restricted to the arts alone. Material objects and three-dimensional spaces also served, notes Bridget Vincent, as ekphrastic prompts (2018). Map descriptions in poetry too, argues Jeff Thoss, are instances of a 'cartographic ekphrasis', where these descriptions are verbal representations of another sign system (2016). For Bernadette Fort, critical ekphrasis is a mode of calling attention to the effect on the viewer but also the artistic principles underlying those effects (1996).

The etymology of the term means simply 'to speak out'. But it also implies, notes Bridget Vincent, 'attentive observation and judicious witnessing' on the part of the spectator who will then commit the object or artefact to verbal narrative (374). As Murray Krieger would argue, it is a device to interrupt the temporality of discourse by riveting attention on an object (1992).

In the case of the Indian traveller, it serves to fashion the observant self, and ekphrasis is recast so as to deliver the material object—monuments, ruins, in particular—in terms of its dimensions, aesthetic features (although this is not so pronounced in many) and historical background. Where the critical ekphrasis underscores the artistic principles that evoke certain effects in the viewer, the Indian traveller's ekphrastic narrative often turns to the backstory and history of the object. Resonant with the enumerative picturesque discussed in the early chapter, ekphrasis is transnational in scope in the Indian travelogue and is a narrative device linked to the travelogue's concerns with mapping connected histories and geocultural spaces. That is, ekphrasis is a necessary narrative strategy, given the Indian traveller's intense focus on connected histories because a *statistical and historical ekphrasis* enables the traveller to offer up to the reader detailed accounts of local political and cultural history in the guise of describing the monument or architectural spectacle. The statistical and historical ekphrasis is a component of the globalectic imagination because of the attention to the local within the ambit of a European or global tour.

Jhinda Ram's description of the Roman ruins, Florence and other Italian cities is extensive. He first describes the Dante statue in Florence, giving us its dimensions and artistic features. He uses the occasion to describe Dante's exile as well, thereby linking the poetic oeuvre, the memorial and the biography (120). He describes some of the exhibits of the museum and then the statue of the Rajah of Kolhapur (who died on his travels in the region) and expresses his sadness ('Oh! the poor Rajah, where you were born, and where lie your ashes', 122) at the sight. Passing through the Roman ruins, Ram writes:

> I was looking down on ruin, ruin, ruin, all about me. The disinterred remains of the temples, the houses, the streets, the theatres were showing the mighty pomp of the old Rome, delineating the hollow but majestic civilization of the old Romans, and describing the early struggles of Christianity with heathen superstition. Broken temples, broken tombs, broken walls, broken arches, broken aqueducts which I was seeing all around me were pointing that Rome had once been at the proudest and most gigantic eminence of luxury and power. You read a history in every one of the stones that are scattered there on the ground. (123–124)

The Colosseum reminds him of the cruelty of the ancient Romans (125), even as he recounts the history of its construction: 'commenced by Vespasian in 77 AD and completed by his son Titus in 80 AD' (125). It is, he admits 'the symbol of the greatness of Rome' (125). Ram produces what Jeff Thoss following Kim McMullen terms 'counter-mapping', 'an alternative experience of space to the one offered by cartography' with his ekphrastic account of Rome and its many ruins (2016: 74–75). Unlike a tourist who hurries through the sights and sites following the guidebook's cartographic organization of the tour, the Indian traveller who takes recourse to the ekphrastic narrative *dwells* on the sights he sees. He uses the sight, as evidenced in Ram's account, to slow down his narrative. In this process, he offers us, first his emotional state when viewing the ruins/artefacts and second, the history of the sight/site. Even as he admits that the Colosseum is a symbol of Roman greatness, and delivering the history of this 'object', he opts to recount the other history of the place—a bloody and violent history that, in Ram's words, represents a 'struggle'. He positions himself then as a careful witness, who prefers to meditate on the invisible history of the stones in Rome. Transforming the matter/material of the stone into a 'speaking' monument by reading 'its' history, Ram invokes the etymology of ekphrasis: the stones 'speak out', chronicling their history.

Like Ram, Syed Ahmed Khan at Versailles gives us the history of the palace: Louis XIII locating the place, the architects he commissioned and the dates in some detail (2011: 135). Soon after there is the account of the dimensions of Louis XIV's courtroom, bedchamber, and the nearby opera house (137), all instances of statistical and historical ekphrases.

We know, from Bridget Vincent's work that

> Ekphrasis is a fertile medium for these questions because it allows the poet to respond not only to the artwork itself but also to lived processes and behaviors of which the finished work is a trace (attentive observation, judicious witnessing, or conversely, disregard or misrepresentation). These processes can involve not only the actions of the artist but also the people depicted, and this detail is particularly significant in scenes of violence. (2018: 374)

This is precisely what Ram sets out to do. See, for instance, this account of Ram:

> Then I went to see the 'Forum,' the most memorable spot in the history of Europe. How one's mind is filled with indignation at the merciless and cruel vandalisms perpetrated on this place. For a thousand years the edifices of ancient Rome were employed as quarries from which churches and secular buildings alike derived their materials; costliest marbles were recklessly burnt for the purpose of supplying lime; the magnificent slabs and alabaster which had once been used as seats by senators, kings, emperors, bakers, meat-sellers, coblers [sic] for displaying their wares ... After the systematic destruction of the 'Forum' its remains were gradually buried beneath the rubbish and debris, only a few isolated columns protruding from the accumulation of rubbish formed a reminiscence of its departed glory. Thus it remained until the 19th century when it was excavated. Here popular assemblies were wont to be held. Here some of the most famous scenes of the Roman republic were enacted. Here Caesars from their thrones

> used to rule the destinies of nations … Temples, public buildings, monuments, basilics, streets and pavements have been excavated—of course all ruins. (1893: 127)

Ram goes on to describe several such ruin-sites (127–131).

Ram's historical ekphrasis enables him to stop in his peregrinations *and* in his narrative of the peregrinations in order to meditate on the violent and exploitative history of the ruins. Roman history, for Ram, embodied in the material remnants is marked by the violence of gladiatorial contests and the battles of Christianity with 'heathen superstition'. Ram would elsewhere point to the historical shifts *within* the character of these ruins, by pointing out that some Roman structures were first 'dedicated to a god' and 'afterwards consecrated … as a Christian Church' (131). And elsewhere:

> No language can describe my feelings when I conceived for one moment in my mind this whole great pile before me [the Colosseum], as it used to be, with thousands of eager faces staring down into the arena to look at the Gladiators' fight …
>
> I was treading on the spot where the heroes had trod, where the blood of martyrs had flowed without moving the hearts of the fierce and cruel Romans. I saw before my eyes the spirits of the victims of the old butchery of Rome, rising and haunting the very ground on which I was treading. (125)

Ram therefore not only tells us about his feelings when viewing the ruins but also the problematic social, religious and political histories of the places: paganism versus Christianity, imperialism (Caesars 'rul[ing] the destinies of nations'), social iniquities and violence, among others. In like fashion, Durgabati Ghose gives us an account of the Colosseum, gleaned, she says, 'from the guides' (2010: 93):

> The wild animals … kept starving for seven or eight days in a room ... when the starved beasts would pounce on them [runaway slaves, prisoners and sometimes strong men] then some of them would die … Warriors and kings, the rich and the noble, even the aristocratic ladies, would sit and enjoy such a cruel entertainment. (93)

Such an extended historical ekphrasis invokes for us not ruins but ruination, as Ann Laura Stoler would term it: the process of ruining. 'Imperial ruins', writes Stoler, are 'racialized markers on a global scale' (2013: 13). Thus, when Ram invokes the ruination of *imperial* Rome via references to the battles of/in religion, social order and politics—including slavery, the conquest of other regions—he is, in fact, reflecting on the ends of Empire on a global scale. Slowing down his route in order to speculate on the effects of history on his own mind is, therefore, a self-fashioning wherein he undertakes a reflection of the 'ends of empire', so to speak, not restricted to the Roman one alone.

That the imperial ruin signals the many cruelties of Empire is not overtly visible in Romesh Dutt's account of the Roman ruins he visits. (Dutt's sections on the Roman anticipate in uncanny ways Ram's, including quotations from Byron and descriptions of how Edward Gibbon may have sat down in these ruins and was inspired to write his magnum opus!) Here is Dutt on the Colosseum:

> This vast structure is an elliptic, its longer axis being 584 feet and the shorter 468 feet, and the arena inside is 278 feet by 177 feet. It was commenced by Vespasian on his return from the war against the Jews, was dedicated by his eldest son Titus in 80, and was completed by his youngest son Domitian. It was calculated to hold about 1,00,000 people to witness those cruel sports which delighted the populace of Rome, 5,000 wild beasts and 10,000 captives are said to have been slain at the inauguration of the structure by Titus; and for centuries after, thousands of prisoners. Christians or gladiators or captives from the far East and West, died a cruel death and stained this ground with their hearts' blood, to make a spectacle for the rabble of Rome.
>
> Two aqueducts were scarcely sufficient to wash off the human blood which a few hours' sport shed in this imperial shambles. Twice in one day came the Senators and matrons of Rome to the butchery; a virgin always gave the signal for slaughter. Roman virtue and Roman heroism have passed into bye-words in history and in tale; but every nation has its vice, and no civilized people of whom there is any record in history were so brutally cruel, so savagely and passionately fond of witnessing suffering as the Romans. It is said, indeed, that the truly

> brave are never cruel; but to that assertion the Roman amphitheatre gives the lie. (1896: 324–325)

Like in Ram, this ekphrasis is both historical and critical. It tells us, first, the history of the place. Then it informs us of the unspeakable horrors perpetrated in the Colosseum when it was still a functioning space and not a ruin. Neither Ram nor Dutt are any longer describing artefacts, architectural marvels or tourist spots. They are no longer describing ruins either, but ruination, to invoke Stoler's distinction (although Stoler's focus is on the 'Imperial projects [that] are themselves processes of ongoing ruination, processes that "bring ruin upon," exerting material and social force in the present', 10).

We see this shift from ruins to ruination in Lala Baijnath as well. At the Colosseum, Baijnath records:

> It is a Colossus amongst buildings, 'grand even in decay' as Europeans say; but to a native of India, it is a heap of ruins with nothing but its fearful associations of fights of gladiators and martyrdoms of the early Christians, and it can offer but little attraction ... Where emperors sat and noble ladies feasted their eyes on bloodshed, are now the nests of the owl and the bat amidst clusters of grass and creepers. (1893: 214–215)

An attention to the inequalities and their attendant brutalities that are inscribed into the stones and ruins of Rome constitutes a politically edged historical-critical ekphrasis by the imperial subject. They refuse to be mere tourists. They slow down their pace of travel and reflect upon the ruins they see. Deflecting attention away from the ruin *per se* and its materiality onto the 'inscription' of historical processes and events therein is to generate an order of indexical signification: material ruins now speak of and alert us to the ruins they brought upon some races and peoples. They do not, as is commonplace in such contexts, evoke melancholy at the ruins of an Empire alone: they also invoke their sadness and shock at the ruins the Empire wrought on others. Examining the subject of ruins and the compulsory melancholy they evoke, Stoler writes:

> Melancholy, compassion, and pity nourish imperial sensibilities of destruction and the redemptive satisfaction of chronicling loss. We

> are schooled to be alert to the fact that ruins hold histories, that ruins are the ground on which histories are contested and remade. Still, the nominative form of a 'ruin' does less work than 'to ruin' as an on-going process. Ruins can represent both something more and less than the sum of the sensibilities of people who live in them. Instead we might turn to ruins as epicenters of renewed collective claims, as history in a spirited voice, as sites that animate both despair and new possibilities, bids for entitlement, and unexpected collaborative political projects. (2013: 14)

In line with Stoler, I suggest that Ram, Baijnath and Dutt reprise their role as viewers. Baijnath in fact foregrounds, unlike Ram and Dutt, his Indianness when he views the Colosseum's remains, thus underscoring his imperial subject status and his globalectic imagination at the site of the older Empire's ruins. None of them function as melancholic tourists saddened at the sight of ruins but as participating in a *specific* historical recall of what the Roman Empire effected—and thus refashion their brand of tourism as a political project. Disputing the glories of the ancient Roman Empire and the bravery of Roman kings and warriors—which are also, supposedly, inscribed into the ruins they see—Ram, Baijnath and Dutt in their historical-critical ekphrasis are reclaiming the ruins for an entirely different order of signification. The ruins are, in the travellers' ekphrasis, signs of ruination, barbaric cruelty and violence.

*

The globalectic imagination in the Indian traveller enables them to refashion their tourist role. With considerable attention to entangled histories and imperial legacies—the transnational ekphrasis as a narrative strategy that effectively supplements both of them—the Indian traveller fashions himself less as an imperial subject than as an informed cosmopolitan who refuses to see European history as a monolithic or insulated process. By disputing meaning, as we have seen, the Indian traveller also refuses to accord extant meanings any hegemonic valence, choosing, instead, to contest any such prevailing jurisdiction. The traveller positions himself as one aware of the contestations, contradictions and compromises that have marked European history, offers his own interpretations of events and people and continually draws attention to entangled histories. In the process the imperial-subject traveller emerges as a person informed by the globalectic imagination, refusing any hegemonic readings of history, particularly European ones.

Notes

1. For studies of the linkage between Christianity and Empire see Stanley (1983), Comaroff and Comaroff (1991), Thorne (1999), among others.
2. Burke argues:

> He [Warren Hastings] has told your lordships in his defence, that actions in Asia do not bear the same moral qualities as the same actions would bear in Europe. My lords, we positively deny that principle ... we are to let your lordships know that these gentlemen have formed a plan of geographical morality, by which the duties of men in public and in private situations are not to be governed by their relations to the great governor of the universe, or by their relations to men, but by climates, degrees of longitude and latitude ... as if, when you have crossed the equinoctial line, all the virtues die ... (2019)

3. Mukharji then offers us instances from the *Mahabharata* to show that a code of conduct in war exists in India:

> As regards international warfare the European nations would do well to study a little of the *Mahabharata* and learn what was done in India some five thousand years ago. They of Kurukshetra fame would not send a rifle bullet into the heart of an unarmed or unequally armed savage, would they? (1902: 148)

Conclusion

The Antinomies of Travel in the Age of Empire

The exploration of the interlinked but distinct features of the Indian travelogue—aesthetics, exoticism, cosmopolitanism and the globalectic imagination—has revealed, as signalled briefly at the end of the chapter on cosmopolitanism, the antinomies within which the traveller found himself.

The vernacular cosmopolitan traveller imbued with a globalectic imagination, tutored in the grammar of European aesthetics, appears to hold within himself an antinomy, where both a nationalist-nativist stance and a global-cosmopolitan aspiration are valid. Drawing on very different and equally relevant, even necessary, paradigms of nationalist and cosmopolitan aspirations, the vernacular cosmopolitanism serves to underscore the unequal social relations in which the traveller finds himself, but struggles against nevertheless. This antinomy is characterized by several features. There is a normalizing of imperial relations by 'proving' the superiority of the English economy, culture and even civilization (as in the case of T.N. Mukharji). Yet the traveller returns periodically to the inequality between the nations, the absence of a global prestige of being 'Indian' (as Romesh Chunder Dutt recounts when he meets the Europeans and Americans singing their respective national songs) or India's older cultural and religious traditions (as Lala Baijnath does). Often, the travellers even demonstrate a 'connection' with European loyalty (as Jagatjit Singh or the Rajah of Kolhapur do). The antinomy signals the struggle between two paradigms of their individual and racial/national identities.

Following Tejumola Olaniyan in his analysis of Fela Anikulapo-Kuti's music, I see 'antinomy' as a more productive concept than 'contradiction'. Olaniyan writes:

> The first invests Fela with an absolute autonomous individual subjectivity, which no human being really has, and the second completely divests him of it. The best way, it seems to me, is at the interface of these two, that is, to see the 'contradictions' as located at the juncture of Fela's individual subjectivity, and the structural conditions that produces it. I have borrowed 'antinomy' to tap into that sense in which, given the historically determinate choices confronting a subject, a 'contradiction' between two necessary choices may be inevitable. (2001: 82–83)

The antinomy of nationalist aspiration and cosmopolitan yearning and a fascination for European/English grandeur, but inflected with an intense *awareness* of the exploitative, even cruel, and creolized foundations (of which India is an integral part) of this grandeur marks all the travellers discussed. Thus, Dutt's or Baijnath's despair at not being able to take his place in the comity of nations as a representative of a free country is in antinomic relation with the pride of being *Britain's* colony. Unable to opt for one or the other, the Indian traveller remains divided and undecided.

Olaniyan productively links the tension of the antinomic condition, for example of the 'friend-enemy economy', with the enchantment that is characteristic of modernity:

> This multifaced, undecidable nature is *enchanting*, an aporetic situation in which modernity is simultaneously railed at as an alien, oppressive, and bewitching illusion (a *dis*-enchantment), and as a catalyst for further striving (a *re*-enchantment) … It is untamable, but it is also inescapable. (83, emphases in original)

This argument offers a productive way of treating the antinomies of imperial travel as a productive process rather than a simple contradiction, even as it enables us to see a self-fashioning undertaken across the two paradigms (nationalist-nativist and colonized-cosmopolitan).

When the Indian traveller explores the European landscape, people and cultures, he is initially fascinated by the sights. Whether the object is the crowded street of London, the art gallery or the rolling landscape viewed from a distance (such as a train window) or from close quarters, the travellers uniformly express awe, wonder and enchantment. The fact that this is the land he has longed to visit—visiting England was a 'step [that] appears to be a completely natural one, falling in the proper line of evolution' (Bhuyan 1938: 138)—as many of the travellers admit, is a crucial one. It prepares the ground for the state of emotional fulfilment, of having arrived in England. The enchantment that is tangible in these texts is a key component of the imperial subject's subjectivity. It is marked by its emphasis laid on the colonized subjectivity, conditioned to look up to the Empire, pre-programmed through an acquaintance with European aesthetics such as the picturesque and the sublime to appreciate the landscape in certain ways. This assimilated aesthetic ensures that the imperial subject is a proper subject of the Empire.

When he then proceeds to analyse the constituent objects of his emotional, admiring response, an awareness of the subaltern or the foreign within this admirable European landscape asserts itself. While 'disenchantment' might be too strong a word to describe a certain deflationary move in these travelogues (studied in this book in the sections on the subaltern picturesque and moral cosmopolitanism, for example), there is a fair amount of qualified enchantment, or what I have termed 'informed enchantment', with England/Europe. When speaking of other histories that are woven into the European one, or the capitalist dimensions of the Empire when observing, say, the Australian landscape and landholdings, we can sense this deflationary enchantment, proceeding from the awareness of social inequalities and uneven power relations between the European races and the others. The Indian traveller does not, in Olaniyan's terms, 'rail' against the inequalities but he definitely erodes the enchantment with Europe by also marking it up with the horrific exploitation or unethical practices that enable Europe to become what it is.

When the Indian traveller then proceeds to demonstrate that Europe becomes Europe through entangled histories, crossovers, and a dependency/connections with the rest of the world, and builds discursive solidarities with other enslaved or colonized nations/races, it generates the globalectic imagination. This globalectic imagination is a re-enchantment, and is itself antinomic. It is generated, in the form of its first strand/paradigm, through and by a sense of their (Indian) shared histories with, say, Australian natives or the Maoris, of being a subject race. It is also constituted by a sense of the global role of Europe and its constitutive Others, such as Asians or Aboriginals. Reinscribing the ruins of Rome or Europe within a history of ruination and the oppression of people does not reject the enchantment of these ruins but qualifies it in moral ways. This is a re-enchantment, and the globalectic imagination is central to this process because it demonstrates the Indian traveller's interest in and knowledge of a global historical tendency to render some people or races precarious, disposable and unwanted. Through the historical ekphrasis of a transnational ambit (studied in the chapter on the globalectic imagination), we see the second strand or paradigm of the globalectic's antinomy emerge.

Re-enchantment is neither a return to the older form of enchanted viewing of Europe/Europeans by the (loyal) imperial subject nor a complete reversal by the fervent nationalist-nativist. Re-enchantment is qualified enchantment, infused with a deep historical sense, an ethical recognition of Europe's others and a clear awareness that Europe did not and does not possess an acceptable or hegemonic narrative of its greatness or solitary splendour. If anything, this narrative demands an attention to the subtext of imperial conquest or European barbarism in its ancient past. For instance, the glory of the Colosseum enchants the imperial-subject traveller, but he also recalls the bloody sports played out by hapless gladiators in this arena, a sport witnessed by so-called 'civilized' Romans. This awareness of the spectacle of sport staged for the pleasure of specific sections of society and at the cost of the poorer peoples who were butchered in the arena qualifies the greatness of the architectural marvel that is the Colosseum. The antinomy that plays out here is between the appreciative imperial subject and the ethical subject aware of the inequities that are embodied in that same architecture.

Travel writing in the age of Empire, for the imperial subject, is the crafting of a self out of this antinomic condition. Unlike a 'contradiction', the antinomy is constructive. It enables him to balance, precariously perhaps, the subjectivity bestowed upon him by the condition of colonial rule *and* the subjectivity he acquires through an informed engagement and qualified enchantment with Europe. Self-fashioning here is the construction of a self by this balancing of the two strands/paradigms, seeking to retain a national-cosmopolitan attitude and working through the imperial subjectivity of the social conditions of being colonized.

In a sense, the antinomic self-fashioning I propose as the outcome of the travel resonates with Mary Louise Pratt's idea of transculturation but approaching it from a different angle. Pratt famously argues:

> While subjugated peoples cannot readily control what emanates from the dominant culture, they do determine to varying extents what they absorb into their own, and what they use it for. Transculturation is a phenomenon of the contact zone ... While the imperial metropolis tends to understand itself as determining the periphery (in the emanating glow of the civilizing mission or the cash flow of development, for example), it habitually blinds itself to the ways in which the periphery determines the metropolis—beginning, perhaps, with the latter's obsessive need to present and re-present its peripheries and its others continually to itself. (2007: 6)

For Pratt, the 'contact' is a

> perspective [that] emphasizes how subjects are constituted in and by their relations to each other. It treats the relations among colonizers and colonized, or travelers and 'travelees,' not in terms of separateness or apartheid, but in terms of copresence, interaction, interlocking understandings and practices, often within radically asymmetrical relations of power. (7)

My argument posits the antinomy of the imperial-subject traveller as a necessary condition of the contact, one where the hegemony of the centre is partially conceded by the periphery—if we accept the binary of centre/periphery—but subsequently modified to demonstrate this copresence (as entangled histories) and the *material* subtext of capitalism, racism and unequal social orders. That is, the Indian traveller's antinomy in the contact zone, by way of enchantment, disenchantment and re-enchantment, points to something underlying the European identity. His transculturation is the recognition of difference at the heart of Europe, its history of entanglements with and dependence on other nations and the subaltern at the core of its social order and social processes. This antinomic self-fashioning may be tantamount to a subaltern identity, but I hesitate to forward this thesis because then it implies that at the conclusion of his travel, the Indian traveller has retained his sense of colonized subjectivity—something I do not see occurring in these texts.

Given the fair amount of narrative authority when commenting on, say, European art or when invoking the picturesque, in these travellers—albeit much of it gleaned from their Western education—there seems little point in treating them as docile consumers of European glory solely because they are colonized subjects. They resist the pressures of handed down imperial meaning-making when they disrupt received histories through their subaltern picturesque or moral cosmopolitan perspectives, but also through a conscious alertness to their own cultural antecedents.

The imperial-subject traveller, in short, fashions an antinomic self, when he refuses to be fully assimilated into and enchanted by either the colonized role or the nativist one, but positions himself at the intersection of both.

Bibliography

Primary Texts

Anon. *A Moral and Religious Guide to the Great Exhibition*. London: Longman, Brown, Greens, and Longmans, 1851a.

Anon. *Official Catalogue of the Great Exhibition of the Works of Industry of All Nations, 1851*. London: Spicer Brothers, 1851b.

Appasamy, A.J. *Student Life in the West*. Madras: Christian Literature Society for India, 1929.

Baijnath, Lala. *England and India: Being Impressions of Persons and Things English and Indian and Briefe Notes of Visits to France, Switzerland, Italy and Ceylon*. Bombay: Jehangir B. Karani, 1893.

Banerjee, Kshitish Chandra. *My Impressions of the West*. Calcutta: Phani Bhusan Roy, 1938.

Bhuyan, S.K. *London Memories*. Guwahati: Publication Board, 1979.

Burke, Edmund. *Edmund Burke on the Impeachment of Warren Hastings (1788)*. A History of India. Available at: http://cw.routledge.com/textbooks/9780415485432/26.asp [Accessed 20 October 2019], 2019.

Doss, N.L. *Reminiscences, English and Australasian: Being an Account of a Visit to England, Australia, New Zealand, Tasmania, Ceylon, &c.* Calcutta: M.C. Bhowmick, 1893.

Dutt, Romesh Chunder. *Three Years in Europe, 1868–1871, with an Account of Subsequent Visits to Europe in 1886 and 1893*. Calcutta: S.K. Lahiri & Co., 1896. 4th ed.

Ghose, Durgabati. *The Westward Traveller*. Trans. Somdatta Mandal. Hyderabad: Orient BlackSwan, 2010.

Haldar, Rakhal Das. *The English Diary of an Indian Student, 1861–62*. Dacca: The Ashutosh Library, 1903.

Jessawalla, Dosebai Cowasjee. *The Story of My Life*. Bombay: Times Press, 1911.

Khan, Syed Ahmed. *A Voyage to Modernism*. Trans. and edited, Mushirul Hasan and Nishat Zaidi. New Delhi: Primus, 2011.

Mahomed, Hajee Sullaiman Shah. *Journal of My Tours Round the World 1886–1887 and 1893–1895, Embracing Travels in Various Parts of Africa,*

Australia, Asia, America and Europe. Bombay: Duftur Ashkara Oil Engine Press, 1895.

Malabari, Behramji M. *The Indian Eye on English Life, or the Rambles of a Pilgrim Reformer*. Bombay: Apollo, 1895. 3rd ed.

Mozoomdar, P.C. *Sketches of a Tour Round the World*. Calcutta: S.K. Lahiri, 1884.

Mukharji, T.N. *A Visit to Europe*. Calcutta: Bangabhasi Steam Machine Press, 1902. 3rd ed.

Natarajan, S. *West of Suez*. Bombay: Indian Social Reformer, 1938.

Nowrojee, Jehangeer and Hirjeebhoy Merwanjee. *Journal of a Residence of Two Years and a Half in Great Britain*. London: W.H. Allen, 1841.

Pandian, T.B. *England to an Indian Eye, or English Pictures from an Indian Camera*. London: Elliot Stock, 1897.

Pillai, G. Parameswaran. *London and Paris through Indian Spectacles*. 2006 [1897]. New Delhi: Sahitya Akademi, 2006.

Rajah Ram Chuttraputtee, Maharajah of Kolhapur. *Diary of the Late Rajah of Kolhapoor, during his Visit to Europe in 1870*. London: Smith, Elder, 1872.

Ram, Jhinda. *My Trip to Europe*. Lahore: Mufid-I-Am Press, 1893.

Roy, Amrit Lal. *Reminiscences English and American: Part I: Three Years among the Americans*. Calcutta: Roy, 1888.

———. *Reminiscences English and American: Part II: England and India*. Calcutta: S.B. Das, 1890.

Singh, Jagatjit. *My Travels in Europe and America, 1893*. London: George Routledge, 1895.

Sorabji, Cornelia. *India Calling: The Memories of Cornelia Sorabji*. London: Nisbet & Co., 1934.

Tagore, Rabindranath. *The Diary of a Westward Voyage*. Trans. Indu Dutt. Asia Publishing House, 1962.

———. *Journey to Persia and Iraq: 1932*. Trans. Surendranath Tagore and Sukhendu Ray. Santiniketan: Visva-Bharati, 2003.

———. *Letters from a Sojourner in Europe*. Trans. Manjari Chakravarty, ed. Supriya Roy. Santiniketan: Visva-Bharati, 2008.

Secondary Texts

Alavi, Seema. *Muslim Cosmopolitanism in the Age of Empire*. Cambridge, MA: Harvard University Press, 2017.

Anderson, Amanda. *The Powers of Distance: Cosmopolitanism and the Cultivation of Detachment*. Princeton University Press, 2001.

Andersson, Johan. 'Landscape and Gentrification: The Picturesque and Pastoral in 1980s New York Cinema', *Antipode* 49.3 (2017): 539–556.

Andrews, Malcolm. 'The Metropolitan Picturesque', in Stephen Copley and Peter Garside (eds), *The Politics of the Picturesque*. Cambridge: Cambridge University Press, 1994.

Aravamudan, Srinivas. 'Response: Exoticism Beyond Cosmopolitanism?', *Eighteenth-Century Fiction* 25.1 (2012): 227–242.

Arnold, David. *The Tropics and the Traveling Gaze: India, Landscape, and Science 1800–1856*. New Delhi: Permanent Black, 2005.

Baker, Josephine J. 'Hawthorne's Picturesque at Home and Abroad', *Studies in Romanticism* 55 (2016): 417–444.

Balachandran, G. 'Subaltern Cosmopolitanism, Racial Governance and Multiculturalism: Britain, c. 1900–45', *Social History* 39.4 (2014): 528–546.

Banerjee, Sukanya. *Becoming Imperial Citizens: Indians in the Late-Victorian Empire*. Durham and London: Duke, 2010.

Barrell, John. 'The Public Prospect and Private View: The Politics of Taste in Eighteenth Century Britain', in John Barrell (ed.), *The Birth of Pandora and the Division of Knowledge*. London: Macmillan, 1992. 41–62.

Bashford, Alison. 'Terraqueous Histories', *The Historical Journal* 60.2 (2017): 253–272.

Baumgartner, Karin. 'Packaging the Grand Tour: German Women Authors Write Italy, 1791–1874', *Women in German Yearbook: Feminist Studies in German Literature & Culture* 31 (2015): 1–27.

Behdad, Ali. 'The Politics of adventure: Theories of Travel, Discourses of Power', in Julia Kuehn and Paul Smethurst (eds), *Travel Writing, Form, and Empire: The Poetics and Politics of Mobility*. New York and London: Routledge, 2009. 80–94.

Bennett, Jane. *The Enchantment of Modern Life: Attachments, Crossings, and Ethics*. Princeton, NJ: Princeton University Press, 2001.

Bennett, Tony. *Pasts beyond Memory: Evolution, Museums, Colonialism*. London and New York: Routledge, 2004.

Bennett, Tony, Fiona Cameron, Nélla Dias, Ben Dibley, Rodney Harrison, Ira Jacknis and Conal McCarthy. *Collecting, Ordering, Governing: Anthropology, Museums, and Liberal Government*. Durham and London: Duke University Press, 2017.

Bhabha, Homi K. 'DissemiNation: Time, Narrative, and the Margins of the Modern Nation', in Homi K. Bhabha (ed.), *Nation and Narration*. London and New York: Routledge, 2002. 291–322.

———. 'Unsatisfied: Notes on Vernacular Cosmopolitanism', in Gregory Castle (ed.), *Postcolonial Discourses: An Anthology*. Cambridge, MA: Blackwell, 2001. 39–52.

Black, Jeremy. *The British and the Grand Tour*. London: Croom Helm, 2011.

Boehmer, Elleke. *Indian Arrivals, 1870–1915: Networks of British Empire*. Oxford University Press, 2015.

Bohls, Elizabeth A. *Women Travel Writers and the Language of Aesthetics, 1716–1818*. Cambridge: Cambridge University Press, 1997.

Bramen, Carrie Tirado. 'A Transatlantic History of the Picturesque: An Introductory Essay'. *Nineteenth-Century Prose* 29.2 (2002): 1–19.

Brockway, Lucile H. *Science and Colonial Expansion: The Role of the British Botanical Gardens*. London: Academic, 1979.

Brydon, Diana, Peter Forsgren and Gunlög Fur. 'What Reading for Concurrences Offers Postcolonial Studies', in Diana Brydon, Peter Forsgren and Gunlög Fur (eds), *Concurrent Imaginaries, Postcolonial Worlds: Toward Revised Histories*. Leiden and Boston: Brill-Rodopi, 2017. 3–32.

Burgess, Miranda. 'The Scottish Regalia and the Scottish Nation, 1999/1822', in Caroline McCracken-Flesher (ed.), *Culture, Nation, and the New Scottish Parliament*. Bucknell University Press, 2007. 113–128.

Burton, Antoinette. 'Making a Spectacle of Empire: Indian Travellers in Fin-de-Siècle London', *History Workshop Journal* 42 (1996): 127–146.

———. *At the Heart of the Empire: Indians and the Colonial Encounter in Late-Victorian Britain*. New Delhi: Munshiram Manoharlal, 1998.

Butler, Judith. *Precarious Life: The Powers of Mourning and Violence*. London: Verso, 2004.

———. Frames of War: When is Life Grievable? London: Verso, 2009.

Buzard, James. 'The Grand Tour and after (1660–1840)', in Peter Hulme and Tim Youngs (eds), *The Cambridge Companion to Travel Writing*. Cambridge: Cambridge University Press, 2002. 37–52.

Campbell, Mary Baine. *The Witness and the Other World: European Exotic Travel Writing, 400–1600*. Ithaca and London: Cornell University Press, 1988.

———. *Wonder and Science: Imagining Worlds in Early Modern Europe*. Cornell University Press, 1999.

Cannadine, David. *Ornamentalism: How the British Saw Their Empire*. London: Penguin, 2001.

Cantor, Geoffrey. *Religion and the Great Exhibition of 1851*. Oxford: Oxford University Press, 2011.

Caquard, Sébastien and Jean-Pierre Fiset. 'How Can We Map Stories? A Cybercartographic Application for Narrative Cartography', *Journal of Maps* 10.1 (2014): 18–25.

Caquard, Sébastien and William Cartwright. 'Narrative Cartography: From Mapping Stories to the Narrative of Maps and Mapping', *Cartographic Journal* 51.2 (2014): 101–106.

Carter, Paul. *The Road to Botany Bay: An Essay in Spatial History*. London: Faber and Faber, 1987.

Chard, Chloe. *Pleasure and Guilt on the Grand Tour: Travel Writing and Imaginative Geography, 1600–1830*. Mancehster: Manchester University Press, 2000.

Childers, Joseph. 'Outside Looking In: Colonials, Immigrants, and the Pleasure of the Archive', *Victorian Studies* 46 (2004): 297–307.

Chrisman, Laura. *Postcolonial Contraventions: Cultural Readings of Race, Imperialism and Transnationalism*. Manchester: Manchester University Press, 2003.

Codell, Julie. 'Reversing the Grand Tour: Guest Discourse in Indian Travel Narratives', *Huntington Library Quarterly* 70.1 (2007): 173–187.

Comaroff, Jean and John Comaroff. *Of Revelation and Revolution: Christianity, Colonialism, and Consciousness in South Africa*, vol. 1. Chicago and London: University of Chicago Press, 1991.

Constantine, Mary-Ann. *John Hassell, Wales and the 'Industrial Picturesque'*. Picturing Places. Available at: https://www.bl.uk/picturing-places/articles/john-hassell-wales-and-the-industrial-picturesque#authorBlock1 [Accessed 8 October 2019], n.d.

Cosgrove, Dennis E. *Apollo's Eye: A Cartographic Genealogy of the Earth in the Western Imagination*. Baltimore: Johns Hopkins University Press, 2001.

Crary, Jonathan. *Techniques of the Observer: On Vision and Modernity in the Nineteenth Century*. Cambridge, MA: Massachusetts Institute of Technology Press, 1990

Cromley, Gordon. 'A Narrative Cartography of the French Indo-China War: A Journalistic Perspective', *Cartographica* 52.4 (2017): 293–309.

Crosby, Alfred W. *Ecological Imperialism: The Biological Expansion of Europe, 900–1900*, Cambridge: Cambridge University Press, 1995.

Dauphinee, Elizabeth. 'The Politics of the Body in Pain: Reading the Ethics of Imagery', *Security Dialogue* 38 (2007): 139–155.

Dawes, James. 'Human Rights in Literary Studies', *Human Rights Quarterly* 31.2 (2009): 394–409.

Diouf, Mamadou. 'The Senegalese Murid Trade Diaspora and the Making of a Vernacular Cosmopolitanism', *Public Culture* 12.3 (2000): 679–702.

Drayton, Richard. *Nature's Government: Science, Imperial Britain, and the Improvement of The World.* London and New Haven, CT: Yale University Press, 2000.

Eaton, Natasha. 'Nostalgia for the Exotic: Creating an Imperial Art in London, 1750–93', *Eighteenth-Century Studies* 39.2 (2006): 227–250.

———. 'Glimmer of Empire: Academy, "Alchemy," Exotic', *Eighteenth-Century Studies* 52.1 (2018): 13–18.

El-Sherif, Mona. 'Rethinking the Eurocentric Gaze in Narratives of Urban Modernity: The *Shaykh*, the *Flâneur*, and the Orientalist in *Takhlīṣ* al-Ibrīz and '*Alam al-Dīn*', *Middle Eastern Literatures* 21.1 (2018): 28–43.

Fabricant, Carole. 'The Literature of Domestic Tourism and the Public Consumption of Private Property', in Felicity Nussbaum and Laura Brown (eds), *The New Eighteenth Century: Theory, Politics, English Literature*. New York: Methuen, 1987. 254–275.

Fassi, Anthony J. 'Industrial Ruins, Urban Exploring, and the Postindustrial Picturesque', *CR: The New Centennial Review* 10.1 (2010): 141–152.

Fisher, Michael. 'Early Indian Travel Guides to Britain', in Tim Youngs (ed.), *Travel Writing in the Nineteenth Century: Filling the Blank Spaces*. London: Anthem, 2006. 87–106.

Flyn, Tom and Tim Barringer (eds). *Colonialism and the Object: Empire, Material Culture and the Museum*. London: Routledge, 1998.

Folliot, Laurent. 'Early Wordsworth: Towards the Limits of the Picturesque', in Pascale Guibert (ed.), *Spatial Practices of Anglophone Countries*. Brill, 2011. 193–208.

Fort, Bernadette. 'Ekphrasis as Art Criticism: Diderot and Fragonard's "Coresus and Callirhoe"', in Peter Wagner (ed.), *Icons-Texts-Iconotexts: Essays on Ekphrasis and Intermediality*. Berlin and New York: Walter De Gruyter, 1996. 58–78.

Fulford, Tim. *Landscape, Liberty and Authority: Poetry, Criticism and Politics from Thomson to Wordsworth*. Cambridge: Cambridge University Press, 1996.

Fur, Gunlög. 'Concurrences as a Methodology for Discerning Concurrent Histories', in Diana Brydon, Peter Forsgren and Gunlög Fur (eds), *Concurrent Imaginaries, Postcolonial Worlds: Toward Revised Histories*. Leiden and Boston: Brill-Rodopi, 2017. 33–58.

Johansen, Emily. 'Imagining the Global and the Rural: Rural Cosmopolitanism in Sharon Butala's *The Garden of Eden* and Amitav Ghosh's *The Hungry Tide*', *Postcolonial Text* 4.3 (2008).

Ganguly, Debjani. 'Vernacular Cosmopolitanism: World Historical Readings of Gandhi and Ambedkar', in Debjani Ganguly and John Docker (eds), *Rethinking Gandhi and Nonviolent Relationality: Global Perspectives*. Routledge, 2007. 245–263.

Giblett, Rodney James. *Postmodern Wetlands: Culture, History, Ecology*. Edinburgh: Edinburgh University Press, 1996.

Gibson, Margaret. 'Melancholy Objects'. *Mortality* 9.4 (2004): 285–299.

Goodlad, Lauren. 'Cosmopolitanism's Actually Existing Beyond; Toward a Victorian Geopolitical Aesthetic', *Victorian Literature and Culture* 38 (2010): 399–411.

Greenblatt, Stephen. *Renaissance Self-Fashioning: From More to Shakespeare*. Chicago: University of Chicago Press, 1980.

———. *Marvelous Possessions: The Wonder of the New World*. Oxford: Clarendon, 1991.

Grigson, Caroline. *Menagerie: A History of Exotic Animals in Britain, 1100–1837*. Oxford: Oxford University Press, 2016.

Gupta, Jayati. 'Modernity and the Global "Hindoo": The Concept of the Grand Tour in Colonial India', *The Global South* 2.1 (2008): 59–70.

Hållén, Nicklas. 'Travel Writing and the Representation of Concurrent Worlds: Caryl Phillips' *The Atlantic Sound* and Noo Saro–Wiwa's *Looking for Transwonderland*', in Diana Brydon, Peter Forsgren and Gunlög Fur (eds), *Concurrent Imaginaries, Postcolonial Worlds: Toward Revised Histories*. Leiden and Boston: Brill-Rodopi, 2017. 59–76.

Hanh, H. Hazel. 'Exoticism, and Violence: Representing the Self, "the Other," and Rival Empires in the English and French Illustrated Press, 1880–1905', *Historical Reflections/Réflexions Historiques* 38.3 (2012): 62–83.

Herrington, Susan. 'Frames Again: The Picturesque Aesthetics of Contemporary Landscapes', *Landscape Journal* 25.1–06 (2006): 22–37.

Hill, Rosemary. 'Keats, Antiquarianism, and the Picturesque', *Essays in Criticism* 64.2 (2014): 119–137.

Hoskins, William George. *The Making of the English Landscape*. London: Hodder and Stoughton, 1955.

Jenkins, Eugenia Zuroski. 'Introduction: Exoticism, Cosmopolitanism, and Fiction's Aesthetics of Diversity', *Eighteenth-Century Fiction* 25.1 (2012): 1–7.

Johansen, Emily. 'Imagining the Global and the Rural: Rural Cosmopolitanism in Sharon Butala's *The Garden of Eden* and Amitav Ghosh's *The Hungry Tide*', *Postcolonial Text* 4.3 (2008): 1–18.

Johnson, Patricia. 'De-constructing the Cosmopolitan Gaze', *Tourism and Hospitality Research* 10.2 (2010): 79–92.

Khair, Tabish. 'Travel Writing: India', in Shobhana Bhattacharji (ed.), *Travel Writing in India*. New Delhi: Sahitya Akademi, 2008. 7–10.

Knellwolf, Christa. 'The Exotic Frontier of the Imperial Imagination', *Eighteenth-Century Life* 26.3 (2002): 10–30.

Komara, Ann. 'Concrete and the Engineered Picturesque: The Parc des Buttes Chaumont (Paris, 1867)', *Journal of Architectural Education* 58.1 (2004): 5–12.

Kontsevaia, Diana B. 'Mass Graves and the Politics of Reconciliation: Construction of Memorial Sites after the Srebrenica Massacre', *Totem* 21.1 (2013): 13–31.

Krieger, Murray. *Ekphrasis: The Illusion of the Natural Sign*. Baltimore and London: Johns Hopkins University Press, 1992.

Leask, Nigel. *Curiosity and the Aesthetics of Travel Writing, 1770–1840: 'From an Antique Land.'* Oxford: Oxford University Press, 2002.

Lefebvre, Henri. *The Production of Space*. Trans. Donald Nicholson-Smith. Oxford: Blackwell, 1991.

Lisle, Debbie. *The Global Politics of Contemporary Travel Writing*. Cambridge: Cambridge University Press, 2006.

Long, Graham. 'Moral and Sentimental Cosmopolitanism', *Journal of Social Philosophy* 40.3 (2009): 317–342.

Lozanski, Kristin. 'Encountering Beggars: Disorienting Travellers?', *Annals of Tourism Research* 42 (2013): 46–64.

Mackintosh, Will B. 'Mechanical Aesthetics: Picturesque Tourism and the Transportation Revolution in Pennsylvania', *Pennsylvania History: A Journal of Mid-Atlantic Studies* 81.1 (2014): 88–105.

Majeed, Javed. *Autobiography, Travel and Postnational Identity: Gandhi, Nehru and Iqbal.* London: Palgrave-Macmillan, 2007.

Marchetti, Silvia. 'De-colonizing Italy: Migration Literature and the Tradition of the Picturesque', *The Italinist* 29 (2009): 400–424.

Martin, Daniel L. *Curious Visions of Modernity: Enchantment, Magic, and the Sacred.* Cambridge, MA: MIT, 2011.

Martin, Michael S. 'Picturesque America Comes to Appalachia: David Hunter Strother, Henry Colton, and the Visionary Traveler of the Mid-Nineteenth-Century Appalachian Expedition Narrative', *South Atlantic Review* 80.1–2 (2015): 62–81.

Mathur, Saloni. *India by Design: Colonial History and Cultural Display.* Hyderabad: Orient BlackSwan, 2011.

M'Baye, Babacar. *Black Cosmopolitanism and Anticolonialism: Pivotal Moments.* London and New York: Routledge, 2017.

Macccubin, Robert P. and Christa Knellwolf. 'Exoticism and the Culture of Exploration', *Eighteenth-Century Life* 26.3 (2002).

McBratney, John. 'Reluctant Cosmopolitanism in Dickens's *Great Expectations*', *Victorian Literature and Culture* 38 (2010): 529–546.

McClintock, Anne. *Imperial Leather: Race, Gender and Sexuality in the Colonial Contest.* London and New York: Routledge, 1995

Milkova, Stiliana. 'From Rome to Paris to Rome: Reversing the Grand Tour in Gogol's "Rome"', *The Slavic and East European Journal* 59.4 (2015): 493–516

Mukherjee, Pablo. 'Touring the Dead Lands: Emily Eden, Victorian Famines, and Colonial Picturesque', *Critical Survey* 21.1 (2009): 34–38.

Murphy, Ann V. 'Corporeal Vulnerability and the New Humanism', *Hypatia* 26.3 (2011): 575–590.

Murphy, Patrick D. 'Community Resilience and the Cosmopolitan Role in the Environmental Challenge-Response Novels of Ghosh, Grace, and Sinha', *Journal of Modern Literature* 50.1 (2013): 148–168.

Nancy, Jean-Luc. *L'Intrus.* Trans. Susan Hanson. Ann Arbor, MI: Michigan University Press, 2002.

Nayar, Pramod K. *English Writing and India, 1600–1920: Colonizing Aesthetics.* London and New York: Routledge, 2008.

Nayar, Pramod K. *Colonial Voices: The Discourses of Empire*. Malden, MA: Wiley-Blackwell, 2012.

———. 'Colonial Subjects and Aesthetic Understanding: Indian Travel Literature about England, 1870–1900', *South Asian Review* 33.1 (2012): 31–52.

———. 'Beyond the Colonial Subject: Mobility, Cosmopolitanism and Self-fashioning in Sarat Chandra Das' *A Journey to Lhasa and Central Tibet*', *New Zealand Journal of Asian Studies* 14.2 (2012): 1–16.

Nelson,William. *Fact or Fiction: The Dilemma of the Renaissance Storyteller*. Cambridge, MA: Harvard University Press, 1973.

Neumann, Dietrich. 'Instead of the Grand Tour: Travel Replacements in the Nineteenth Century', *Perspecta* 41 (2008): 47–53.

Ngũgĩ wa Thiong'o. *Globalectics: Theory and the Politics of Knowing*. New York: Columbia University Press, 2012.

Nussbaum, Felicity A. 'Between "Oriental" and "Blacks So Called", 1688-1788', in Daniel Carey and Lynn Festa (eds), *The Postcolonial Enlightenment: Eighteenth-Century Colonialism and Postcolonial Theory*. Oxford: Oxford University Press, 2009. 137–166.

Olaniyan, Tejumola. 'The Cosmopolitan Nativist: Fela Anikulapo-Kuti and the Antinomies of Postcolonial Modernity', *Research in African Literatures* 32.2 (2001): 76–89.

O'Quinn, Daniel. 'Tears in Tehran/Laughter in London: James Morier, Mirza Abul Hassan Khan, and the Geopolitics of Emotion', *Eighteenth-Century Fiction* 25.1 (2012): 85–114.

Ovington, John. *A Voyage to Surat, in the Year 1689*. London: Jacob Jonson, 1696.

Paquette, Jonathan and Aurélie Lacassagne. 'Subterranean Subalterns: Territorialisation, Deterritorialisation, and the Aesthetics of Mining', *Culture and Organization* 19.3 (2013): 242–260.

Paulson, Ronald. *The Beautiful, Novel, and Strange: Aesthetics and Heterodoxy*. Baltimore and London: Johns Hopkins University Press, 1996.

Pinney, Christopher. 'Creole Europe: The Reflection of a Reflection', *Journal of New Zealand Literature* 20 (2002): 125–161.

Poovey, Mary. 'Figures of Arithmetic: Figures of Speech: The Discourse of Statistics in the 1830s', *Critical Inquiry* 19 (1993): 256–276.

Porter, Dahlia. 'Maps, Lists, Views: How the Picturesque Wye transformed Topography', *Romanticism* 19.2 (2013): 163–178.

Pratt, Mary Louise. *Imperial Eyes: Travel Writing and Transculturation*. New York and London: Routledge, 2007. 2nd ed.

Prince, Gerald. 'The Disnarrated', *Style* 22.1 (1988): 1–8.

Pyyry, Noora. 'Learning with the City via Enchantment: Photo-walks as Creative Encounters', *Discourse* 36.1 (2016): 101–115.

Ramaswamy, Sumathi. *Territorial Lessons: The Conquest of the World as Globe*. Hyderabad: Orient BlackSwan, 2018.

Reddy, Sheshalatha. 'The Cosmopolitan Nationalism of Sarojini Naidu, Nightingale of India', *Victorian Literature and Culture* 38.2 (2010): 571–589.

Ridley, Glynnis. *Clara's Grand Tour: Travels with a Rhinoceros in Eighteenth-Century Europe*. Grove, 2004.

Rogers, Brandon. 'The Politics of the Picturesque: The Marches Settle Van Rensselaer's New York City', *American Periodicals* 12 (2002): 75–88.

Roque, Ricardo. 'Stories, Skulls and Colonial Collections', *Configurations* 19.1 (2011): 1–23.

Rosenthal, Laura J. 'The Queen of Sorrow and the Knight of the Indies: Cosmopolitan Possibilities in *The Recess* and *The New Cosmetic*', *Eighteenth-Century Fiction* 25.1 (2012): 9–35.

Rothberg, Michael and Yasemin Yildiz. 'Archives of Holocaust Remembrance in Contemporary Germany', *Parallax* 17.4 (2011): 32–48.

Rothberg, Michael. 'From Gaza to Warsaw: Mapping Multidirectional Memory', *Criticism* 53.4 (2011): 523–548.

Rousseau, G.S. and Roy Porter. 'Introduction', in Rousseau and Porter (eds), *Exoticism in the Enlightenment.* Manchester: Manchester University Press, 1990. 1–22.

Rubiés, Joan-Pau. 'Travel Writing and Ethnography', in Peter Hulme and Tim Youngs (eds), *The Cambridge Companion to Travel Writing.* Cambridge, MA: Cambridge University Press, 2002. 242–260.

Saha, Poulomi. 'Singing Bengal into a Nation: Tagore a Colonial Cosmopolitan?', *Journal of Modern Literature* 36.2 (2013): 1–24.

Schiebinger, Londa and Claudia Swan (eds). *Colonial Botany: Science, Commerce, and Politics in the Early Modern World.* Philadelphia, PA: University of Pennsylvania Press, 2007.

Schiebinger, Londa and Claudia Swan. 'Introduction', in Londa Schiebinger and Claudia Swan (eds), *Colonial Botany: Science, Commerce, and Politics in the Early Modern World.* Philadelphia, PA: University of Pennsylvania Press, 2007.

Schmidt, Benjamin. *Inventing Exoticism: Geography, Globalism, and Europe's Early Modern World.* Philadelphia, PA: University of Pennsylvania Press, 2015.

Segalen, Victor. *Essay on Exoticism: An Aesthetics of Diversity.* Trans and ed. Yaël Rachel Schlick. Durham: Duke University Press, 2002.

Sell, Jonathan A. *Rhetoric and Wonder in English Travel Writing, 1560–1613.* Aldershot: Ashgate, 2006.

Sen, Simonti. *Travels to Europe: Self and Other in Bengali Travel Narratives, 1870–1910.* Hyderabad: Orient Longman, 2005.

Shears, Jonathon (ed.). *The Great Exhibition, 1851: A Source Book.* Manchester: Manchester University Press, 2017.

Siganporia, Harmony. *I Am the Widow: An Intellectual Biography of Behramji Malabari.* Hyderabad: Orient BlackSwan, 2018.

Simpson II, Tyrone. *Ghetto Images in Twentieth-Century American Literature: Writing Apartheid.* New York: Palgrave Macmillan, 2012.

Small, Helen. 'George Eliot and the Cosmopolitan Cynic', *Victorian Studies* 55.1 (2012): 85–105.

Smethurst, Paul. 'Introduction', in Julia Kuehn and Paul Smethurst (eds), *Travel Writing, Form, and Empire: The Poetics and Politics of Mobility.* London and New York: Routledge, 2009. 1–18.

———. *Travel Writing and the Natural World, 1768–1840.* London: Palgrave-Macmillan, 2012.

Spary, Emma Chartreuse. 'Of Nutmegs and Botanists: The Colonial Cultivation of Botanical Identity', in Londa Schiebinger and Claudia Swan (eds), *Colonial Botany: Science, Commerce, and Politics in the Early Modern World.* Philadelphia, PA: University of Pennsylvania Press, 2007. 377–410.

Stafford, Barbara Maria. 'Thoughts Not Our Own: Whatever Happened to Selective Attention?', *Theory, Culture & Society* 26.2–3 (2009): 275–293.

Stanley, Brian. '"Commerce and Christianity": Providence Theory, the Missionary Movement, and the Imperialism of Free Trade, 1842–60', *Historical Journal* 26.1 (1983): 71–94.

Stewart, Susan. *On Longing: Narratives of the Miniature, the Gigantic, the Souvenir, the Collection.* Durham and London: Duke University Press, 1993.

Stoler, Ann Laura. 'Introduction: "The Rot Remains": From Ruins to Ruination', in Ann Laura Stoler (ed.), *Imperial Debris: On Ruins and Ruination.* Durham and London: Duke University Press, 2013. 1–37.

Tait, Sue. 'Pornographies of Violence? Internet Spectatorship on Body Horror', *Critical Studies in Media Communication* 25:1 (2008): 91–111.

Teltscher, Kate. *India Inscribed: European and British Writing on India, 1600–1800*. Delhi: Oxford University Press, 1997.

Tester, Keith. 'Introduction', in Keith Tester (ed.), *The Flâneur*. London and New York: Routledge, 2006. 1–21.

Thorne, Susan. *Congregational Missions and the Making of an Imperial Culture in Nineteenth-Century England*. Stanford University Press, 1999.

Thoss, Jeff. 'Cartographic Ekphrasis: Map Descriptions in the Poetry of Elizabeth Bishop and Eavan Boland', *Word & Image* 32.1 (2016): 64–76.

Turner, Bryan S. *Vulnerability and Human Rights*. Philadelphia: Penn State University Press, 2006.

Valkeakari, Tuire. 'The Photographer-Flâneur as Facilitator of Urban Connectivity in John Edgar Wideman's *Two Cities*', *Critique: Studies in Contemporary Fiction* 60.2 (2019): 222–235.

Van Renen, Denys. 'Decomposing the Picturesque and Re-collecting Nature in Dorothy Wordsworth's Scotland', *Journal of Narrative Theory* 45.2 (2015): 165–192.

Vandevoordt, Robin. 'Moral Cosmopolitanism and the Everyday Life: How Students Encounter Distant Others', *Media, Culture and Society* 40.2 (2018): 195–210

Vardy, Alan. 'Joseph Cottle and Reminiscence: The Picturesque Gone Awry', *Romanticism* 19.2 (2013): 188–196.

Vincent, Bridget. 'Object Lessons: Derek Mahon's Material Ekphrasis', *Interdisciplinary Literary Studies* 20.3 (2018): 371–384.

Wagner, Peter. 'Introduction: Ekphrasis, Iconotexts, and Intermediality—The State(s) of the Art(s)', in Peter Wagner (ed.), *Icons-Texts-Iconotexts: Essays on Ekphrasis and Intermediality*. Berlin and New York: Walter De Gruyter, 1996. 1–42.

Werbner, Pnina. 'Vernacular Cosmopolitanism', *Theory, Culture & Society* 23.2–3 (2006): 496–498.

Whiteley, Giles. 'Cosmopolitan Space: Political Topographies in "Lord Arthur Savile's Crime"', *Victoriographies* 7.2 (2017): 124–142.

Youngs, Tim. 'Strategies of Travel: Charles Dickens and William Wells Brown', in Tim Youngs (ed.), *Travel Writing in the Nineteenth Century: Filling the Blank Spaces*. London: Anthem, 2006. 163–177.

Zeng, Minhao. 'Subaltern Cosmopolitanism: Concept and Approaches', *The Sociological Review* 62 (2014): 137–148.

Index

F

G

H

I

P

R

About the Author

Pramod K. Nayar teaches at the Department of English, University of Hyderabad, India. His most recent works are *Ecoprecarity: Vulnerable Lives in Literature and Culture* (2019), *Brand Postcolonial: 'Third World' Texts and the Global* (2018), *Bhopal's Ecological Gothic: Disaster, Precarity and the Biopolitical Uncanny* (2017), *Human Rights and Literature: Writing Right* (2016) and the edited collection, *Indian Travel Writing, 1830–1947* (2016). His essays have appeared in *Modern Fiction Studies, South Asia Review, South Asia, Narrative, Celebrity Studies, Asiatic, Journal of Postcolonial Writing, Prose Studies, a/b: auto/biography studies, Biography, Image and Text* and *Postcolonial Text*, among others. Forthcoming is a book on Human Rights Graphic Novels.